LEARNING AND LIVING

ACADEMIC ESSAYS

LEARNING AND LIVING

ACADEMIC ESSAYS

BY

EPHRAIM EMERTON

WINN PROFESSOR OF ECCLESIASTICAL HISTORY
IN HARVARD UNIVERSITY
(*EMERITUS*)

Essay Index Reprint Series

BOOKS FOR LIBRARIES PRESS, INC.
FREEPORT, NEW YORK

First Published 1921
Reprinted 1967

LIBRARY OF CONGRESS CATALOG NUMBER:
67-30209

PRINTED IN THE UNITED STATES OF AMERICA

PREFATORY NOTE

TO find a suitable title for these essays written at different times and under widely differing circumstances has been no easy task. Each of them was the result of some special impulse pointing to some rather special treatment. They have grown out of a long and varied experience covering important changes in method, an enormous material expansion, a portentous professionalizing of the university career and an almost complete revision of the academic vocabulary.

It is these changes and these expansions that have most sharply caught the attention of the intelligent public. The constant struggle to maintain the higher ideals of education, to separate the permanent from the whimsical and the transient, escapes observation and passes unrewarded. If these scattered academic essays are read together there appears through them all the reflection of this struggle. This does not mean, I trust, that they are the echoes of a forlorn conservatism trying to hold its own against the resistless march of change. On the contrary, they try to point the way to changes still more radical because they go down to the ancient roots of all sound human culture.

The threads that run through them all are: the value of hard work done "as by God's law"; the freedom of the teacher to teach and of the learner to learn; the discipline of the remote aim and the responsibility for reaching it; the folly of educational tricks and short-cuts; finally, the justification of all educational effort by its bearing upon the associated life of men. In the continuous interrelation of Learning and Living lies the hope of the Republic.

E. E.

CAMBRIDGE, MASSACHUSETTS
June, 1921

CONTENTS

LEARNING AND LIVING

·ACADEMIC ESSAYS

THE ACADEMIC LIFE

I CANNOT claim any qualification for speaking of the academic life except that I have lived it and loved it and believed in it during a working lifetime. I have passed through all its varied experiences of preparation, candidacy, probation, recognition, promotion and finally of honorable retirement. I have shared in its drudgery, have felt its temptations, been thrilled with its enthusiasms, perceived its limitations and enjoyed its modest rewards. I have borne my share in the obvious criticisms to which the academic person is always subject, but have never for a moment doubted that, after all allowance has been made for such adverse comment, enough is left to make this kind of life worth living. More, I think, than most careers that of the university man involves a continual adjustment of the claims of the individual and of the society in which he forms a part. These claims are always in apparent conflict. As our universities are at present constituted the two pursuits of scholarship and teaching are necessarily combined, not only in the institution itself but also in the life of the individual member. The university is both a society for the advancement of science in its manifold activities and a school for teaching. So the academic person is at once an investigator in the peculiar field he tries to make his own and also a teacher of youth.

This persistent dualism has not failed to attract the attention of all observers, and numerous attempts have

been made to resolve it. Such attempts have assumed
as a matter of course that it is in itself an evil. Schemes
to get rid of it appear as solutions of a problem that has
impeded true progress in both science and education.
Certain catch-words have come to indicate the line
of reform: "endowment of research," "research professorships," "relief from teaching," all alluring
phrases pointing toward an academic millennium.
There is probably no university man who has not at
times felt deeply the strain of this double duty, and
yet, with all the arguments in mind, I doubt whether
on the whole the dualism is quite the evil thing it appears. The reform measures I have referred to have
affected sometimes the learned society, sometimes the
individual scholar. Separate institutions have been
founded with the deliberate purpose of fostering the
scientific spirit through unlimited practice of investigation and publication. It would be rash to say that
such institutions have actually fallen behind their dual-
ist compeers in the amount and value of their contributions to science; but so far the scholarly standards
of our best administered older universities have not
been lowered in view of this competition.

Other reforms have touched the individual. There
have been endowments for the maintenance of research or for securing time to the teaching professor
for the publication of his results. "Sabbatical years"
have made possible many productive activities that
otherwise would have been indefinitely postponed. All
these have helped, but they have not yet gone so far
as to draw the line sharply and permanently between

the teaching and the learning sides of the scholar's work.

Another device has been employed, perhaps with greater success. It is one of the commonplaces of academic comment that equally valuable university men may be distinguished by wide diversity of gifts. One is obviously, as we say, "a born teacher," another seems specially qualified for the work of investigation, while a third takes his peculiar satisfaction in the problems of administration. The solution of the whole matter, therefore, would seem to lie in the widest possible differentiation among these several functions. Let the teacher teach, the investigator study and write books, and the executive person run the machine. Each, it is supposed, would be happier doing the thing for which he is by nature best fitted, and, because he is happier his work will be the better done, and the university as a whole will be the gainer.

This argument is attractive, but I do not find it convincing. It proves a little too much. The life of the university is not like that of a manufactory where the accomplished product is the result of so many separate contributory processes. The three functions I have named cannot be separated from each other without detriment to the product. Freedom from class-room routine is a very alluring prospect to the eager scholar; but that very freedom brings with it its special dangers of introspection, of over anxiety in detail, of hesitation to form conclusions, which are the snare of the student temperament. It is a wholesome thing for such a mind to be compelled at frequent intervals to give out what it has been taking in, to restate its results so that they can be understood by unprepared minds, to get out of the receptive and into the outgiving attitude. The ultimate product in the printed book will be so much the more widely appealing.

And the same thing in the reverse sense is true of the specially gifted teacher. His work as teacher cannot be of the best unless it be continually fed at the source by wide and serious study. A colleague of mine, speaking of a certain schoolmaster, said with a sad smile: "I suppose he has learned his lessons for the rest of his life." As he said it he was thinking grimly of the long vista of weary days and nights that stretched out before himself as he looked ahead over the years of professional activity before him. Such a man loves the work of teaching. He feels its stimulus in the rest of his academic service, but he knows, certainly after some experience, that it would be fatal to his success here if he were to be cut off by any kind of university restriction from the continuous pursuit of his own private and personal scholarly interests.

These same considerations have still greater force when we come to the administrative side of the academic profession. "So-and-So likes to run things; let him run them! So much the more time for me to give to my laboratory or my library or my classes." Such is the not infrequent comment of the zealous scholar or teacher on the vexed question of the distribution of university work. "College *work* seems to me rather more important than college *business*" said an elder colleague of mine a good many years ago. His thesis was unanswerable in that form, but the result in his case was sadly instructive for our present purpose. In pursuance of his doctrine he withdrew himself completely from the discussions of the Faculty, which in just those years dealt with the most important problems of university policy. Instead of making his own contribution to these discussions and keeping himself informed on the gradual movement of thought within the university he put himself into the attitude of criticism toward those of his colleagues who felt that their duty and their interest as well called for their steady and active participation in the monotonous, often dreary and seemingly unprofitable debates by which the course of things was after all determined. He got what he thought he wanted, exemption from the distractions of "college business," but in the end "college work," even his own work, suffered thereby instead of gaining.

The moral of this is that the scholars and teachers of the university cannot look with complacency on the development of a separate class of university administrators, and this for two reasons: they need a certain experience of this kind for their own sakes, and if they try to escape it they are sure to find themselves caught in the toils of a separated administrative system that will block them in their highest endeavors. There is no greater danger before the university world to-day than precisely this. The portentous growth of our larger institutions has seemed to demand ever more and more administrative activity, and the smaller have thought they must follow in the same road. A colleague of mine burst out in the midst of a debate on the details of college discipline: "What we need is to enlarge the Dean's office. One dean is not enough. We ought to have three or four of them!" There were others who thought that the Dean's office administered as it was with a fatal zeal and fidelity and self-sacrifice, was precisely the evil that needed remedy, not by increasing it, but by lopping off the greater part of its functions. Needless to remark that their views did not prevail; for administrative machinery grows by what it feeds upon. In the university, as in the nation, the executive is in danger of crowding the other elements of the community into a willing obscurity and inactivity. Administrative standards are bound to be on a lower level than those of the really important workers; standardization, uniformity, bookkeeping regularity, a semblance of discipline without its reality, quick and obvious results, these are the ideals sure to appeal to the administrative mind. These are the things easily understood by the "university public" upon which the institution has to rely for its material support. And yet these are just the things against which the true scholar and wise teacher has to struggle with all his might if his work is not to slip constantly backward and downward toward the level of the things that are seen and away further and further from the "things that are not seen."

This is a large and weighty subject worthy of treatment by itself. I have touched upon it here only to show its relation to our definition of the academic life as inevitably a complex one. The youth who looks forward to this career cannot too thoughtfully consider this aspect of it. He will have to make up his mind that he cannot be merely either a scholar or a teacher or a man of affairs, but must be prepared to distribute his energies over all three of these activities. In what proportion, will depend upon circumstances; the point now is that any one of these functions will suffer if the others are too far neglected. The individual will suffer, and the institution will in so far be less well served. The rational policy of a university government would seem to be to draw a just line of division between the diversities of gifts on the one hand and the demand upon all its servants to give as they can of their services in each of the several fields of academic usefulness on the other. For the man who is merely a teacher or merely a scholar or merely a good office head there is no permanently useful place in a university.

The academic profession in America is comparatively a new one. Less than two generations ago a young American of scholarly tastes considering what he should do with his life had before him hardly more range than a choice among the three so-called learned professions, the law, medicine, and the Christian ministry. If his tastes excluded medicine and inclined rather to the practical sides of life he was led naturally into the law, not because he cared specially about law, but because it might eventually give him some opportunity to carry out the more purely scholarly ambitions which, after all, were the real guiding motive of his choice. If, on the other hand, after eliminating medicine he still found himself unattracted by the sterner conflicts of affairs he might find refuge in the ministry of religion as promising him in the long run the largest share in the purely intellectual life. At that time it probably seldom occurred to a youth of parts to aim definitely and from the beginning at the university career as a life work.

The teaching profession, as a profession, had then hardly come into existence. Teachers were mainly accidents, drawn or driven or drifting into their work through failure or necessity or inertia. The line between the teacher in a school or in a college was not sharply drawn, and men passed from the lower to the higher grade without violent change of quality or intellectual outlook. Our young man standing in the valley of decision, if the thought of the academic career occurred to him at all, may have dreamed about it as of something immeasurably beyond him to which he might conceivably be called by some mysterious process, but not as a legitimate object of his own exertions. He liked to think of his professors as men of monstrous learning, though it must be confessed that the methods of instruction of that time tended more to conceal than to display whatever equipment they may have had. That they had ever been much younger than they were, or less the autocrats of their world of knowledge, he could scarcely believe.

As to the younger instructors, the suggestion of an open profession of learning could hardly come with any greater weight from them. They were largely experiments, temporary makeshifts taken out of one or another professional school and utilizing their teaching appointments only as helps toward their ultimate aims, furthering their own ends at the expense of the luckless youth intrusted to their ignorance and indifference. Only here and there did he encounter among these younger men one and another actuated by the true scholar's purpose, perhaps already trained in some foreign school or gifted with the insight that led him straight toward the academic goal. From some such pioneer the young man may have received suggestion and encouragement to follow his higher leadings and make a way for himself into the kind of life that, however vaguely, appealed to the best there was in him. Seen through the veil of mystery that beclouded it, the professor's life may have seemed to him the most attractive of all lives, but how to reach it was still to him a perplexing puzzle.

All this was quite natural, for, if it is true that there was no recognized profession of teaching, still less could it be said that there was a recognized career for the "liberally" educated scholar. Obviously there could be no easily perceived way to a non-existent profession. The case of Henry Adams, recently described by himself in his "Education," is a typical one. A man of thirty-two, untrained in any regular fashion for the work of teaching or of historical investigation, living at the time in England as private secretary to the American Minister he was suddenly invited to take the position of an Assistant Professor of History in Harvard College. To his protest that he knew little history and least of all in the period he was expected to teach, the far-seeing President replied that if he would name any one better prepared he would appoint him. The plain fact was that there were no technically prepared men ready to take up the work of teaching history in America.

What was true of history was pretty nearly true of other subjects. A contemporary of mine, a brilliant classical scholar while in college, finding himself in Europe a year after graduation with the world before him, conceived the unusual idea of becoming a well-fitted college teacher. He had a modest income which made some years of study possible, but he was proposing to earn his way in the world. He wrote to the great college he had recently left stating his case. He was willing to follow any course of study and submit to any tests the college might prescribe. All he asked was a reasonable certainty that upon the satisfactory completion of such a course the college would give him a chance to try his hand. Unaccountably to him his letters remained unanswered, and, after waiting a reasonable time, he threw himself heart and soul into the study of the law. Several years later, just after he had begun a successful practice in a distant city, quite suddenly, without a word of warning, he received from his *alma mater* the offer of a classical tutorship. Of course it was too late, and a man of real genius was lost to scholarship and to the academic life because as yet there was no well-marked road leading thither.

To-day the whole situation is in this respect pretty radically changed. A young man of this type would now be singled out from an early stage of his studies as a prize for whom in a few years universities would be competing. There is to-day in America a well-defined academic profession. The roads leading up to it are almost too clearly marked, and yet it may be doubted whether there is any other profession, unless it be that of the stage, about which the intelligent public knows so little. The real life of the professor, like that of the actor, is lived behind a curtain and is revealed to the public only by occasional glimpses at moments of special readiness for exhibition. The processes of his work are wholly concealed. He works at different times and in different places from those affected by other workmen. He is seldom seen abroad except at his play times, and his public appearances as an expert are limited to audiences interested for the moment in his special field of learning. His own particular college community knows him hardly more intimately. To his students he is a more or less mysterious being who, at stated intervals during the week, emerges from his obscurity and imparts to them something of the results of his habitual seclusion. Their scraps of tradition about his personality and his history are more often than not grotesquely inaccurate.

True, the professor of to-day is in these matters somewhat more happily placed than his predecessors of two generations ago. He is, or at all events likes to fancy himself, more of a man of the world. He is a more movable person. He stands in closer relation with his professional colleagues all over the world. He goes to frequent gatherings of men of his own kind and thus gains a more just measure of himself and his surroundings. He is more apt to feel that he owes certain duties to the community at large and lends himself more readily to this or that form of public service. But after all allowance has been made for this change of attitude, the hard fact remains that all these things have to be treated as so many interruptions to the regular business of his life. If he allows them to fill too large a space, this real business, namely his teaching and the study that supports it and supplies the sources of his contribution to the world's learning, will suffer in proportion.

I have dwelt thus upon the seclusion of the academic life because this is one of the first things which our young man looking forward to it ought carefully to consider. It makes one of the charms, but it forms also one of the chief limitations of the university career. The young scholar, conscious of power and eager, as he should be, to make it felt in the world has his visions of what learning can do among men. Perhaps he thinks, albeit unconsciously, of the university as the medium between himself and a waiting world. He will use the university as his stalking horse to capture fame and opportunity. "When I began my work" said a colleague after a quarter of a century in the service, "I used to see before me my *Complete Works* in thirty-seven volumes octavo standing in beautiful order on the library shelf. And now!" He had done a man's work, and the volume of his publication was respectable, but that fair vision of a waiting world had resolved itself into the full sight of a world that could still afford to wait.

I would be the last person to dim by any shadow of

experience the splendor of youthful vision, but if any beginner starts with the idea that he can use the university for his own ends, he is on a false trail. There is a far greater chance that the university will use him and will do it so effectually that there will be little of him left for other service. The law is proverbially a jealous mistress, and though the university profession in America is hardly old enough to have a set of proverbs of its own, it can without hesitation apply to itself the claim of the law to the undivided allegiance of its votaries. It is true that a healthful interchange between the university and the active world outside sometimes takes place to the great advantage of both. The university occasionally draws its teachers from the professions and sometimes, though more rarely, the professions are enriched by the transfer to them of men who have gained their early strength in the more theoretical school of the university. At present mobility seems to be one of the characteristics of the academic person. We hear much of "university extension" "exchange of professors," "utilizing the plant" and other devices whereby the ingrowing tendencies of the university body may be checked and its influence in the larger community be increased. All that is well if due limits be observed. What we have to guard against is that wider usefulness may not become distraction, that the call to new activity may not become a sign of mere restlessness. In so far as this is the case the regular, solid movement of academic life will be interrupted, its true foundations of quiet study and productive reflection will be weakened and the long result will be dimin-

ished. With the greater development of the university
career as a profession by itself the process of interchange between the university and "the world" is not
likely to be greatly extended. Young men will go into
this new profession in the hope of promotion as the
natural reward of success, and if they are to see their
way to promotion barred by the introduction of men of
larger reputation who have climbed up by some other
way, they are going to think several times before they
incur the risk.

A few years ago the academic community was not a
little stirred by the discussion of the advisability of
establishing "prize professorships" with salaries ap-
proximating the incomes of highly successful business
or professional men and to be filled by drawing into the
service of the university men who had already "arrived" in their several fields of action. It was interesting to note that in this discussion it was not the obvious
financial difficulty, but the probable effect upon the
university profession that was most dwelt upon. It
was felt that such exceptional chairs would inevitably
become rather decorations than positive forces and
that their establishment could act only as discourage-
ments to modest effort within the university limits.
Rather, it was said, let the university do all in its
power to develop in its own carefully selected members the kind of eminence in science that seeks and
finds its best reward in the obscure but precious rec-
ognitions of those best qualified to judge.

The candidate for university honors must make up
his mind from the start that he is entering on a career

that will claim all there is of him and that this claim
will not relax as years go on, but will rather increase in
intensity and in variety of forms. That is his first sacrifice, to give up once for all the kind of ambition
which looks forward to making a great place in the
world. His life is to be mainly a life of seclusion, filled
chiefly with a more or less monotonous routine and
giving him only now and then points of contact with
other interests. Again, he must be prepared to sacrifice every prospect of worldly advantage. As things
go now he can hardly look for permanent employment
much before the age of thirty, and he is fortunate if at
that time his salary is two thousand dollars. At some
point between forty and fifty he may reach a permanent position with an income of from three to six
thousand, but beyond this he is not likely to go. Wife
and children under these circumstances are obviously
something to be postponed to an age well beyond the
normal. And yet nothing ought to commend an otherwise promising young man to permanent employment
in the academic world than precisely the fact that he
has given his hostages to fortune early and wisely.

The figures just given will vary, of course, with place
and grade of standing, but they are fairly indicative of
what the young man thoroughly trained by years of
expensive preparation may reasonably expect. They
represent doubtless the average appreciation of learning on the part of the great American public. They
mean sacrifice of many kinds, but they do not mean
poverty. They place the university man, so far as
money is concerned, below the average moderately

successful tradesman or industrial manager or professional practitioner. On the whole they compare pretty
well with the figures in other countries, and since the
noble foundation of Andrew Carnegie, this comparison
is still more favorable to America. Still the cold fact
remains that our academic population, in so far as it
depends upon its salaries, is living always on the verge
of distress if any misfortune befall the wage-earner
of the family. To make such provision for the future
as will enable him and the rest to meet old age with
approximately the same resources as they have enjoyed during his active years involves continual sacrifice of a kind which inevitably reacts upon the value
of the work on which the whole establishment depends. It means inconvenient lodging with perhaps no
suitable working place for the worker of the family. It
means a diminished table with consequent depression
of working power. It means lack of books, the tools of
the worker's trade. It means denial of recreation, the
necessary condition of successful work. It means often
a kind of social deprivation especially wearing to a sen-
sitive nature. Finally, and worst of all, it means the
acceptance of "extra work," that insidious allurement,
that "one thing more" which the man always thinks he
can do, but which crowds him just so much closer to the
wall — the private pupil, the course in a secondary
school, or, latest and most fatal product of the educational machine, the Summer School.

This is no plea for the maintenance of a privileged
class of scholars. Access to the scholar's life should be
difficult, and progress in it should be determined solely

by the tests of personal fitness; but it is well that our public should understand what chances of satisfaction in life it is offering to men from whom it demands the highest service of character and laborious devotion to an exacting ideal. It is doubtless true that the public can always count upon a certain supply of academic material, for the scholar's life has its own attraction sure always to outweigh many material considerations. The question is how far the public can afford to speculate in the scholar's readiness to take chances. It cannot in the long run be satisfied with men in academic positions who make positively low demands upon life. It ought to expect them to seek suitable mates at a reasonably early age, to live easily and in a civilized manner. The home of the academic man ought to be a center of light to the youth who are privileged to enter it. The public owes it to itself to see to it that its university service be well done, and it cannot be well done by men who are under the continual stress of personal anxiety.

It is, of course, impossible here to name any exact standards, but it is not extravagant to ask that the position in life of the academic man be not made greatly inferior to that of the picked men among lawyers and physicians. Somewhat inferior it is sure to be, for it would be a millennial conception to place the interests of men's minds or souls upon as high a level as the interests of their bodies or of their pockets. But, taking into account the element of comparative security essential to scholarly success, the standard I have suggested can hardly seem unreasonably high. In a community, for example, where a fairly successful lawyer or physician at the age of forty-five would be earning ten thousand a year, it can hardly seem too much to ask that the university professor who has stood all the tests should expect about six thousand. This maximum should ordinarily be reached by stages long enough to give ample guarantee of satisfaction, and governing boards should not be held to have committed themselves to further advance by any action during the earlier stages.

The ways to permanent appointment at maximum pay should be kept as difficult as they are at present, and the candidate for promotion should be made to feel that his fate is in his own hands. The question how far the probationary stage should be extended is a serious one. In a recent conversation with a newly appointed member of the corporation of an important university we discussed the advisability of adding one more stage to the already existing normal steps of approach to the full professorship. He enlarged upon the beneficial moral effect of long probation. "In a very true sense" he said "we are all on probation as long as we live. It is a wholesome thing to feel that we are under inspection and responsible to some superior power for the best exercise of our faculties. To remove that sense of responsibility would be to slacken the tension of our working machinery and lead gradually to less efficient service." I admitted fully the force of these general propositions, but ventured to warn my friend of certain limits to them. I reminded him that the university service is not like that of the business

houses with which he was familiar. The professor is
not the *employé* of a superior individual or corporation.
The controlling corporation is not an employer, but a
trustee bound by the nature of his trust to procure expert service of which he is only imperfectly capable of
judging. The professor on his side serves, not the corporation but the cause of learning and education. He
is a partner with the corporation in this larger service.
His pay comes, not from the corporation but partly
from the students and partly from endowments which
again are not the property of the corporation but of the
community at large which through its lawful agencies
entrusts them to the corporation for the purposes of
their foundation.

This peculiar quality of the university service has
certain consequences. "You and I," said a colleague
with whom I was discussing, as professors will, certain
frailties of the executive branch, "can stand a good
deal of this sort of thing because we love the place."
Our loyalty, tried and proved in many an encounter
was, we believed, proof against almost any strain. But
how about the loyalty of men without these ties of affection and these memories of storm and stress? Can
they be counted upon for unselfish service at critical
moments? Will they withstand the temptation of
higher offers from other institutions? Will they bear
patiently what they feel to be encroachments upon
their rights as members of the university family?
Upon the answer to these questions must depend very
greatly the whole problem of university *morale*. The
creation throughout the whole working staff of this

spirit of loyalty is one of the most important — I had almost said, the most important object of university policy. Without it the movement of the academic life is crippled and hampered at every turn. Mutual misunderstanding and mistrust are sure to creep in and impede that harmony of effort which is essential to a successful administration of the common trust.

Now, what is the bearing of all this upon the question of prolonged probation? It is this: that nothing contributes more effectively to the spirit of loyalty than the sense of confidence that one is no longer under suspicion of any sort whatever. Say what we will about the stimulating effect of a constant supervision, it is infinitely less than the stimulation of confidence. It is not merely the sense of security, great as the relief of that is. It is the spur of finding that one's effort is recognized beyond all cavil. It is the uplifting sense that one is fully admitted to partnership in a great and worthy undertaking. Looking back over my own experience I find that on twelve different occasions I was made to feel that my service was acceptable to the government of the university, and as I recall those occasions I feel anew the glow of satisfaction and the stimulus to renewed effort that accompanied them. And among these occasions one stands out above all the rest — the moment when, quite without any expectation of mine, I was given the duties and responsibilities of permanent appointment. It cannot have been the material advancement, for that was set at an irreducible minimum; it was certainly no overpowering conviction of my own value, for never before or since was I in a more humble frame of mind. It was the sense, almost greater than I could bear, of loyal determination to prove that so far as depended upon me the corporation had not made a mistake.

I draw from that experience and from long observation of many men the principle that university governments should be concerned with the question, "how short" rather than with the question, "how long" ought they in a given case to make the period of probation. Whenever they are satisfied that, barring accidents, the man is of the kind they need, it would generally be wise policy to bind him to their service by giving him the fullest possible share in the responsibilities of membership in their company of scholars. At present the only effective reminder to them of such wisdom is a "call" elsewhere. Into that painful subject I will not go. The ins and outs of it are familiar to all academic citizens. It may well be maintained that the loss of a good man in this way is readily made up by calling another equally good man in his place, and that such interchange of services is on the whole a wholesome incident of our academic system. This is all true, but it is not the whole truth. Back of all these outward considerations lies the appeal to that spirit of loyal coöperation among the several elements of the university body with which we are here concerned. Probation is good; but the deliverance from probation is better.

In making the comparison between the academic profession and those of the law and medicine I ventured to use the expression "picked men." Lest that

comparison should seem exaggerated it is well to remind ourselves that the modern professor is a picked
man in a very literal sense. He is picked first by some
natural endowment, in virtue of which he may be expected to be more successful in his chosen line of work
than others. He is picked again by a very long and
very arduous process of selection, and this process is
carried on by experts who watch at every step for indications of fitness and of unfitness for the career he has
in view. As his preparation advances the strain of this
constant inspection becomes more intense. One after
another the candidates fall out of the race. The sur-
vivors plod along through their repeated tests until
finally with more or less reluctance their judges grant
them the certificate which admits them, not to any
great reward, but only to the privilege of beginning a
still more arduous struggle. If they are fortunate
enough to obtain temporary positions they are again
subjected to long and expert observation. The community sees the cases of success; we on the inside know
the story of a long procession of silent failures, of
worthy men slipping quietly out of the competition
and accepting occupation, often more lucrative, in
other lines. Comparisons are always dangerous, and
one hears sometimes such as this: "Professor So-and-
So may be a very competent man, but what kind of a
lawyer or doctor would he have made?" There is only
one answer to this kind of comparison, and that is:
"What kind of a professor would your successful lawyer or doctor have made?" They have been picked by
the process which brought out their special endow-

ment. The professor has been picked by the process suited to his needs. It is fair that they should all be judged on an equal scale.

It is a pleasure to record that on the whole the tendency of things academic is in the direction of a policy of largeness and confidence in the treatment of the teaching staff. Truth requires us, however, to face the fact that the material rewards of scholarship are still not such as to weigh very heavily in the balance of a young man considering his chances in life. As we are venturing upon comparisons another distinction between academic and·other rewards may be pointed out. In other professions there is a certain direct and obvious relation between work done and the return. The lawyer or the physician undertakes a case; he expends so much effort and may claim so much compensation. Extra work counts for extra pay in something more than direct proportion; for success here brings not only immediate reward but draws more and more demand with a steadily increasing scale of prices for specialized service. A rising young city physician of my acquaintance was called to visit a patient at a summer resort and was kept in attendance during a long illness. Meanwhile another similar case presented itself in the neighborhood, and our young man returned to the city with six thousand dollars in his pocket. The college teacher, worn out as he is almost sure to be with his year of work, yields perhaps to the temptation of the Summer School, goes on wearing himself out still more and droops at the end with two or three hundred dollars to his account.

The best work of the scholar has no equivalent in material things. The book on which he spends his spare time and his reserves of strength for years brings him no money return. The text-book, often most successful when it is stripped of every scholarly quality, may prove an investment profitable in proportion to the lowness of the grade it reaches. The real contribution to learning, the laborious investigation, the long self-denial of years bring no other reward than the sense of a thing well done and the precious approval of the few who can understand. I shall never forget a remark made to me in the last year of his life by an elder colleague the fragrance of whose life was well typified by the roses he loved: "I have always dreamed of having a nice little place in the country with one of those great big Norman horses to drive back and forth to the station; but I shall never have it now." It was a modest ambition. His life would have been the longer and his work the richer for its realization but he would not sacrifice to it one iota of the precious time and strength he gave without stint to the unrewarded work that has made his name one of the glories of American scholarship.

Every observer of the academic life is conscious of the wear and tear of it, but the explanation of this is not always so clearly perceived. Study, we are told, is a very pleasant occupation. The man of affairs often says in all honesty: "There is nothing I should so much enjoy as a chance to study. In what little of it I can do I find the greatest happiness of my life." The president of a great railway system said to me: "I come home from a long day full of perplexing problems. I throw myself into an easy chair in my library and in the pages of some historian or in a book of travel I forget that there is a railroad in the world." So study, it would seem, is a rest rather than a weariness, and the life of the professional student is one prolonged repose. As to the teaching: we are well accustomed to the somewhat pitying expression that comes over the face of our man of affairs when he hears that we are, as he might say, "on duty" not more than six or eight or ten hours a week and that duty only the telling over again of a story we know so well that we could tell it in our sleep.

Well, study *is* a pleasant thing, but it is a pleasure to be compared, not to the irresponsible comfort of the railroad president "off duty" in his evening chair, but rather to the joy he feels when he has just made a successful "deal" or overcome some great engineering problem. Teaching too is a pleasure, but, done with the whole man, it is a pleasure like that of the lawyer before a court, which fills him for the moment with a glow of excitement but leaves him for some time thereafter a nerveless wreck. Study and teaching both make exacting demands upon the scholar's strength and vitality; but this is not the whole of it. The real strain, year in and year out, comes from a peculiar cause less urgent if not unknown in other professions, and, so far as I know, not reckoned with in the numerous popular descriptions of academic life. I mean the expenditure of force in keeping the mental machinery up to working pitch. Much of the work of the world can be done mechanically, and the more mechanically such work is done the better, because it leaves the worker so much the fresher for the severer effort. The scholar's work cannot be done in this way. If it is not done heart and soul, it is not done at all.

Again cautious comparison may help us. The lawyer, having finished one case turns at once to another that is calling him. The physician makes his daily round in obedience to definite calls. The clergyman has his weekly sermon to prepare and is besides summoned hither and yon by immediate calls he must obey. Even the business man, after his business is fairly started, is kept going by direct and peremptory demands of trade. All, of course, chafe at times under this incessant pressure from the outside, but they little realize how much help it is to them in overcoming the inevitable dead points in the rotation of human energy. It is a common saying that when a man has on hand a long job and a short one, it is always the short job that gets done. That is because it makes a definite, tangible demand, whereas the longer job, the work *de longue haleine*, can always be indefinitely postponed. The professor's work is of this type.

So far as his student world is concerned, he can keep himself right with that by a minimum of effort. His few regular appointments during the week he meets with little inconvenience to himself. During about four months of the year he can, without attracting any special comment, absent himself entirely from the scenes of his regular activity. All this sounds like a life of absolute liberty, a charmed existence free from the strain and fret of most human things. In reality he is the servant of a master more jealous than any clientele of the successful man of the world. Body and soul he has given himself to his profession, and his only aim is to get out of himself all he can in fulfilment of this obligation. Whatever his vices may be, laziness is not often one of them. The inalienable right to grumble he retains like other men, but the form his grumbling takes is usually that his powers or his opportunities for work are not what they ought to be. I cannot recall a case of complaint of overwork on the part of a colleague, unless it were of work of such a kind that it interfered with what seemed to him his highest professional activity. In many ways, to be sure, he is like any *employé* owing service in return for pay, but his service is so much the more exacting in that it is a service of honor. He has no master's eye upon him to check him in a momentary weakness. He may absent himself from his functions occasionally at will without giving account of himself. He may, for a long time, be neglectful of many details of his study without criticism. He is not controlled in the use of his time outside the regular tabular view. He may work in the morning or he may sleep till noon and sit at his books till daybreak. His original output is not produced at any word of command. It has to be wrought out of his innermost self by the force of personal self-control. There is never any positive reason why a given piece of work should be done at one time rather than at another. His only safety lies in making for himself a rigid division of his week and holding to it in the face of the

numerous distractions which the collective life of the
university continually offers. He has to be his own
taskmaster, and only those who have tried this know
what it means. It is almost as if an engine had not
only to do its work but to furnish also the energy by
which it is set in motion. That would be perpetual motion, and indeed the life of the professor, like the
proverbial life of woman, comes as near that impossible
achievement as is possible under human conditions.
His work is never done. It goes to bed with him at
night and rises with him in the morning. It can never
quite satisfy his own exacting standards, and he always
sees around the borders of the accomplished a wide and
never diminishing margin of the unattainable.

That brings us again to vacations. Ah! Happy professors! For three months of the year they are free to
wander as they will. They hie them to mountain and
seashore, and there, lying under the spreading shadows of the forest or floating on the surface of summer
seas they dream away the time until they are called
back to their pleasant labors of the autumn. Such is
the fancy picture so often drawn and firmly believed in
by those who see the academic life only from "the
front of the house." In fact there are very few members of a college staff who give themselves anything
like a full summer of idle recreation. Almost everyone
has work on hand which he has been putting off from
day to day in the pressure of term time and for which
he now sees, or thinks he sees, a clear space before him.
The academic stay-at-home finds no lack of companionship. He has sent off his family and entered upon

that "peace, perfect peace, the loved ones far away" which invites him to long hours of quiet work. He goes to the library, and, as he turns the corners of the bookstacks, one after another his colleagues appear, until he wonders if the whole Faculty is not in the same conspiracy. Others are with their families but within easy reach of library or laboratory. Others again have betaken themselves to their more distant summer homes armed with boxes of books and ready to attack the unfinished manuscript, the new edition of a classic text, the new course of lectures for the coming winter.

The establishment of summer schools has brought a new and very serious kind of pressure upon the university teacher. He is urged to this additional task by the sense of loyalty to his college and by the prospect of adding a pittance to his income. He is really worn out by the work of the year, or if not he ought to be, but the effect of that strain is not immediately felt. There is a certain exaltation of weariness which keys its victim up to new exertion. Every physician will bear witness to this fact. The tired teacher enters gaily upon his summer work, but he will almost certainly droop under it. Other forms of summer occupation have at least the merit of a change of work and of scene. The teacher is tied to the same spot and subjected to the same kind of strain as at other times. He is prevented from making any further profitable use of his vacation and goes back to his work of the next year with a diminished vitality that must tell upon his usefulness. Colleges ought to consider very seriously whether the good results of the summer term really outweigh this sapping of the energies of their best men. If the summer term is a necessity, if as the phrase now is "the plant must be kept going at capacity," there should be some system of "shifts" whereby the teaching force can be more evenly distributed and the wear and tear of the individual be measurably diminished. To suggest that in the intellectual life periods of complete rest, with that possibility of calm reflection which alone can place things in a true perspective, are actually periods of productivity is to invite the undeserved reproach of dilettantism. The razor's edge sharpens itself while lying idle, through the adjustment of the particles that compose it.

Therein lies the true value of the vacation. It is not, and it ought not to be a period of idleness, but of that *otium* which through wise activity keeps the mind in readiness for renewed action in the routine of daily service. Viewed in this way the incident of long vacations becomes indeed an attraction of the academic life, a legitimate attraction which may well influence a young man in striking the balance of opportunities before him. As for the shorter holidays at Christmas and Easter: they have almost entirely disappeared through the extraordinary growth of learned associations, the meetings of which every university man now feels it his duty to attend. These associations have proved of immense value during the past generation in creating and maintaining a quite new sense of common professional interest. They offer a medium of publication for the results of investigation; their meetings give valuable opportunities for comparing notes on methods and conditions of work; older men have there the chance to review the field of talent coming forward in their profession, and younger men gain a useful personal knowledge of those to whom they have been looking up as leaders in the way they are going. None can afford entirely to neglect these organizations, but even a very moderate devotion to them suffices to consume the entire time of the shorter holidays. To those who take an active part in the reunions of many sorts that properly and usefully accompany them they prove stimulating indeed, but not altogether refreshing. It is proverbial that three days of convention require at least a week of recovery.

Thus far we have been giving our attention mainly to those aspects of the academic life which may well cause the youth who is considering it among the possibilities of his future to pause upon the threshold and ask himself very seriously whether this is indeed the kind of life he wishes to lead. The sacrifice of public recognition; the narrowness of income; the long probation; the persistent pressure of work demanding a constant strain on the conscience and with no corresponding external advancement — these are all things to be weighed most carefully before a decision is made. The decision will after all have to rest upon that instinct for the right which even in a very young man gives the truest counsel as to what life is for. I remember asking a venerable German professor how it was that university authorities could allow a candidate for his profession after long years of training, and after

he had given every evidence of fitness, to serve the
university, perhaps for years, without pay or other
academic recognition. His reply was: "We regard the
position of university professor as so desirable and so
honorable that we propose to make the approach to it
as difficult as possible."

For Germany that was a perfectly satisfactory answer. Would it be equally so for America? With allowance for difference of conditions, I think it would.
The kind of obstacles we have been considering are not
such as daunt the spirit of an ambitious youth conscious of power and willing to work. Rather they are
likely to stimulate ambition and give him the feeling
that the work is worth doing because it will eventually
give him the things he values most highly. The desir-
ability of any position depends in the last resort upon
its social distinction. Sometimes this distinction expresses itself in terms of money and what money can
buy, and if the things so bought are worthy things,
then this is an honorable distinction and money-mak-
ing becomes a worthy pursuit. But there is a social
regard which money cannot buy, and it is a just source
of pride that on the whole, in civilized America, the
scholar, definitely excluded from consideration on the
ground of wealth, is respected for his calling. In fact
the scholar who inherits wealth or acquires it by mar-
riage falls under a certain suspicion of slackening in the
motive power of his life and must justify himself by an
increased tension of application.

Many years ago a rich young man of great promise
just finishing his college course came to me for advice

about further study. He outlined his plans with becoming modesty and added that his circumstances would permit him to spend as long a time in preparation as he might choose. I heard him through with interest, gave him what help I could and closed our conversation with a word of warning: "If you expect to succeed in the scholar's life you must make yourself believe that you are a poor man." He took my warning kindly, perhaps forgot it, but followed its spirit. He began at the bottom, took his punishment with his mates, earned his advanced degree, avoided the distractions that so easily beset the foot-free student abroad, started on the lowest round of the academic ladder and rose to the highest with the cordial esteem of his colleagues and the growing approval of the authorities.

Quite different was the attitude of another candidate, a man with his living to earn, who came to America after a residence of some years at a foreign university where his personal and social gifts had won for him an enviable reputation. He desired, as he might have phrased it, to "adopt the university career," but there was one hopeless flaw in his reckoning — he wanted to begin at the top. He would not put himself down to the task of building up from the bottom the foundations of patient study on which a serious candidacy could be based. So the university career refused to adopt him, and he drifted into more congenial occupation.

Neither wealth nor the absence of it has any specific relation to the consideration enjoyed by the academic person. His social status depends upon the regard for learning in the community in which his lot is cast. A young man of parts coming to a great eastern university said to me: "You cannot imagine the relief it is to be in a place where people are not all the time asking me why I am such a fool as to be spending my time over books when I might be making big money in some decent business." That state of things has distinctly changed with the wider spread of civilized conditions. On the whole it is safe to say that to-day the college citizen may assume that he will be *persona grata* in any society which may seem to him worth cultivating. If such association involves the spending of more money than he can afford he cannot have it, as he cannot have many other pleasant things; but ordinarily this is not the case. The man of learning, provided, of course, that he is otherwise acceptable, can look forward to as "good society" as the community affords. He can accept hospitality as it is offered and can return it in such fashion as fits his purse without fear that any one worth considering will think the less of him. A recent magazine gave a would-be pathetic sketch of the social miseries of a young couple in their first year of academic life. The pathos fell flat because the couple were silly persons, each in his own way, and the academic community was represented by a clique of hopeless snobs. Those are not normal American conditions. No person has a right to any more social regard than his personal quality can command, and academic society is the last place for the display of fictitious superiorities.

An evidence of popular respect and confidence is to
be found in security of tenure. Americans are proverbially jealous of long tenures of public office. Only
here and there has this jealousy been so far overcome
as to admit of life appointments for judicial officers.
It is, therefore, a matter for congratulation that life-
tenures for university professors are as widely established as they are. True, such appointments for life are
seldom or never guaranteed, but practice, and a sentiment stronger than any contract have made them the
rule in most of our older communities, and the newer
are falling into line as they come more and more to appreciate the importance of education in the making of a
state. Nearly a generation ago a western university
president of long experience and accumulated wisdom
gave to a young candidate for a university presidency
this advice: "Don't turn out *all* your professors in
the first year." To-day that advice would hardly be
needed. Insecurity of tenure is the natural accompaniment of ill-advised appointment, and all those
factors in the preparation of candidates which we have
been considering as so many deterrent agencies show
their value also as so many guarantees of good appointment and therefore as justification for security of
tenure. We have every reason to hope that as appointments become increasingly difficult, and probation is
more effectively enforced, the conditions of tenure will
improve in proportion.

Another evidence of public consideration is the increasing readiness of communities to look to the universities for expert service of many kinds. Passing by

the monumental instance of a president of the United States who served his apprenticeship as a university professor and then as university president, one recalls without effort professors of law appointed on legislative commissions for the reform of procedure, professors of economic science on state tax commissions, professors of geology in charge of state and national surveys, and a long series of professors serving on school boards and otherwise doing public duty in educational matters. The list of university men who have been employed by our government upon long and arduous and delicate negotiations with foreign powers is a striking and honorable one. It may fairly be said that it depends only upon the quality of the man how far he may be brought into relation with public affairs.

I speak of this here only to illustrate the consideration of our public for the profession of the scholar. I am not referring to it as a motive for the ambitious youth looking forward to the academic life. It would be a misfortune if his mind were to be directed to any other goal than that of the highest distinction possible to him within the limits of the profession itself. To make his profession a means of attaining distinction elsewhere would be to belittle it in his own eyes and in the estimation of the community in general. It is a wholesome sign that the community should turn to the university for expert service, and universities will do well to make it possible for their members to respond to such calls for brief periods. The reaction upon their proper work cannot fail to be beneficial, provided only that they be not thereby led to think of this proper work as something less important or less worthy than the "larger" service.

But these are all external and material considerations. There are others involving more nearly questions of the inner life. If the academic career can seldom offer the attractions of the world of affairs, it has the charm of freedom from its anxieties and its strifes. In most other occupations there are inevitable competitions and rivalries full of stimulation to energy but bringing men down every now and then to the primitive law of the survival of fitness with its heart-breaking accompaniments. What one gains another loses; the weakest to the wall! *Vae victis!* In the academic life there is indeed competition, plenty of it, from bottom to top; but it is never a competition in which the gain of one is a loss to another. In the world of knowledge the success of each contributes to the advancement of all. The rivalries of the scholar are the wholesome strife in which both parties are always victorious. He who makes the final discovery, deciphers the precious manuscript, or solves the riddle of the historian, conquers, not those who have striven with him in the same endeavor, but the obstacle itself. His rivals are his colleagues and his friends, and they profit by his success as much as he. In the rivalries of commerce the discoverer or the inventor of some new thing hastens to protect himself by law against the encroachments of competitors. In science the discoverer seeks only to proclaim his results as soon as they are established, that others may build upon them and rise to still greater heights. Now and again, to be sure, one meets a scholar, it may be a very eminent one, who finds his special satisfaction in belittling and begrudging the success of another, but such a man is the pariah of the academic society, not its type.

More too than in most other occupations the rewards of the scholar and teacher are found in the work itself. He is drawn into his profession primarily by some special attraction it has for him, and this attraction grows naturally greater as he goes deeper and deeper into his subject. The inevitable drudgery and monotony of his routine he comes to think of as the price he has to pay for the privilege of doing the thing in which, on the whole, he takes the greatest delight. His problem is to keep the routine from obscuring the larger and higher satisfactions of his life. Sometimes, under the stress of the daily round, it seems to him as if life were very much of a treadmill with an immense amount of treading to a very small proportion of power gained. But then, quite unexpectedly, some little turn of the wheel opens up a new glimpse of possibility. He feels the power really working and accomplishing something. Long standing puzzles seem to be clearing themselves up. Results are actually visible. Something may be put aside as really done at last, and one goes on again with the routine enlarged and brightened by the vision of success.

Academic rewards are few and slow in coming, but they are extremely precious. Their value comes, not merely from their rarity, but because they are unmixed with any alloy of baser motive. One goes on teaching week in and week out, putting one's whole life into it and wondering from day to day at the unresponsiveness of youth. A sense of failure haunts one's thoughts and makes one question whether it is worth while after all. But then, it may be years afterward, there comes to one out of that same unresponsive group, a word of gratitude, a reminder of some chance remark of ours which has turned the current of a young man's thought, and we are ashamed of our depression and our little faith.

One often hears this perpetual contact with youth referred to as one of the chief dangers of the academic life. Youth, we are told, is so uncritical, so ready to take us for more than we are worth. We must suffer from it as the clergyman proverbially suffers from over much dealing with admiring women. All this is partly true. The teacher like the clergyman feels at times the temptation to lean too hard upon his official character and too lightly upon the legitimate sanctions of his subject and his own interpretation of it. I doubt, however, if academic teachers who appeal directly and naturally to the student mind find it an uncritical mind or one over ready to take them at their price rather than at its own. In mere knowledge, of course, the student world owns its inferiority at once; but as to every other academic quality it has its own standards and enforces them at times with the remorseless cruelty of the youthful savage. Well for the superior person if early in his career he touches upon this stratum of primitive humanity in his students and learns to respect it. But woe to him if he presumes too far upon their simplicity! At some unexpected moment he will find his assumed superiority toppling over in hopeless ruin.

But in fact this is such an obvious danger that it must be a very dull person who should surrender himself easily to it. The man of sense recognizes it at the start and begins at once to feel it as only another aspect of what ought to be one of the greatest charms of his academic experience. This continual contact with minds that are all facing forward is a happiness we can thoroughly appreciate only when our own minds begin to be divided between the forward looking and the backward looking views of life, with a certain increasing tendency toward the backward. It is then especially, if we are wise, that we learn to refresh our sometimes failing hope and courage at these ever renewed springs of energy and faith.

One of our most devoted teachers and most famous scholars used to say in his moments of semi-depression: "We shall never have a university here till we get rid of all the students." Another expressed the same sentiment: "If it weren't for these plaguy lectures what a pleasant life this would be!" Now neither of these eminent men meant quite what he said. For the moment each was feeling rather heavily the burden of his teaching as a check upon the other and to him more precious work of pure scholarship he was trying to do. For that moment each had lost sight of the debt his scholarship itself owed to the reaction of the young life that had surrounded it. Certainly neither of them would have been willing to miss the tributes of grateful affection which brightened the closing years of their academic lives.

The obvious corrective against an overplus of youth is to be sought in the companionship of elders and equals in age, and, after all is said, it is here that is to be found the greatest happiness of the university career. The scholar gives up the great world, but he enters into a little world as free from the meaner passions as any human society is likely to be. In his study he enjoys the immense privilege of an inviolable solitude, but when he leaves his study he feels himself at once an active member of a society of kindred tastes, of quick response to the best that he has to offer and with professional aims for which he has comprehension if not understanding. He may make what excursions he can into the larger world, but it is here that he will have to look for the intimate associations and the real satisfactions of his life. True, in these days of specialization he can hope to enter into the technical detail of the work of but a few of his colleagues, but our day is no more remarkable for its specialization than it is for its marvelous revelation of the essential unity of method in all science. If specializing tends, as it certainly does, to divide men pretty sharply into technical groups, it is one of the functions of the academic unit we call the university to remind them in every way that they are but parts in a something greater than the several sciences they represent.

Membership in this unit brings with it the privilege which the isolated scholar can never enjoy of constantly verifying the method of one science by comparison with others. The historian learns from the physicist, and the biologist from the philosopher, many a thing that will illuminate his own science. The man who withdraws himself from such association suffers inevitably. A mathematician once confessed to me early in his career that he had so confined himself to the mathematical process that he had lost the power of following an ordinary train of reasoning by other than mathematical principles. A very eminent philologian who had spent the best years of his life in making a dictionary was accustomed to deplore his incapacity for logical and continuous thought. In both these cases it was conspicuously true that the usefulness of the man in his own sphere was sadly diminished by his limited conception of his function as a scholar. The free give and take of the university offers ample scope for specialization, but tends to preserve the specialist from the worst dangers of learned narrowness. If the university man fails to see his opportunity, buries himself in his books, willing to let the devil pipe to his own, that is his own mistake and, consciously or not, he is the worst sufferer from it.

In retrospect the dominant feeling in regard to the academic life is not of its burdens or its limitations, but of the happiness of it. To the young man weighing the chances of the future I would leave no better message than this: It is a happy life.

WHAT TO DO WITH A BOY?

A FRIEND of mine, a man of wealth and real culture living in an agreeable suburb of a large western city, wrote me to inquire as to the very best school
at which his sons might, as the phrase is, prepare themselves to enter Harvard College. The inquiry was in
several ways characteristic of the American state of
mind in regard to the education of a boy between the
ages of ten and eighteen. The father used the phrase
"prepare for Harvard College" because that was the
idea uppermost in his mind as he thought of the immediate future of his sons. The boys were to enter
Harvard College; that was the one fixed point in his
outlook. They would enter at about eighteen, and the
handiest summary of their life during several years
previous to entrance was that of a "preparation" for
college. It probably never occurred to the father, as it
seldom occurs to American fathers situated as he was,
to consider that precisely these years of the boy's life
had most important bearings upon his whole future,
and that this relation to the whole future was of far
greater moment than their relation to the immediate
future of the college course.

Furthermore, it was not merely the college that filled
the foreground of this anxious father's thought. It was
one particular college, and it was with a view to getting
light upon the best way of preparation for entrance
there that he did me the honor to consult me as a supposed expert. That there was such a "best" way, he

did not doubt, and the form of his inquiry showed that he thought I could answer it promptly and very briefly. In this respect also I think he was typical of his kind. The same question: what to do with a boy? arises in hundreds of American homes, and in every case the search is for some "first best" school, where all the highest requirements of the modern favored boy shall be met. In fact, my answer was rather longer than one ordinarily can make to such inquiries, and I was much interested in its reception. For some time I received no word from my friend; but then came an almost pathetically grateful response. The delay, he wrote, was because my letter had been sent around through the various family connections most concerned, and the effect of it had been a feeling of general relief. The gist of my advice had been that the boys should, if possible, be kept at home. Deep down, this had been the wish of the family also, but they had supposed, unwillingly, that the "preparation" thus to be obtained would not be of the "best" variety and were correspondingly relieved by my "expert" opinion. The sons were kept at home until the last year before their entrance into college, and were then sent to a school of the type to which I had given a certain qualified approval.

It has seemed to me possible that the reasons for the advice given then to a personal friend might be of interest to a larger audience. That the general question: what to do with a boy? should interest so many American families is a fact at once significant and hopeful. It is significant first of the absence of any general standards in regard to the education of our youth. Comparing class for class with any civilized European country the difference here is most striking. The "best" way for the well-to-do English boy is clearly marked from the beginning. He will be sent to a so-called public school, which means an endowed school not conducted primarily as a business enterprise by a private person. Such a school stands ordinarily in some relation with one of the two great universities of Oxford and Cambridge, so that the progress of the youth from school to college is at least indicated pretty clearly from the outset. The British public freely criticizes its educational system, and this criticism produces gradual changes in administration; but on the whole the system itself has remained singularly uniform and continues to appeal powerfully to those elements of society which give tone to English life.

Much the same may be said of Germany and France. There too there is a distinctly best course for the normal youth. It is determined to a far greater extent by governmental activity. It is much more definitely related to professional life; but its appeal to the ordinary studious youth is equally strong. In no other way can he reach the results he and his family naturally set before themselves in planning his career. It is only in the case of exceptionally endowed or exceptionally incapable individuals that any acute problem arises. Ordinarily the successive stages of the national schools are passed through without any special crisis at which the question of method presses for an answer.

In America no such universally accepted standard exists. We pride ourselves indeed upon our system of public schools in which, we like to tell the foreign visitor, every boy and girl in the land may receive an education in the rudiments of learning without cost. We point to splendid buildings equipped with every device for this universal training. We show the figures of state appropriation for this purpose and regret only that they do not bear a still larger proportion to the rest of the public outlay. We conceal from ourselves and others that there are vast areas of our country into which the blessings of free education have not penetrated, and we readily forget the alarming percentages of illiteracy revealed whenever, as in the case of the recent war, our adult population is subjected to rigid statistical inquiry.

But, taking our public school system at its best, we Americans are inclined to treat it as we treat many another privilege that lies close to our hand. We praise it as the palladium of our liberties, the essential instrument in that mysterious process we call "americanization," the glory of our free institutions, the noblest witness to that idealism we like to think of as our chief national trait. It stands to us as the most vivid expression of that democracy we all worship in the abstract and so few of us practise in the concrete. For the curious fact is that, in spite of all our glorification of the public school, one of the first instincts of the American parent, the moment he feels himself well enough off in this world's goods, is to deny his children the precious privilege of sharing its blessings. He continues to defend it in theory. For other people's children it is a magnificent asset. For his own there must, he feels, be

something better. Just as he will give them better
clothes, a better house, better social surroundings, or,
as he would say, a better "chance," so he begins to cast
about him for a better education.

Wherein this improvement is to consist he has not a
glimmer of an idea. He only knows that while the
thing near at hand is undoubtedly good enough for the
multitude, he has won for himself through his effort in
life the right to something different. Especially if this
parent has himself been obliged to be content with the
means of education offered by public provision, he is
likely to be all the more determined that his children
shall not be subjected to the indignity of this handicap.
Only the best will do for them, and the best is according to the standards familiar to him, that which costs
the most — costs in money and in sacrifice. It is a
noble instinct; the logic of it is plausible, and the excuses for its exercise are readily found. It rests upon
that sound principle to which we owe all the best in
American life, the principle that the welfare of a community depends upon a constant effort to improve,
never to be content with what we have, but to strive
constantly for something that eludes us, to be willing to
experiment and not be discouraged by failure.

As long as parents are saying "I want to give my
child every advantage in the game of life, and especially
those advantages I lacked myself" there is hope for the
Republic. It is a spirit no wise adviser would wish to
quench. The critical question it raises is, what "advantages" are. The parent means by the word, positive and direct helps for his boy toward the ends he has

in view. He thinks most of all of the removal of what he feels to have been obstacles in the way of his own progress. He says to himself "if only I had had this or that kind of help at the right moment, how much easier it would have been for me to do what I wanted to do." Now in this reflection of his mature life he is probably wrong. The chances are a thousand to one that what he now conceives of as obstacles were really so many spurs to his own energy. Not in spite of them, probably, but because of them, he has reached that measure of success which now enables him to do for his children what he thinks he wishes somebody had done for him. The world moves; everything is being improved; the new must be better than the old; nothing short of the newest, and therefore the best, will do for the favored youth in whose welfare he is most concerned.

Moved by some such reasoning as this, the conscientious but perplexed parent begins his inquiries as to where he can find the solution of his problem. The names of a few well-known schools are familiar to him, but they are only names. Why one should be preferable to another is not clear to him. The one thing clear is that he must send the boy away, and here is where I should be glad, if it is possible, to say to him what I wrote to my inquiring friend, and perhaps to give him an equal relief. As a general proposition, I believe it to be true, that for the normal American boy, the best place is the normal American home. By the normal boy I mean just what the word implies, one who is not distinguished by any such gifts or deficiencies as indicate the need of any special treatment. By the normal home I mean one in which there exists no specific obstacle to the reasonable development of a child.

These definitions suggest two cautions against errors of judgment frequently observed in those responsible for the education of a boy. The first is against the notion that the boy is "peculiar," a favorite delusion of parents, encouraged and even deliberately cultivated by educational doctors of many types. In a sense, we may almost say that every boy is abnormal. Every one has qualities that mark him from all the rest, and authorities differ as to the wisdom of cultivating these qualities or trying, as far as possible, to repress them. On the one side we shall be told that only through the full development of these special characteristics can the most complete personality of this individual be attained. On the other we shall be warned that this course will produce a warped and one-sided character, lacking in all that belongs to a well-rounded ideal of a human being.

The wholesome attitude of the parent toward his hopeful son is that in all probability he is very much like other boys, a puzzling mixture of good and evil propensities, of capacities and incapacities. The puzzle is not going to be solved by any rule of thumb, by any prescriptions of educational experts. It is going to untangle itself gradually through the growth of the boy in body and in mind. Sooner or later the boy will classify himself, roughly at first, more precisely afterward, but this process of classification will in all probability be a long one. It will probably cover a period much longer

than any which the parent has in view, and for that
reason he need not greatly concern himself with it. He
will do the best for his son if for the present he thinks
of him as quite an ordinary human being, a bundle of
possibilities, but not much more. It will be well if all
the evidence of his phenomenal qualities during the
nursery years can be forgotten. My friend the Dean
used to say: "If only these office mothers wouldn't tell
me what beautiful babies their scapegrace sons used to
be!"

A word here as to expectations arising from inheritance. The man of business who sees a vision of his
son following his lead, succeeding to his own interests
and building up the fortunes of his house to still greater
heights is a familiar figure in our literature. His disappointments furnish the pathetic element in many a
romance of American life. Even more pathetic is the
attitude of the man of learning, the scholar, the clergyman, the lawyer, the writer, who dreams of a son who
shall carry on still further the tradition he has made
honorable. Such a man is especially likely to plan the
education of his boy from the beginning with a view to
this consummation. He assumes that the same impulse
which led him to sacrifice everything to the cause of
learning is going to reappear in the next generation
and do the same work. Let such a parent stop and cast
about him for illustrations. Here and there is a family
that for several generations has seemed marked by a
striking continuity of taste and capacity. Certain
special aptitudes "run" as we say, "in the family," but
these indications do not go very far as guides in the

planning of a boy's school life. Far safer to disregard them and treat the youth as a very commonplace individual, much like his mates in the average of his qualities, however much he may seem to be distinguished from them by certain superiorities or certain defects. Of one thing the parent may be quite sure: if heredity, through the accumulation of generations, is going to affect greatly the course of his boy's life nothing that he can do will have very much effect in the long result. Our knowledge of heredity is still but elementary. Its working is too subtle to be reduced to any workable formulas. As we watch our children it seems at times to be determining absolutely their tastes and their accomplishments, but again these seem to be just as completely opposite to everything heredity would lead us to expect.

To say that we often confuse the influence of heredity with that of environment is to state a commonplace, but the remark may be of service here. In a condition of society where class distinctions are fairly fixed, the son succeeds the father almost as a matter of course, and then we say that the son inherits the tastes and capacities of the father. In reality it may not be a matter of inheritance at all, but only the perpetuation of a tradition too firmly fixed to be easily changed. It is a social or an economic phenomenon, not a physical or a psychic one. At the present time one may almost say that there are no such fixed traditions. Classes cross and recross with the utmost freedom. I asked a famous German theologian in the days before the war whether any of his seven children were preparing to follow in his footsteps. "Only one," he answered sadly, "and that a daughter. The boys all want to be engineers!" A few days ago the university granted a high degree in theology to a youth who had begun life as an engineer. And so it goes. Heredity may determine moral qualities, but the parent who should allow his mind to dwell very much upon the possibilities in this respect is doomed to many and great disappointments.

The second caution touches the phrase "the normal home." To enlarge a little upon the brief definition already given: I do not mean a home which is in any special sense a center of light and leading, where the intellectual life is specially cultivated or even where the virtues are illustrated with any special brilliancy. The more of all these good things, of course, the better, but the absence of them in some degree does not disqualify the home as the place where the boy is best off during those formative years we are here considering. His parents may not be the models his maturer judgment would select as the best for him to follow. This might be a better world if we were all permitted to select our parents, but it would certainly not be this world. The grim fact is that the boy belongs to these parents, and they belong to him. All that he is and all that he has comes to him through them. He begins to see the world through their eyes, and only gradually comes into the critical attitude toward them. He enters from the start into the motives that animate them, he shares their struggles in the conflicts of life, feels their sacrifices, understands something of their

ambitions, suffers with them in their failures and triumphs in their successes. His measure is a different
one from theirs, but so far as it goes its standards are
the same. Everything tends to deepen and strengthen
the impression conveyed by the one phrase, that they
belong together.

And what is true of the parents is equally true of the
place in which the boy's lot is cast. It also need not
provide him with precisely the environment he would
have chosen, but, as the master hand of English romance wrote, "We cannot choose our duties," and his
duty lies here and not elsewhere. It is not a primary
question whether the place of his origin provides a
"best" school or natural surroundings best fitted to
give him scope for his ranging spirit, or great libraries
to feed his curiosity, or a society that may — or may
not — teach him the manners we should like him to
have. These are all secondary requirements. The essential point is that this is where the boy belongs. He
belongs to the place and the place belongs to him, for
him to make use of in all the ways his growing powers
and expanding nature demand. It is a false pedagogy
which calls upon families to send out their boys searching by external processes for the things that can come
only through the awakening of the inner impulse, and
which, if that impulse is once awakened, will come. It
is idle for the dweller in a cabin to push his boy out
looking for electric lights to read the latest and best by.
Let him throw a pine knot on the open fire and see
what the boy will do with a dogs-eared primer after his
day's work as a member of the family!

Exceptions? Of course there are. Families are broken up; homes are desolated by selfish passions; fathers lose themselves in the mad race for more and more wealth to feed the insatiable call of mothers for more spending. Mothers sink into the empty whirl of "society" and make the word "home" a travesty of everything it ought to mean. From such homes as these the remote school may be deliverance. Or again, specific requirements for admission to a college may make a year or two of residence at a school almost imperative. Provision must be made for exceptional cases, but what I am insisting upon is that the separation of the normal boy from his normal home should frankly be understood as an exceptional and in itself an undesirable thing.

This insistence is made necessary at the present time because there is a widely spread and growing sentiment among our well-to-do classes that precisely the opposite is true. The boarding school, no matter how remote, is represented as the ideal place for the making of a man. The local school is scorned, not primarily because it is inadequate, but simply because it is local. There are schools with long waiting lists upon which the names of candidates are entered as soon as they are born. Not to succeed in placing their boy in such a school would seem to these parents a failure in their highest duty toward him. They think of it, not as a necessary evil, but as the greatest good. They do not act upon a reasoned consideration of what the boy is to lose, but only upon a vague notion of something he is to gain. They know little of the

actual conditions of boarding-school life and are probably about equally ignorant of the advantages or
otherwise of the schools near at hand. They are governed by considerations primarily social, and "social"
is in these days a word of very elastic meaning.

My thesis on this point is that the very greatest
"advantage" an American boy can have is to strike
his roots deep down into the soil of some place which
he can call his own. Every gardener knows that the
worst thing you can do in a dry time is to sprinkle the
surface of your ground. That treatment draws the
roots upward, and exposes them to the blasting rays of
the pitiless sun. The wise gardener stirs the surface
and only at long intervals digs down deep beneath the
roots and fills the lower earth with water to draw the
thirsty roots farther and farther downward. The root
system of a man responds to similar treatment. Keep
the tiny fibres near the surface and they grow constantly weaker; send them down into the moist, cool
spaces of the under soil, and they will gather strength
and throw out new branches to seek still new life and
transmit it to stem and leaf.

It is of the highest importance to the future citizen
of the American democracy that he should feel himself from the first a member of a true social unit. First
of the family, then of the neighborhood, then of the
town and the state. I say, a *true* social unit, and what
makes it true is that the boy comes into it by natural
processes, without reflection of his own or the conscious planning of any one else. It is all his, just as his
body and his soul are his. That means that he has to-

ward this social unit certain obligations. As a member
of the family he is bound to help in carrying forward
the work of the home, to be responsible in his degree
for his part of the family life. As a member of the
larger community he is bound to respect its laws, to
help make it a cleaner, a safer, and a happier place. In
a natural community, where there is wholesome mingling of industry and trade and rational living, the boy
feels himself from his earliest years part and parcel of
all these things. The movement of the community
catches him up into the current of its varied life and
carries him on to happy usefulness.

Contrast this opportunity with that of the best endowed, best equipped, best organized, best intentioned
boarding school. After all that can be said, this proud
aggregation of "bests" is an institution, and the boy
adjusted to its well-oiled machinery is an institution-
alized being. It is only by a fiction that he can be
called a "member" of the institution at all. To be a
member of anything means to be a living, organic part
of it, with functions that no other member can perform, so that if this member be injured the function
ceases, and "all the members suffer with it." Cut off
the orphan from the asylum or the boy from the boarding school and nothing happens, but if the boy be cut
out from the family, or the neighborhood, or the town,
there is a loss that can never quite be repaired. The
reason is that the boarding school has no soil for the
roots that go to nourish the life of the individual as a
member of a true community. The youth entrusted to
its fostering care may be supplied from above and from

without with all the nourishment for body and soul he seems to require, but the tap-roots will not run down far because there is no water there.

It is a singular fact that institutionalism in education should have taken on such an extraordinary development at the very time when it is being repudiated in every other field of social effort. Our organizations for charity and for the physical and mental welfare of the community have long since come to see that the best results are obtained by distributing the persons needing help as widely as possible. We do not now send the dependent orphan into an "asylum," but into a family. We do this precisely because we want him to feel the pressure of necessity in the supply of his daily wants. We do not wish him to have food and clothing shed upon him like the gentle rain from heaven; we want him to take his little part in the struggle for existence. The older method we stigmatize as "pauperizing." Only in the education of our "best" youths we are more than ready to pauperize. We deliberately deprive them of the very advantages we are so anxious to give to our really dependent classes. We pull them out of the natural relations into which they are happily born and set them into highly organized mechanisms, expecting these to do the work of the free but disciplined will.

But here we are met by the argument from England. Time out of mind, we are told, English boys have been sent away from home as early as possible, at the age of ten or twelve, and they have grown into the men who have made England great. Moreover these men have

not ceased to be home lovers and home makers; they
have gone on generation after generation building those
English homes which have become the home ideal for
all the peoples of the earth. The argument sounds convincing, but like most comparisons with foreign cus-
toms, it does not prove very instructive. There are too
many sides to it, too many questions bound up with it.
The English society which has sent its infant sons
away to school has always been in its essentials a rural
and aristocratic society. It could not keep its boys at
home and educate them in day schools for the simple
reason that such schools did not exist. The public
school in our sense of the word is a recent institution in England, and so far has had but slight effect
upon the general sentiment as to what is best for a
boy.

The English "public school" is above all else a social
institution. The public which supports it desires to
keep its sons aloof from those of another "class" by
placing them where they will meet only, or chiefly,
youths of their own kind. Do we really wish to import
this ideal into American life? If we do, let us acknowledge it frankly and not pretend to be leading the world
in democratic feeling and practice. The conditions
that produced the English system do not exist here.
Our social standards, so far as we have any, are not
rural but distinctly urban. To speak of a man as "in-
land bred" does not convey quite the impression of
culture in America that it did in Shakespeare's England. The city here does not imitate the country, but
the reverse. "Back to the land" means with us to

import into the country the standards of life we have learned to demand in the city. It is one of the results of this demand that our public free schools have penetrated, at least in theory, into every corner. Happily the wholesome practice among the "best people" of sending their sons to these schools has gone far to make them in a very true sense a social institution as well as an agency of learning. They have commanded a type of loyalty in every way comparable to that called out by the English school or by the private schools which have grown up to supplement them here.

We are not driven, therefore, as Englishmen have been, to send our sons away in order to have them as well taught as the standards of our society require, and more than this no system of education anywhere can be asked to provide. The boy in an American home learns to know the friends of his family. He listens to the conversation of his elders and his superiors; he knows what public events are interesting them and comes to feel that he has his part in them. Best of all, he grows up in natural and wholesome relations with women, young and old. The sacred mystery of sex impresses him long before he knows what it means, and in those critical years when he is first feeling its compelling allurement he is given a sweet and healthful sentiment about it that may hold him upright through many a storm of later temptation. There can be no safeguard for the youth so powerful as the constant thought of the women who have surrounded and beautified his childhood. That is an influence which the school cannot supply.

So I say: keep the boy at home, but make the home a consecrated place worthy of the high mission to which it is called. Alarmists are calling our attention to the dangers which to-day seem to threaten the very existence of our homes, and it is idle to deny that there are powerful and subtle influences at work to undermine those sanctities on which the homes of the past were built. But, as one looks about, one sees a steady flow of young lives launching out into the untried responsibilities of the future with the same courage, the same devotion, the same high hopes that sustained their fathers and mothers, and one feels the right to assume that the homes they are going to found will be indeed consecrated places where childhood will find its best development.

Let the home be a sanctuary of tenderness, but not of softness. Give the boy all the freedom of motion that a young growing organism demands. Let him make his own mistakes and, within reasonable limits, take the consequences, but let him feel that his home is the sure haven to which he may always return and where he is certain to find his ideals of justice and sympathy. Let him choose his own friends, but supply him always with the standards that shall help him to choose them wisely. His school will give him all needed security against the perils of coddling. The local school forms for him another center of interest and affection, and year by year the discipline of contact with his mates in the free give and take of school life will develop his independence of thought and action. Home and school work thus naturally together, carrying the boy along up to his sixteenth or seventeenth year in a harmonious development of his capacities and his affections. By that time he will be getting restless, and he ought to be. The limitations of school, the routine of home will begin to gall him a little, and then comes the time to put to the test all that has been done for him hitherto. Then he must spread his wings and fly, but not till then.

I wish that by what I have said so far I might have convinced some American parents that their boys will be better off at home than in any possible remote institution, but I am aware how strong the appeal of the highly organized and amply advertised establishment is. Not every parent has the rugged sense of the western father who made a careful inquiry into his son's conduct of life in a great eastern college because he "didn't want to be spending two thousand dollars a year on a two dollar boy." The typical American father is more than willing to spend money, and the typical mother of every race is ready to spend her affections as the price of bringing a man into the world. I asked the head of a famous boarding school whether the majority of parents sent him their boys gladly. "No" he replied "to most of them it is a heart-breaking experience. They do it because they believe it is best for the boy." The same master assured me that the chief obstacle to the entire success of his school in stamping upon its boys a definite school hall-mark was the unfortunate incident of vacations. For some months of the year the boys were allowed to feel that they had families, homes, relatives, friends, native towns and other inconvenient

belongings not always in entire harmony with the free-
masonry of the school.

So we are not dealing with an imaginary danger.
From both sides, from the side of the community and
from that of the schools the ideal of a separated school
life for boys of twelve to eighteen is in fact being presented to our people. It is commending itself, not by
any scientific definition, but by the subtle process of
social distinction and through the thinly disguised
imitation of foreign ways. Its attraction can be counteracted only by strengthening in every way the conviction here expressed, that, ideal for ideal, the very
theory of such an institution is a false one, and that for
the normal American boy up to the age of seventeen
the best place is a normal American home.

So far we have been speaking of ideals; but it must
be confessed that circumstances often arise which com-
pel a departure from the ideal. Many homes are not
normal, and are not likely to become so. Day schools
even tolerably adequate are not everywhere accessible. There is a legitimate sense in which the query
we are trying to answer becomes a pressing one and
must be answered. I visited in a military school not
far from New York a class of thirty boys of from fourteen to nineteen studying, for the first time in their
lives, the geography of the United States. These boys,
some with bass voices, did not know where the Mis-
sissippi river was, nor what states touched its banks.
In answer to my inquiry, in what uncivilized corner of
the world they had spent their early years the Principal
replied: "Most of them come from New York City, and

if I should tell you their names you would be still more surprised." "The fact is" he went on to say, "their fathers are too busy with business and their mothers too busy with pleasure to know much about them. They are handed over to nurses and governesses until, all of a sudden, the parents wake up to the idea that their children are growing up in ignorance. Then they look about for schools, and we get our share."

Nor can it be denied that, in spite of all the cautions we have been urging, there are boys in whom some peculiar quality of mind or character makes separation from home at an age earlier than the college period desirable. It may, then, be helpful to some anxious parent lost in the maze of glittering advertisements that embellish the pages of our magazines, to hear, even from one who claims no authority whatever for his information or his judgments, a brief classification of the types of school offered for his choice. In making this survey we shall follow as nearly as may be the order suggested by the resemblance of the several school types to the ideal we have set forth above.

To come as nearly as possible to the conditions of a good day school in the boy's own town, it may be worth remembering that in many cities there are excellent public high schools to which a non-resident pupil may be admitted for a very modest fee, and that in such a city it is often possible to find a family where the boy can be placed under conditions so closely resembling those of his home that in all outward respects the difference is hardly worth remarking. It is not, to be sure, his own place, but it becomes his by adoption.

He is in a home, though it be an adopted one; he has the natural surroundings of an orderly society; he is under the wholesome restraints of a community whose interests he may learn to share. The unspeakable loss of his own family life is made up to him by substitutes which are not purely fictitious and are as far as possible from being institutional. I do not hesitate to say that, if the boy must go away, this device is likely to give as good results as any other.

The type of institutional school which comes nearest to the local public or private day school is that venerable New England product, the country or town academy. It is not confined to New England, but wherever found it partakes of the character given to it in the older communities of the East. It owes its foundation often to the piety of some private citizen who gave to it the modest endowment that carried it through the early years of its strictly local usefulness. It served ordinarily as a day school for the town, but received pupils from the neighboring country at a low rate of tuition. It might or might not have dormitories of its own. The traditional method of caring for the outside pupils was to house them with worthy citizens who were expected to stand *in loco parentis* to them. However diligent such supervision might be there was always a certain sense of freedom and its accompanying responsibility that had their educative influence upon the growing boy.

Even more, perhaps, than our colleges these old country academies have contributed powerfully to the intellectual life of their several communities. As time went on and the wave of sentiment in favor of free public instruction swept over the land these ancient foundations were in danger of being completely over-shadowed or replaced by the local high schools. That they have not entirely disappeared is owing to the good sense with which they have been adapted to the needs of the time. Their endowments, often increased by the gifts of successful sons, have been applied to en-large their equipment and thus make them more at-tractive to pupils from abroad. On the other hand the towns fortunate enough to have such an institution among their assets have contributed to its usefulness by adopting it as the local high school, paying it for the work of instruction required by the laws of the state.

In quite recent times many of these older schools have grown with almost dangerous rapidity. Endow-ments have been provided for them, and the increasing resort has enabled them to establish tuition fees com-mensurate with the ever increasing demands. The interesting thing in the development of these old acad-emies is that on the whole they have retained a great deal of their original character as representatives of a sound local sentiment. Some of them have become places of national resort, and in the process have not escaped the inevitable temptations to laxity and excess. These dangers, however, have been perceived in time and for the most part have been overcome. Without abandoning the traditions of freedom wise restraints have been provided, unwholesome tendencies checked and rational standards of living and working main-tained. The famous dictum of the honored head of one such school in his address to new pupils: "There are no rules here until they are broken!" expresses well the spirit of liberty in order which has marked the whole history of these typical products of our early, largely rural society.

In a school of this type the restraints are in many ways comparable to those of a well-ordered home. Just as in the home it is not the restraint of rule and compulsion that really helps in the upbuilding of personal character, but is rather the wise direction of a large liberty, so, in the easy and natural life of a half rural community there are restraints felt more or less unconsciously which may work in the same way. Doubtless the evils of a small community are often greater than those of a larger one, but there is always the wholesome corrective of publicity, and the boy who can persistently defy that is sure to have a pretty hard time of it wherever he is. The sentiment underlying the country academy, as it still exists in the older parts of our country is one of the most admirable incentives to honest work and cleanly living. It is doing well and is likely to do better under the new impulses of our active day. A boy placed under its influence is saved from a premature cosmopolitanism and is brought into a healthy competition with other youths whose opportunities in life may have been greatly superior to his own. Those who are responsible for him may safely feel that in sending him thither they are giving him a rational substitute for a boyhood at home.

Out of this class of local, rural academies there has been developed a group of large and highly organized

schools generally distinguished by the unfortunate
name of "fitting schools." The name is unfortunate
because it emphasizes one function of the school in its
relation to a higher grade of instruction rather than its
own proper mission as a preparation for life. It calls
attention too sharply and too exclusively to the standard of success represented by the passing of examinations for entrance to college and tends to diminish in
porportion all effort not directed to this end. Our
American education can never take the place it ought
to hold among the educational systems of the world
until each of its grades has a standard of its own set
firmly upon the basis of the specific work it has to do.
Elsewhere such standards are fixed by some supreme
authority which represents on the whole the ripest
judgment of those best qualified to judge. Here there
is no such authority, and we can only be thankful that
we have so far escaped the kind of standardization we
must have had if it had been entrusted to the kind of
tribunals we should have been sure to create. Meanwhile the only safe method of securing passable results
in the lower grades is to pull them up by some pressure
from above. To fit the higher to the lower is to drag
the whole structure down to disastrous failure.

The "fitting school," whether we like the phrase or
not is, therefore, a reality in our educational scheme.
The problem of those who have it in charge is to make
it so worthy a thing in itself that it will command the
respect of the community, not primarily because it "is
sure to get the boy into college," but because it is a
good place for a boy to learn to be a man. This prob-

lem has been clearly perceived by far seeing managers. A few years ago we were told with very great authority that our colleges were in danger of being wiped out of existence by the growth of such schools as these on the one hand and the professional schools on the other. This calamity has not happened, and we hear but little about it now. The warning interests us only as showing that the greater academies were becoming to a threatening extent the resort of boys whose liberal education was to end there. In other words that they were to that degree not "fitting schools" in the usual sense, but independent institutions with standards that appealed to a considerable public. That is as it should be. The parent seeking the best resort for his boy will feel himself freer in his choice if he is not restricted to the idea of getting him "fitted" to the requirements of college. And the school, on the other hand, will be strengthened in its whole attitude by the demand of the colleges for the very best it can do to satisfy them.

To say that the older academies are the outgrowth of the early New England spirit is only another way of saying that they had at first predominantly a religious character. They were but another expression of the uncompromising independence of New England Congregationalism, and that temper they have still largely preserved. Some of them have remained under a nominal denominational control, but even there the spirit of independence has been working with decisive effect. From time to time the religious organization may make a vigorous effort to give to its schools a predominantly sectarian character; but the happy inability of any denomination in these days to bring all of its members under any one description of faith is sure to prevent any such dragooning of the schools. There is a religious body in New England which has its academy, its college and its theological seminary. The academy is expected to feed the college and the college to feed the seminary, and then in turn the seminary is expected to furnish teachers both to the college and the academy. It is a scheme of intellectual inbreeding cleverly calculated to ruin the mind and corrupt the soul of the denomination that controls it. Happily, however, it does not work. The demand for excellence in each stage of education is too great.

An academy which should surrender itself to any such combination would find itself lagging behind in all the competitions that test its quality, and there would soon be enough clear-sighted men in the denominational ranks to insist upon fresh blood and a larger ideal. Indeed, the more strict the nominal control of a denomination, the more loudly its leaders to-day are wont to claim for it a thoroughly liberal administrative policy. It is safe to say that in the great academies of the East the denominational element is of little account so far as the instruction and discipline of the place are concerned. It is brought out on state occasions as a means of appealing to the loyalty of graduates and others upon whom its material support depends, but it may well be questioned whether a boy not verystr ong on his catechism would know whether he were under Baptist or Methodist or Congregationalist or even Unitarian influence. It is greatly to the credit of all concerned that, on the whole, the main effort of the past generation has been to make good schools rather than to hold them within precise theological limits. There have been notable fights, but the tendency is clear. With an increasing supply of well-trained teachers, not produced by theological seminaries, these well-endowed schools have been able to pick their men. They have been learning to respect the scholarly ambitions of their teachers and thus to raise the tone of their own scholarship. It is a pleasure to record here the extraordinary insight and self-control of the late Dwight L. Moody in the management of his school at Mt. Hermon, Mass. Although a religious place in a very emphatic sense, this school gave to its teachers and its pupils a freedom of thought and action quite in advance of that allowed at many a place of larger opportunity and loftier pretensions.

So far as the scholarly side of the question is concerned parents need have no hesitation in entrusting their boys to any of the schools we have here been trying to describe. The question of discipline, taking that word in its widest meaning, is the serious one. The principle of largest liberty, absolutely sound in the abstract, has to be administered, in the case of boys under eighteen with the greatest caution. A boy of fourteen — not to say of twelve — dropped into a community of from one to four or five hundred youngsters is put upon a strain for which a previous tempering is an essential. If the experiment works well, it may work very well; if ill, very ill indeed. The sound nature meets the strain and grows stronger under it. The feeble will, the pleasure-loving, self-indulgent temperament, not roused to interest either in work or play, is lost in such a place. If the boy ever finds himself it will be through the awakening of some impulse drawn out by the eager young life around him.

The best that can be said of the discipline of a great academy is that it is based upon the natural and spontaneous working of young human instincts, with faith that they will justify themselves if let alone. Of course the application of this principle will vary greatly in different hands. There is enough that is distinctive in it to mark off the large schools where it prevails into a class by themselves. The parent who selects such a place for his boy must do so with the full consciousness that the boy has his own salvation to work out. Such a school has no formula for the making of a man. It will take the boy, keep him at work, give him a chance to play, take care of his health and bring him up short when he has gone too far out of the straight way. But it is not seeking to put a stamp on him. It has no stamp which it recognizes as a guarantee of quality. It is satisfied if he does his work, keeps his health and goes no farther wrong than he can make good by repentance and honest effort.

This brings us naturally to another category of schools, which differ from the great academies chiefly in the fact that they do, more or less avowedly, seek to impress upon their pupils a certain stamp. These schools are in connection with the Protestant Episcopal Church in America, but are not, as a rule, under its

official control. Their principals and many of their
teachers are men who have advanced to one or another stage of that ministry. Their religious services
are conducted under the forms of the Anglican worship, and whatever religious influence they have is
toward conformity with these traditions. We may,
therefore, without prejudice describe them as Church
Schools.

They have also another quality which marks them
off into a class by themselves: they are based very
largely on English models. Their vocabulary is enriched with English words, they encourage the English
spirit in their sports; they have to a greater or less extent the English theories of self-government among
the boys. Unsympathetic critics would find in all these
matters a certain danger of affectation. Doubtless
each and all of these schools would repel with some heat
the charge of Anglicanism or of exclusive sectarian influence. They would defend their Americanism and
their liberality in religious matters to the last breath.
And in this defense they would be perfectly honest.
Their directors are not foolish enough to imagine that
American boys can be made into English men, or that
any one type of religious life can be made to include all
that there is of hope and safety for the future of our
society. The day is gone by when a school aiming at
the largest usefulness could venture to require of all its
pupils more than a formal conformity to its religious
usages or make itself the agent of any very active
propaganda.

Still the fact remains, that the group of schools we

are now considering has, in a sense quite different from
the other groups, a fairly definite ideal to which it
would be glad, if it could, to make its pupils conform.
The Church School is not quite satisfied that its graduates should have learned "to speak the truth and ride
horseback." It would like to fix upon their minds a
certain definite form of truth and to see them riding
horseback after a model approved by a great and ancient, even if it be a measurably foreign, tradition. It
will not force these things upon them; it will honestly
refrain from prescriptions and directions which might
call attention too sharply to the end in view. But, on
the other hand, it would be unfaithful to its trust, if it
did not, by every proper means, in the thousand and
one little details of daily life, gently and steadily build
up in the mind of the boy the ideal it has set before
itself.

Much more easily than the old-fashioned free
academies, the Church School may come to regard itself as a desirable substitute for even the best of homes.
It aims to get its boys young, so that, in their tenderest
years, while the affections of the child are still active,
it may win him to its plan and stamp its mark inef-
faceably upon him. It aims to make his relation to the
school the governing thing in his life. Its tendency is
to make him sink his individuality in the school ideal,
to work for that and through that. The principle of
liberty must necessarily play a lesser part in such a
plan of school life as this, and that is really what the
parent has to consider when he is thinking what to do
with his boy. It is not a question of this or that little

matter of detail in study or discipline, but whether, on
the whole, he desires to place his boy under the experiment of fitting him to any given ideal standard whatever. He may comfort himself with the reflection that
his boy will be strong enough to stand the strain or,
perhaps, indifferent enough not to perceive that any
strain exists. But then comes the further question,
whether the reaction against a system which, if not
successful, must appear tyrannical, would not be a
doubtful blessing to a growing boy. Under conditions
of greater freedom the youth who finds himself chafed
by one or another feature of his school discipline can
probably adjust himself without great difficulty; but
in the Church School the system as a whole counts for
so much, that, if it once began to gall, it seems as if life
under it would hardly be tolerable to a boy of independent spirit.

On the other hand, it cannot be denied that, if one
does respond to it, the attraction of the Anglican ideal
is very great. The regular and orderly movement of
this mass of well-meaning lads from their uprising in
the morning, through all the routine of study and play
to their lying down at night, without friction and with
utter good feeling is a most charming thing to look
upon. Even the absence of that occasional solitude
which many believe to be one of the most essential
elements in the making of a sound imagination, may
be overlooked in the wonderful charm of the whole.
Such schools have generally been fairly endowed and
through tuition fees higher, doubtless, than their
directors could wish, have been able to maintain a

standard of simple refinement of living which seems to reflect or to surpass the standards of the best homes.

As to scholarship, the danger which we have already described as "inbreeding" lies especially near to the avowedly Church School. Happily various causes have contributed to prevent this danger from becoming serious. For one thing, these schools have been anxious to draw pupils from as wide an area of population as possible, and with this in view they could not venture to draw their teachers exclusively from their own denominational ranks. They have had to seek the best wherever they were to be found and to make the conditions of residence as attractive as possible. It is a positive asset for them to be able to say that neither pupils nor teachers are to be subjected to rigid religious tests. Then again, they have had to prepare their pupils to enter the best colleges whether these were or were not in sympathy with their methods. They have had to face the wholesome competition of schools quite positively opposed to their theories, and this competition is not limited to college entrance examinations. Still more, in the far more serious tests of the college years the Church School has had to be always on its mettle to show that boys trained in its way can stand the strain intellectually and morally as well as any others.

It is not the place here to pass judgment upon the value of this comparatively new contribution to the resources of our country in the matter of secondary education. As the older academies were the outgrowth of Congregationalism with its spirit of independence, so these schools have grown out of a new emphasis upon ecclesiasticism with its spirit of conformity. The problem of the parent is to determine under which of these ideals of life and duty he prefers to bring his growing boy.

Another class of schools includes the private academies or "fitting schools" without endowment and without the backing of any special sentiment, religious or local. These are frankly business undertakings in which, as in all other business, the question of profit and loss must take precedence of all others. This is not to depreciate the sincerity of the effort made by conscientious masters to maintain high standards of scholarship and discipline. In the long run such standards are sure to prove the best investment; but the run may be a very long one indeed, and meanwhile the pressure toward lowering of standards is inevitably greater than where the safeguards of endowment or of corporate interest exist. The quality of such a school is absolutely dependent upon the personality of its principal. It is, therefore, impossible to lay down any general principles by which the claims of one or another institution of this kind can be judged.

A variety of the private academy is the so-called military school. Here the existence of a daily drill, the wearing of a uniform and the general military organization of the place are supposed to do for the boy very much the same kind of service which is expected from the less picturesque theory of the Church School. They are intended to cultivate a corporate spirit, a high standard of personal honor, a dignity of bearing and a sense of the responsibility of each for the welfare of all. It would be absurd to suppose that these admirable traits do not prevail in any of the military schools, but one may be permitted to doubt whether this is not owing to the personal quality of some individual rather than to any intrinsic merit in the system itself. The answer made to the writer by the principal of a military academy: "Without the military organization I would not undertake to run this school for a moment" seemed to be the all-sufficient explanation of its wretched quality. The incompetent man found in the military system a crutch by which he managed to keep himself going. It is possible that a competent man might find it a useful tool, but for him it would certainly not be an indispensable one. It is not machinery of any kind, military or otherwise, that will save the soul of a boy. Beyond that there is not much to be said.

The same is true, even in a higher degree, of still another class of schools, the strictly limited Home Schools, of which the name is legion. Here the personal element is the all-determining factor. The attraction of such a place to the inquiring parent is the hope that his boy may receive there the kind of "personal attention" which he fancies may be the best substitute for the influence of his home. The limited numbers seem to insure continuous watchfulness and helpfulness. On this point we have already said enough to show the danger of the whole theory of "special treatment," but there remain cases where, to use a medical phrase, such treatment seems "indicated," and it is a function of the home school to supply it. One of its chief advantages is that the boy may here be brought into wholesome relation with women of refinement and find thus, in some measure, a compensation for the unspeakable loss of his home life. It hardly needs to be said that, just in proportion to the greater intimacy of the home school, greater care is needed in its choice. As to this, there is no resource but the parent's sense for what is best and soundest in a home. One is tempted to say that a parent who knew how to select a home school for his boy would thereby prove himself the best person in the world to make a home for him.

This suggests a device rather more common a generation ago than it is now, by which parents of large means and generous intentions thought to avoid the ills of remote boarding schools for their sons by keeping them strictly at home and employing resident tutors for their instruction and entertainment. At first thought and in view of all that has been said here this might seem the very most desirable plan. It would seem to be supplementing all the good of family life by introducing into it a stimulating and broadening influence. The young tutor thus brought into close relations with the family is supposed to be a kind of elder brother to the younger fry, leading them in study and in sport, setting their minds to work on the glories of the distant college life to which they are destined and meanwhile encouraging them at every stage of their progress thither. All this under the watchful eye of parents ready with curb or spur to correct any immediate danger of excess. It is a pretty picture; but one has only to consider the almost infinite difficulties of the situation thus created to realize how small are the chances of success. The selection of a young man to whom one would be willing to entrust such responsibility is a problem of the utmost delicacy. The wrong man will do far more harm than can come from almost any influence in a school of any type whatever. Little frictions are sure to grow greater. The triangular relation of family, boy and tutor is prolific of causes of stumbling. The wear and tear on the tutor is bound to be reflected in the nervous tension of the boy and the hypersensitiveness of parents.

But even supposing the best of conditions, there remains the question of the value of the system for the boy. My own feeling, based on considerable observation and a little early experience is that it should be resorted to only as a necessity, certainly not as a luxury. It tends to exaggerate to the utmost the evils of "special attention." It separates the boy from the wholesome competitions of his mates. It unfits him for the rough and ready contacts that surely await him whenever he is released from this gentle surveillance. It gives him fictitious standards of values. I dislike to say that it is "undemocratic," because that is a word which may mean something or nothing according to the point of view, but perhaps after all this is the word which best conveys to the most hearers the fatal danger of this private tutorial method. It may be necessary, but that is the best that can be said for it.

Finally there is one other device against which I should like to register an even more serious warning, and that is the sending of young boys to Europe for what is called "a foreign education." I have tried elsewhere to set forth with some detail the reasons why this should not be done.[1] Here I would touch only upon the argument in favor as it presents itself to the parent of large, or sometimes even more forcibly to one of small means, who wishes to do the best for his, or more often for her boy. The first step is that European schools are better than American schools. This idea is probably based upon little more than a vague notion that, since European civilization is older than American, and has done many greater things, the schools which form a part of that great result must be better than those which have grown up as a part of our own more rapid and more casual progress. I am afraid we must admit that in certain respects this impression is a true one. The school systems of England, France, Germany, and Switzerland rest upon a kind of valuation of the teacher's profession which has so far been unhappily lacking in America. Let us grant this superiority and accept the conclusion that, for the boys of those countries, these systems are the best available.

The question is whether they are desirable for our boys. Of course all that has been said hitherto against sending our lads away from home applies with double force to this much greater experiment. The inexperienced parent, often a mother confronted suddenly with the responsibility of decision, is caught by the glamor of the argument. Her boy shall have the opportunity denied to less favored youths. She is prepared

[1] Pages 197 *sqq.*

to make the sacrifice — if such it be, of breaking up her home and plunging into the glittering uncertainties of foreign residence. But what does she find? The regular schools, the only ones really worth considering, are far from easy of access to the foreign pupil. Those of the Continent are generally closed to him by the barrier of language. It is not the business of these schools to teach their own language to the foreigner. Only after he has acquired a really adequate speaking knowledge of it can they accept him as a regular member of their classes.

This implies·an interval in which the luckless boy is to be subjected to the tortures of isolation from the sound of his own speech. The length of this interval will depend upon the completeness of the isolation. The chances are that it will be spent in one of the numerous hybrid schools that have sprung up to meet precisely this demand. There the American boy will meet other American boys mingled with English, German, Italian, Russian, all supposed to be learning the language of the country, but all, boylike, dodging their opportunities and snatching every occasion to speak and hear the dear native tongue and to cultivate hatred of the odious foreign things about them. Such schools are purely commercial enterprises, depending upon numbers for their success and consequently interested to prolong the residence of their pupils as far as possible. As to the moral conditions likely to prevail in such a place: I leave that to the intelligence of the reader.

Fancy the holidays of a boy thus torn up by the roots! If his parents are in Europe he spends his free time in the wretched luxury of hotels or lodgings or in the aimless wanderings miscalled "travel." If, through the apprenticeship of the mixed school he succeeds in entering one of the regular government schools he will certainly have the opportunity to learn certain lessons of thoroughness and seriousness that are in themselves valuable, but at what a sacrifice of the things worth most to him as a future American citizen! I heard only the other day an American mother of good intelligence, but limited experience, say that the best educated men she had known had been educated abroad, and for that reason she was prepared to transplant her little son to Europe. I doubted her premise and deplored her conclusion. The value of what foreign study and residence can give can be realized only after the youth has got the best he can out of what is offered him at home.

To sum up: keep the American boy at home up to his seventeenth year; but make the home all that it ought to be for his sake. If it is becoming anything less than this, do not sacrifice the boy, but sacrifice the thing, no matter what it is, that is making the home less worthy of him. Send him to the best available day school, and as a good citizen do all you can to make the school what it ought to be. If he must go away consider, not "social opportunity," not any single detail of school life, but what on the whole offers him the best chance of a full and harmonious development in body, mind, and feeling, the best preparation, not for a college course, but for the life of a citizen of the Republic.

THE DISCIPLINE OF A UNIVERSITY
COLLEGE

THE nomenclature of American education is so far from uniform, is so much a matter of local usage and is so destitute of common standards that, before employing even its most familiar terms we must define them anew. For our present purpose I mean by a "college" what has always been meant by it in our best educational traditions, a school of liberal culture following in due succession the school of preparation in the elements of sound learning and preceding the schools for training in the several professions. Precisely what such general culture ought to be is matter for discussion, and will, it is to be hoped, always continue to be so; for in such discussion lies the best guarantee of rational progress, the best hope for the continuous adjustment of the educational process to the needs of the time. All that we require for the moment in our definition of the college as distinguished from the technical school is that it stands for a period of "liberal," that is unprofessional study, the aim of which is the development of intellectual character and capacity through occupation with the things that so far have been proved useful to this end.

The college is the peculiarly American educational institution, not precisely the equivalent of any foreign one, varying greatly in detail, but preserving, now for several generations, a marked character of its own.

The object, during the generation just passing, of attacks and encroachments from many sides, it is still recognizable under its changes of form as essentially a "liberal" school, not afraid of the word, but aiming to give to it always a larger and a more vital meaning.

By the word "university" we mean here a school or group of schools of advanced learning, whose object is such fundamental training in the principles of professional activity as shall fit young men to begin practice with the greatest advantage. This definition would exclude on the one hand the great mass of so-called universities which vary in their standards from those of a good high school to those of an average college and on the other those examining or certifying boards without teaching functions which are intended to regulate the educational machinery of a state. It is a misfortune that the looseness of our terminology has so often confounded the two words "college" and "university," and this confusion has not been one of words alone. Colleges have striven to become universities, and universities have been compelled to perform collegiate functions, until the public mind is really in a pretty hopeless muddle about the whole matter. Its conclusion is likely to be, that the distinctions we are trying to make here are, to use one of the public's favorite terms of opprobrium, "purely academic." I hope to show that they are real distinctions and that they are fundamental to our purpose.

Their value becomes clearer when we put them together in the form chosen in the title to this essay. The phrase "university college," while it brings the two words into a closer and more integral relation, compels us to know even more precisely what we mean by them. We mean a school of liberal culture standing in an organic connection with a university. As to the wisdom or unwisdom of such a connection we are not now concerned. That is a point upon which opinions differ widely and fortunately. It would be a pity if Americans were not to be at liberty to experiment or should ever be brought to sacrifice the advantages of diversity to the cheap attraction of uniformity. Our concern for the moment is with the fact that there are colleges thus intimately bound up with the larger life of the university and that such colleges are thus brought into certain peculiar relations to the problems of collegiate administration.

Even where this close relation between the university and the college exists it is the college which has possessed and still possesses the strongest hold upon the affections of the graduates, and it is these graduates of the college who still form the main portion of the public which supports and, because it supports, claims a large share in directing the policy of the institution as a whole. The college, in spite of all the advances in technical professional training, remains the most important and the most interesting stage in our educational scale. It is the most important because to the great majority of our academic youth it is the final stage. It is the most interesting because its problems are so wide-reaching, so varied and so promptly reflective of every advance in human thought. Professional training has always been fairly well taken care of by the professions themselves, and in the nature of things it must be so cared for. The college needs the continual guardianship of all those in every walk of life to whom liberal culture means a something effectively different from professional training of any sort.

During the past generation the American college has been the subject of continuous attacks, chiefly in the house of its friends. We have had dangled before our eyes the bugaboo of its inevitable annihilation between the advancing standards of the secondary schools and the steadily increasing claims of professional preparation. To this pressure the colleges have been forced to make certain concessions, by no means to their injury, a slight addition here, a little amputation there, a reduction in what one of my colleagues used to call "frills" and a strengthening in the essential parts. Yet, in spite of all these changes, it remains the greatest proof of the value of the college as an element in American life that it has held its own and that whenever, as happened a few years ago in the case of one of our most typical New England colleges, the body of graduates has expressed itself, its voice has been in favor of the traditional studies and the well-tried forms, allowing always for such modifications as advancing knowledge and wider experience shall suggest. Both the upper and the nether educational millstones have been grinding away during this most exacting generation, but they have not yet reduced the college to any such straits as seriously to alarm its defenders. Rather, they have stimulated them to renewed energy in proving anew the right of the college to its own existence. As these words are written come reports from every hand of an unparalleled crowding of our most typical colleges. In those farthest removed from cities the housing problem has become almost fatally serious. Some are considering plans for a systematic limitation of numbers on the basis of a more careful selection of candidates. The supply of competent teachers has already become a question of the highest importance.

And now, by "discipline" is meant whatever in the life of the college, apart from the actual study, tends to form the youth into that being whom, for lack of a better term, we call an "educated man." Discipline is indeed the final object of the whole college organization. It ought to be kept in sight at every moment by those who shape the details of administration. No measure of any sort should be passed until its bearing upon this supreme object has been duly weighed. The discipline of an army we in these days have learned only too well to understand. It means, not merely the outward form, the salute, the drill, the punctuality, the instant and unquestioning obedience, but also the change in the recruit's whole attitude from the more diverse and scattered interests of the civilian to the intense and concentrated loyalty of the soldier to his single task.

Some such attitude toward his work is what is here meant by the discipline of the student, but the comparison, just now being made with increasing frequency, is likely to be misleading. Already voices are beginning to be heard calling attention to the swift results and the amazing efficiency of military discipline and more than suggesting that the happily brief experience of our academic youth under military supervision ought to be indefinitely extended. That, however, is not at all what we are here aiming at. Nothing could be much worse than to bring the methods of the military academy into our colleges. These methods presuppose one uniform aim for all students and one well established body of instruction to be conveyed by teacher to pupil. The method of instruction is naturally that of the standardized text-book learned and repeated with daily and hourly insistence upon the regular performance of allotted tasks. That is indeed discipline, but in the lowest sense of that inspiring word. It may well have its effect on the youth by starting him in useful habits. It will doubtless convey to him a mass of useful information. It will give him a certain facility in exercising over others the kind of authority he has himself been forced to respect — or appear to respect.

All these are results of the greatest value to the soldier in the special service he will be called upon to perform; but in the higher sense they do not mean discipline at all. Essentially this is all external in its method and its spirit. It is not primarily directed toward rousing into activity that inner impulse which, working outward expresses itself in action under the domination of the disciplined will. The very essence of military discipline is the absence of will: "theirs not to reason why." Yet the highest achievement in human life comes only from the constant will toward the best, and our academic aim should be directed wholly toward the highest. Not the quickest process, not the most "direct" application of effort, but the slow ripening of the intellectual and the moral character is the academic, but not the military, ideal.

The university college differs from the separated college mainly in its closer contact with what we have called the larger ideals of the university. Our first question, therefore, concerns the inevitable reaction upon the college of the university life in the midst of which it stands and with which it is organically connected. The essential principle of university discipline is the principle of freedom. The university man is a free agent. He lives and comes and goes as he pleases. The opportunities offered him he takes or leaves at his discretion. When he is ready to submit himself to the tests of scholarship required for his degrees he does so; but no one in authority reproaches him if he does not or if he fails to stand the tests. His general conduct of life is subject only to the rules of a civil society.

It is inevitable that this freedom of the university should react powerfully upon the associated college. Many restrictions which might well be set in a college apart cannot be maintained here without injurious friction. In the university college even the lowest undergraduate cannot entirely escape the influence of the continuous contact of the collegiate with the university ideals. Even the conscious effort of the authorities cannot quite bring this to pass. They may shut up the Freshman in buildings swarming only with his kind; they may feed him at the same table, move him through the same class-rooms, subject him to the same degrading system of academic bookkeeping which masquerades under the name of "discipline," but they cannot quite hide from him the most important educational fact in his whole situation, namely, that he is a member, however humble, in a "society of scholars." No matter how remote from him the higher regions of scholarship may be, some faint glow of their radiance must penetrate into the mists of his inexperience and his indifference.

It is this contact of two educational ideals which underlies the whole problem of the university college. To some persons this contact seems so dangerous that it may rather be described as a conflict. To others it offers the most valuable aid possible in the attainment of the highest academic results. The efficient head of one New England college used to say that he would not tolerate a graduate student on the *campus*. He thought that advanced study belonged only at the university and that its mere presence in the college tended to create an atmosphere unfavorable to the steady pursuit of purely collegiate aims. In other equally typical colleges there has been a persistent effort to create something of what we call the "university spirit" because it was believed that this would further the more specific purpose of the college. In the university college this contact is, for better or worse, already present, and the problem of administration is to utilize it.

It is a very pretty illustration at once of the importance and the difficulty of this problem, that while some of the separated colleges have been trying to lift themselves up by introducing studies and methods supposed to belong to "graduate" instruction, there has been a constant pressure upon the university colleges to withdraw themselves more and more from the baleful influence of such advanced ideas, or, in other words, to draw the line more sharply between undergraduate and graduate methods. Graduates, we are told, are men; undergraduates are boys and must be treated as such. The kind of discipline suited for men is not fit for boys. In fact, say these counsellors of imperfection, it is doubtful whether men profit much by any other kind of discipline than that which boys need to hold them to their tasks.

This is a fundamental antithesis and needs a little more clearing up. Let the word "boy" be our starting-point. We use it carelessly in a half affectionate, half depreciatory way to express our feeling toward these youths of eighteen to twenty-two. To us they seem but just out of their cradles. We think of their follies, their waste of time, their confused notions of right and wrong, their contempt of authority and precedent, their generous enthusiasms and their *blasé* affectations. We turn away our heads to hide our tolerant smiles and say to each other: "Boys! dear boys! When will they begin to be men!" And so, putting our feelings into terms of education, we hail with a new sensation of relief each new effort of the college to safeguard these precious pledglings of our affection and our sacrifice. Fond parents and alarmed schoolmasters and easily excited social reformers rush to meet half way the amiable deans and canny presidents who offer them all kinds of plausible panaceas against laziness and viciousness and social neglect. "Revive class-feeling, and all will be well!" shouts one. "Publish abroad the grades of scholarship" says another, "so that even he who can run a mile in x minutes may read the lesson that it pays to learn what is set before him, and you will be offering to these ' boys ' the only kind of motive they are able to understand." "Look after them more sharply" insists a third, "provide them with hordes of ' advisers,' deans and assistant deans, tutors, student counsellors and what not, and this irresponsibility which is of the very nature of the ' boy ' will be so hedged about that it will no longer be harmful to him." "Herd your boys together as much as possible, and all those wicked invidious distinctions that work against a true democracy will disappear."

Now all this multitude of conflicting counsels rests upon our persistent misuse of the word and the idea, "boy." To call our youths of eighteen to twenty-two merely boys is as false as it would be to call them merely men. They are *young men* not *old boys*. What is manly about them is the essential and the formative. The boyish things are the transient, the outgrown, the disappearing things. As in all human affairs it is the growing, forward-looking, upbuilding aspects that are important, so is it in the highest degree with the making of a man. A popular weekly presented recently on its cover a pathetic picture of a sturdy urchin in the barber's chair, his face radiant with the broadest of grins as his golden curls fall thick around him while behind stands the poor, proud little mother pressing her handkerchief to her lips to check the sobs that protest against the sacrifice of her baby to the insistent claim of the boy. The passage from the boy to the man calls for no less pathetic sacrifices on the part alike of parents and of the community. Cost what it may the "boy" must be sloughed off, and the man must have his chance. The picturesque elements of boyhood must be as relentlessly abandoned as the baby curls are surrendered to the cruel shears.

If we are to do justice to our growing youth we must first conquer our own blinding affections. We must first of all get it into our working consciousness that this being whom we have been taking as a joke is a joke no longer, but a stubborn, persistent, individual fact. The clouds of glory he has been trailing about with him are darkening into threatening masses of shadow, whose silver linings are pretty steadily turned the other way. It is a severe trial of our faith, and it is not strange that our faith often fails us and we grasp at anything that seems likely to give us a hold upon realities we can understand. Our fixed point must be the fact of the freedom involved in the university contact. The theory of the university college must include a considerable measure of freedom; the practical questions are: how much freedom? in what directions? and at what stages of advancement?

To begin with the last of these questions: at what point in the life of the college youth should he begin to be subjected to the trials and introduced to the joys of academic freedom? I reply: at the moment of his entrance into the academic community. About this there has been much discussion, and many experiments have

been tried. It sounds reasonable that a "boy" just released from the necessary restraints of school should be
led over gradually into the responsibilities of university
freedom. But what is this process of leading over? In
practice it means nothing more than prolonging the
period of external control or, in other words, postponing the beginning of the only process by which the
lesson of responsibility was ever learned, namely the
taking of responsibility. It is not a question of age.
The offenders against college morals are seldom the
youngest of their year. The youth of sixteen *plus* who
has passed all requirements for admission to college
has usually shown, simply by this fact, that he is already sufficiently master of his will to be safely trusted
to use it aright. If the moral backbone is not fairly
well set at eighteen it is not a matter of a year or two
longer of irresponsibility that will do it.

In saying this I am making for the college youth no
special claim to superior virtue beyond what belongs
to his quality as a picked man. He will undoubtedly do
a great many foolish things and will try a great many
experiments on himself to see how far he may safely or
comfortably go without disaster. The college can make
no superhuman demands upon him, but it may fairly
expect that when he enters upon its privileges and its
joys he shall also face its special responsibilities. College discipline should be so adjusted as to catch hold
upon every one of his forward and upward looking impulses and to discourage actively and passively every
one of his lapses into flabbiness. It is a difficult and a
delicate problem demanding a clear comprehension of

young human nature and a persistent faith in its ultimate rightness. The especial difficulty in practice is to remember that we are not to expect immediate results. The temptation is to make regulations so that apparent results shall be produced at once. It can be done; but this is the discipline of a reformatory, not of an educating community. The college which applies the principle of liberty must expect apparent failures. They will come at whatever stage the liberty begins to work, and the sooner the better. College life does not in this respect differ from any other form of associated life. It must have its periods of initiation, of experiment and therefore of waste, of error, and of folly. As compared with entrance into any other kind of life, as for instance, into the business community of a great city, entrance into the college is infinitely less dangerous. It is surrounded by natural safeguards in the very character of its occupations and of the men who direct them.

We sometimes hear the defenders of a system of graduated liberties speak with alarm of the "shock" of an abrupt transition from school control to college freedom. Well, it is a shock, but of a kind that is highly educative. There is nothing better for a youth than to run up hard at times against the consequences of his own acts. It is a lonesome but a fortunate moment for him when it comes over him with full force, that he is the person most concerned in his own success or failure. At home and at school he has had some one else to do his suffering for him. Now he has come into a world that seems to care about him not at all. He is a number on an examination slip, a seat in a lecture room, a page in the treasurer's books. It is a shock; but it sets him thinking. A classmate of mine, father of boys and a successful private tutor, said: "The chief difference between our time and now is, that nowadays a student begins his college life with an act of thought." Very likely this unwonted exercise will paralyze him for the moment. Thinking for one's self is a trying occupation. He casts about him for the props that have hitherto supported his wavering will — the family habit of early rising, the helpful but hateful sound of the school bell, the daily report of his study to parent or teacher, the regular, orderly movement of a mass of boys of his own age, the quiet evening and the early sleep all are gone. Of course the college could supply all this machinery. It used to do so. The college bell to compulsory prayers took the place of the family summons to an early breakfast; the regular succession of classes was so planned as to keep up a systematic division of the day; hourly recitations with accurate bookkeeping kept the authorities informed at every moment of the precise "standing" of every student.

That system still commends itself to those who believe that education is primarily a thing of so much work, done under a regular and personal supervision. They think that the conditions of such a regulated life are more favorable to the formation of working habits likely to be of permanent value. The question is still an open one; but so far as the university college is concerned the tendency is clear. The principle of liberty has been accepted, and its application begins more or less sharply with the beginning of college life.

If now we turn to the question of the forms which university freedom may properly take in the college stage, the first and most obvious application is in the choice of studies. Whatever may be thought as to the meaning of a liberal education, no one at this day would undertake to administer a university college upon any other theory than that of a wide election. So general has this conviction become that to most persons not professionally concerned with the subject the two phrases "elective system" and "university freedom" are practically synonymous. Just how wide such election should be at any given moment is again a matter for discussion; but such is the logic of freedom that, if the principle is once admitted, it tends inevitably to cover the whole range of studies as we have seen it covering the whole period of college life. The only logical solution is to open the whole list of "liberal" studies to the choice of all candidates for the "liberal," that is the non-professional degrees. That this conclusion is logical, however, does not prove that it is either practicable or wise.

The theory must justify itself by its results or else it must be modified until it can do so. In fact, such a thing as absolute freedom of election in studies is an impossibility. In many subjects there is a natural sequence of topics which would prevent the more advanced from being studied until after the more elementary. Some subjects demand a certain maturity of mind which would ordinarily exclude the younger students. Any conceivable elective system implies election among such studies as are suited to the student's capacity and previous acquirements.

We are concerned with the disciplinary effect of the free election of studies. That initial act of independent thought may be very crude, based upon very insufficient grounds and subactuated by very trifling motives, but it sets for the young man the note of personal responsibility which henceforth he cannot escape. It has been my fortune as boy and man to live through the whole process of change from a system of absolute uniformity and compulsion to one of almost as complete liberty and then long afterward to another system of regulation intended to retain the benefits and avoid the dangers of both its predecessors. In the light of these changes and of the illuminating discussions that accompanied them, I do not hesitate to say that American education owes more to the expansion of student freedom than to any other cause, perhaps than to all other causes. On the whole the choice of their studies has been taken as seriously by our college youth as could reasonably have been expected. The reaction upon their ways of working and thinking about their work has been most encouraging.

This conclusion is not weakened by the undeniable fact that a great proportion of the graduates of the freest period would have made different choices if the thing were to do over again. The same might be said of most later human decisions. The real question is whether the increase of freedom has strengthened the will, has given larger and truer views of study and increased respect for the intellectual life. That such has been the case is best proven by the practical unanimity with which our higher institutions of learning have accepted the principle and invented devices for securing the best results from it. Within recent years there has been noticeable a certain tendency toward limitation of freedom in this matter of the choice of studies, but so far this has been no more than a healthful reaction against rather obvious exaggerations of the logic of the situation. The principle has been preserved; the details have been modified rather with the object of saving the principle than of working against it.

But the mere fact of a free election of studies is far from being the same thing as university freedom. It is only one aspect of it. It may be so administered as almost entirely to obscure or even to nullify its disciplinary character. There are certain kinds of regulation which tend to enforce the idea of liberty and others which tend to destroy it. This is a distinction which the university college is bound to recognize. It ought to insist that only such forms of control shall be used as will reinforce in the student's mind at every turn that sense of responsibility which is the end and aim of all academic discipline. For example, how to treat the not altogether simple question of attendance at college exercises. It is quite possible for the college to say: "We permit the largest practicable freedom in the election of studies; but, the election once made, the student must be present at every regular exercise of every course. In case of unexcused absence he may be punished by some form of academic censure." But what is the result of this prescription? The discipline of liberty is lost. The attitude of the student toward his instruction remains a false one. He is no longer the recipient of a privilege; he is the victim of a conspiracy to force upon him something from which he is trying to escape. Or, supposing that a certain limit of absence before censure is allowed, he keeps within his limit and fancies he has done all that can be asked of him. He has not caught the spirit of university freedom. In spite of the elective system of studies, the student is still no more of a university man than was the college "boy" under the straitest of compulsory methods.

But now, supposing that no faculty regulation whatever exists as to attendance. There arises at once between teacher and taught a relation appalling in its simplicity to the men of little faith, but inspiring and profoundly educative in its effect. It is the relation which has existed between all good teachers and all willing learners since Socrates and Alcibiades, since Abelard and Arnold of Brescia, since Mark Hopkins and James Garfield. Alcibiades, Arnold, and Garfield are perfect types of the picked youth seeking instruction where best they could find it and bound to their teachers by no other tie than the confidence that their instruction was worth while. In this free relation the teacher is compelled to give such instruction that the student cannot afford to miss it. In most systematic teaching there is a natural continuity which of itself is enough to secure as regular attendance as any university college is likely to require by rule.

The student comes then to his classes, not from any

angelic sense of duty but because it pays. He gets there something which he can get nowhere else and which he must have in order to meet the final purpose of his college life toward which he is continually looking forward. If he is not present with fair regularity he cannot do the work of his class. If he is foolish enough to indulge in long lapses from attendance he meets with perfect naturalness the rational consequence. He is forbidden to enjoy the privilege he has abused. He turns himself out of the company he has not chosen to keep up with. If his negligence covers a great part of his work he simply turns himself out of college. He cannot feel himself the victim of any too rigid regulation; there has been no regulation at all. He has disciplined himself by the process through which youth and age alike are always being disciplined, by the consequences of his own acts. It is the sternest of all discipline, and yet, so curiously are we blinded to the realities of things that to many persons it appears like positive neglect and shiftlessness on the part of those whom such critics like to describe as the "guardians of youth."

Unquestionably there is a temptation on the part of college authorities to administer carelessly a system of liberty. It makes far higher demands upon the insight, the faith, the courage and the persistence of executive officers and teachers than any system of precise regulation. It is far easier to impress the public by showing a fine scheme of rules, no matter how badly they work, than by keeping up a continuous demand upon the reason and conscience of youth, with the inevitable cases of apparent failure. And on the side of the student, youth is not alone in a too willing dependence upon crutches. Nothing is more depressing than the readiness with which students will slump back into irresponsibility as fast as they are permitted to do so. A clever college president has recently spoken of "student activities" by way of contrast with "the passivities of the class-room." The whole problem of discipline is to convert passivity into activity through convincing the youth that intellectual things are really worth his while. The initiative toward this conversion cannot come from the student. His sense of something wrong in the method of treating him can express itself only in vague resistance, not in constructive suggestion. The motive must be supplied by the governing powers, educational and executive together, or it will not come at all.

With all due caution in making comparisons with foreign countries, it is instructive to remember that nowhere in the civilized world are youths of our collegiate age subjected to the kind of super-regulation we accept as a matter of course. Even in England, whose traditions we have more nearly followed than any others, the step from school to college is more sharply accented. Except for certain rather superficial physical restrictions, the English college youth is freer in his movements in all that relates to his studies, a freedom based largely upon his sense of accountability in the remote future. And as to the Continent, the answer of the German student to a stranger asking the way to the university is characteristic: "Excuse me,

Sir; this is only my third semester." Such laxity as that we in America are certainly not prepared for. We are bound to preserve something of the ancient collegiate tradition which made the college accountable to families for the conduct of their sons.

It is the special privilege of the university college to interpret this obligation as liberally as possible, not that it may escape from thought or responsibility, but that it may help the student to the highest form of discipline. How far, then, may it wisely go in the matter of attendance? Its guides in solving this question should be on the one hand, that it is bound to have some knowledge of the student's general fidelity to his regular duty and on the other, that mere bodily presence at college exercises without active participation in them is of no value whatever. A record of attendance may be kept, because such a record is in itself no encroachment upon personal liberty. It is a mere device for procuring statistics. In so far as it is made use of for enforcing unwilling attendance it is a positive evil. If the record of a student shows persistent absence in any one course of study, he should be required to explain it, and every allowance should be made for the undoubted fact that well-considered absence may often be of much more use than unthinking presence. If his acount is satisfactory, as it well may be, he should be let alone. If not, the privilege of attendance at this particular course, which he has not found worth his while, should be withdrawn.

If, however, his neglect in attendance all round shows a settled purpose, it should be accepted as evidence that he is not a useful member of the academic community and he should be required to separate himself from it. Not, be it well understood, as punishment. The university college has no place for punitive discipline. Separation is simply an answer to his own real desire as expressed by his actions. Whenever he can show by other actions a reasonable promise of readiness to use well the academic privilege, it should be opened to him again. There is a phrase hallowed by long usage in a certain academic connection which ought to be published as expressing the sum and substance of university college discipline: "Any student may be deprived of his privileges at any time, if he abuse or fail to use them." It should never be forgotten that the obligation of the student to attend is no greater than that of the teacher to give him something that is worth his while. If he is tolerably certain that at a given point the teacher is not going to fulfil his obligation, then his own is released, and he is perfectly right in finding a better use for his time. Free attendance thus becomes a positive agent in toning up the whole mechanism of instruction. It may be abused, but in the main the control is in the teacher's hands. The motto of the good teacher is: "I want no hearers who do not want to hear!"

The system of freedom, applied with due watchfulness and rational guidance is not an easy one to administer. If this is true in regard to personal attendance, it is even more so in the very complicated matter of academic bookkeeping. Just as there are persons to whom the notion of a regular and orderly mechanical

attendance appeals as evidence of interest and progress, so there is an order of mind for which the idea of
a systematic and "accurate" account between every
student and the college authorities has a deadly fas-
cination. To such a mind the spectacle of a graded list
upon which every member of a college class is duly
credited with so much scholarly accomplishment is an
object of positive beauty. It is not so very long since
all our education from bottom to top was controlled by
this demon of statistics. Even in our colleges every
academic exercise was checked and ticketed off to the
account of every student like the sales in a retail shop.
The function of the teacher was largely one of judging
and valuing the daily and hourly performances of his
students, and his skill and fairness in this kind of academic shop-keeping were of far more immediate importance in their eyes than his learning or his aptness
to teach.

At a great dinner in celebration of a professor's jubi-
lee, it was curious to notice that what drew these generations of former pupils together was not in the least
their recollection of anything he had ever taught them,
but a kind of filial regard for his upright and down-
right character. It was summed up in such remarks as
these: "He never added anything to science. Of
course we never learned anything from him; but he
was always *fair*!" A contemporary of this "teacher"
but of the opposite type, a man to whom learning was
everything and machinery nothing, was driven by the
same foolish conditions upon the other horn of the
dilemma. It was told of him that when a certain stu-

dent of excellent ability in his subject sought correction
of a very low grade on the ground of possible confusion
with a very bad student of the same name, he only replied: "You must take your chance, Sir! You must
take your chance!" The fault in both cases was not in
the man, nor yet in the pupil. It was in the absurd
system and in the false pedagogy that lay behind it.
A classmate of mine applied to a mathematical professor not destitute of humor for revision of grade and
was answered next day: "Yes, Mr. X, I was in error.
I have reëxamined your book and take pleasure in
raising your grade from 67 to 68." One of my colleagues always told his students: "I shall be glad to
reread any examination books, provided you will take
the chance of a reduction in grade." Such anecdotes
could be indefinitely multiplied. They illustrate the
pitiful, pettifogging business in which men of learning
and students of promise were involved so long as they
remained subject to the fundamental error that intellectual accomplishment can be graded and registered
like the output of a factory. One has only to go back a
little further to find a time when moral conduct and
scholarship were tied up together in the college bookkeeping. If a student threw a snowball in the college
grounds, or was late to prayers or got tipsy, his record
of scholarship was docked according to a scale of
prices.

Such blatant absurdity as this was recognized a good
while ago, but we are not yet delivered from the false
principle that lay behind it. In the long warfare between the Faculty and the "Office," it is only eternal

vigilance that can prevent the poisonous gas of the competitive marking system from clogging the arteries and dulling the will alike of teachers and taught. The principle is false not only because it proposes to do the impossible, that is to grade intellectual work accurately, but because it sets a false standard for estimating the final result of the student's academic course. It tends to glorify the man who "has never missed a lecture," or who has never "got" less than ninety per cent in a "course." It helps the man to "get by," who has "half his work above C" or who has only "three D's" to his discredit. Very recently a student graduating with the highest reputation for true scholarship from an important university college was refused "highest honors" because at some time in the remote past of his Freshman year he had "got a C" in an elementary course! Not a word as to his steady growth in intellectual character. Not an inquiry as to his actual command of a subject or his quality as a man of power in the things of the intellect. Only a deadly rule of thumb such as might be useful in making weather statistics or in tabulating the reports of the stock market, but has no place in the process of making an educated man.

Such a case as this brings out into glaring contrast two conflicting ideas of what education is and what it is for. The one presents education as the regular performance of so many allotted tasks with even excellence, with little regard to their relation with each other or to any specific end. The other regards education as first the acquisition of a modicum of knowledge and then the gaining of power to use this or any other knowledge for productive ends. If the former is the right ideal then by all means let us have the marking system in all its perfection, with its percentages, its averages, its small rivalries and its empty triumphs. If the latter is right, then all the weight of discipline should be applied to fix the attention upon the distant goal of some real accomplishment of knowledge and of capacity. Between these two ideals there is no permanent compromise. The lower nullifies the higher; the higher drives out the lower, as a gold standard drives out the silver which tends to degrade it. The university college must make up its mind which of these gods it will serve, and in this choice the influence of the university ought to be decisive. As the university trains for professional ends, so the college should have its equally well-defined though not professional aim, and toward this aim all its effort should be directed. But one objector will say: "That is all very well, but the college "boy" is incapable of working toward distant ends." Is he? Watch him at his games, and find the answer. Where is the motive that leads him to subject himself to the self-denials, the physical hardships, the dreary monotony of months of training? It is the far off goal of the final struggle on field or river. Here no one asks how he rowed six months ago; the question is: how does he row *now*? Is his form good, his heart sound, can he stay *now*? And lately, when the call to arms went singing through the land, where were these "boys" then? They saw the end from the beginning. The vision of themselves leading their mates into battle for the right made them forget the long months of weary preparation, the dangers of camp and field, and they went.

No, if the college follows a lower instead of a higher ideal, it is not the student who is at fault. I rejoice to give my testimony that I have never known a case in which students did not respond to the highest demands made upon them when they were made to understand what such demands meant. On the other hand, I have never known students — or any other class of persons — to fail to slump when low ideals were set before them. It is not the students; it is those who administer the affairs of the college who do not see clearly or seeing have not the spirit to carry through the best they know.

I dwell upon this matter of the marking system because it touches so closely upon the daily thought of the student. It is idle to preach high ideals when we are offering low ones. The high ideals are remote and doubtful; the low ones are close at hand, continuous and certain. If we are content to have the youth "get by," he is not going to trouble himself greatly about the more solid things. A detailed grading system cannot exist together with real academic freedom. It is undoubtedly a convenience in several ways. It gives to the college at every moment the means of answering superficially inquiries as to what we call the student's "standing." It enables parents to receive prompt information of a formal sort about their sons. It answers, in short, all the bookkeeping requirements necessarily involved in a parental system of education. Furthermore it is not unwelcome to the student body as a whole. In our times of weakness we all welcome the formal, mechanical props that aim to replace the more painful support of our own disciplined wills. The difference is that we elders know when we are dodging, and the youth does not. If he does what we "require" he thinks he has a right to feel that he has done enough and may go play with a clear conscience. The whole problem of a sound discipline is to make him feel that it is not we who are "requiring" anything of him, but that it is he and he alone who profits by diligence and loses by neglect. Whatever in our administration of this great trust interferes with that understanding of discipline either on his side or on ours is contrary to the spirit of the university college.

I venture to believe that any rigid system of grading based upon fragmentary bits of work, kept always before the mind of the student and published to the world is such an interference with sound discipline and therefore has no place in university conditions. The pretense of discipline it offers is bad, because it holds up to the student standards which he knows to be fictitious, inexact, and incomplete. He laughs at the fiction, he grumbles at the inaccuracy, and he invents devices for getting round the insufficiency. It is a prop to the idle, because it sets for him a low visible line which he can reach with a minimum of effort and then imagine that he has fulfilled all requirements. It is an abuse of the diligent, because it tempts him continually to apply his diligence to fictitious ends.

There are two practical defenses of a marking system: one, that it is a necessary spur to effort, the other, that it is the only means by which college honors and pecuniary assistance can be wisely assigned. The first argument appeals especially to those who think of discipline as primarily intended to "get work out of students," without special anxiety as to the kind of work or the spirit in which it is done. Now, doubtless men can always be kept at work by a penal system, and they may be fairly happy under it; but in college life there will be certain weak points in its appeal. It is no use to preach the fear of hell to the modern sinner; he calmly replies: "There is no such thing" and sins away as merrily as ever. So the indifferent student, by no means always the least clever, quietly calculates his chances, skims along the edge of the fictitious academic limbo and defies the authorities to "get any more out of him." Really, so far as discipline is concerned, he comes off rather better than the better student. He makes himself no illusions. It is a fair fight between himself and the office, and with a not excessive amount of strategy he is sure of a victory. For here as always, when there is a straight issue between the government and the student, the government will get beaten. Nothing is more idle than to invent devices for getting the better of the student. He is always the cleverer party. Our only safety lies in presenting the aims of academic life to him in their highest and clearest light as privilege and opportunity and then leaving it to him whether he will accept or reject them. That is the sharpest spur there is, and it is the only one he needs.

The subject of "college honors" is too large to be treated here in detail. Such distinctions are warmly defended and violently opposed. In so far as their defense rests, as it usually does, on their value as incitements to scholarship, they come fairly under the head of discipline. The arguments for and against them turn generally upon the usefulness of competition in education. They are usually defended by those who approve of competition, rejected by those who do not. But this does not go to the root of the matter. Competition in education is useful or not according to the spirit of work it may develop. If it is a competition going on from day to day and hour to hour, involving continuous comparison and stimulating to effort merely to get ahead, like the tacking of racing yachts, it is a thoroughly vicious thing. It is vicious because the mind of the student is thereby kept more on the competition than on his actual progress, and he fancies himself to be going straight on when he is only tacking round his rival. This is the kind of competition maintained and encouraged by the marking of daily exercises, by frequent examinations and the publication of continuous rank-lists during a college course. "Honors" based upon this kind of competition deserve all the contempt they have so abundantly received.

But there is a competition quite different from this. It is designed to bring out evidence of special capacity at certain points in the student's progress. All the petty accidents of daily class work are here left out of the account. At stated periods the student is called upon to show what use he has been making of his privileges. This may be by means of examination questions written or oral, or by other written work of various kinds involving special, independent and original inquiry or experiment. This is a true competition, but it is one in which each competitor runs his race alone. It can be so conducted that the work is more in evidence than the rivalry, and this is the more true the longer the intervals of study and the more really significant the tests. "Theses" of considerable length, requiring long periods of research, give an admirable discipline in themselves and furnish one excellent test of individual ability. Liable as they certainly are to great abuses, if rightly managed and fairly judged they come as near to real tests of acquirement as are attainable under academic conditions.

The same may be said on the much disputed question of special prizes for specific pieces of work. Rightly administered such prizes are thoroughly useful as a means of discipline. There is a reality about them that is lacking in so many other forms of college honors. The work thus rewarded may be of many kinds, but it can always be so planned as to offer a chance for real scholarly accomplishment. A long experience in the administration of a group of such prizes given for excellence in "useful and polite learning" has convinced me that foundations for this purpose, holding up as they do from one generation of college youth to another standards of scholarly quality only too likely to be lowered in the mechanisms of daily teaching, are among the most valuable additions to the resources of the university. Our conclusion is, then, that college honors are good or bad according as they help or hinder in enforcing our idea of discipline. They help when they rest upon real, honest, independent work done for its own sake. They hinder when they involve a fictitious competition that tends to obscure the value of the work itself.

The assignment of pecuniary aids to students is a matter of peculiar delicacy. Provision for such aid has been made in America with generous, sometimes with lavish hand. One hears at times wholesale condemnation of the principle itself; but it is safe to say that we are not likely to see in any visible future any sensible diminution in so appealing a form of altruistic effort. The problems are those of method, not of principle, and the most perplexing of them is: to what extent, if at all, should the applicants for aid be distinguished from their more "fortunate" mates? On this point the American instinct is against any formal, officially recognized discrimination. It is true that most of our foundations are specifically or by implication intended for the benefit of "needy and deserving" youths; but in the application of them we shrink from creating a class of students "branded," as some would say, with the mark of poverty. By whatever tests the aid in question is to be granted, we have felt that they ought to be applied to rich and poor alike. To put it in other words, we have not generally been willing to set up special examinations or other tests for applicants for scholarships.

The feeling that underlies this reluctance is fine and generous, but it has had certain consequences affecting seriously our whole subject of academic discipline. It has added one more argument for the maintenance of a general competitive grading system in which the applicants for scholarships should find themselves entered on precisely the same terms as all others. In fact, so far as my experience goes, this argument has weighed more in the minds — or shall we say in the feelings? — of the official defenders of such a system, than all the rest put together. "Show us how to assign scholarships without individual grading on the basis of frequent tests and we will cheerfully abandon the whole scheme," has been the frequent reply to criticism. That brings the issue quite clearly before us. Is it of more importance to maintain a sentiment of doubtful value or to insist upon a principle of discipline that should sustain and ennoble and make vital every incident of the academic life? I say "of doubtful value," because after all poverty in itself is no disgrace. In the generous competitions of youth it is not even a handicap. If we are convinced that special tests for scholarship applicants would relieve the college of a burden it ought not to carry, then it would seem to be a manifest duty to establish them. Properly administered they could be made a thing of honor without a shade of unworthy reflection being cast upon them. If a youth asks for a special privilege, it can hardly seem unjust that he should expect to meet some special conditions. If something like the scheme of examinations described below be assumed, it would go far toward giving the information necessary for scholarship purposes. Special tests at more frequent intervals could be administered without great difficulty for the college and with little interference with the student's proper liberty of action.

So we come to the still more vexing subject of examinations. The holding of more or less frequent tests is defended on two grounds, first, as a means of furnishing certificates of various sorts for practical ends, such for example as promotion to academic grades, transfer from one institution to another, granting of scholarships, paid employment both in college and afterward, and so on; second, as a means of discipline. The "practical" handiness of examinations for these purposes is beyond question. It concerns us here only in this way: is it a compensation for obvious defects on the side of discipline? We insist here only upon one principle: that, where the practical purpose in any way conflicts with the disciplinary, that is, with the formation of the highest type of academic character, it must somehow be made to conform, or it must be abandoned. Nothing can justify any academic machinery which works against the very highest purpose of the university.

We frequently hear examinations spoken of as if they were an unmitigated, if a necessary, evil. If this means that they are a great nuisance to the examiner, a sad consumer of valuable time, an intolerable interruption to the work of study and teaching, and, after all, untrustworthy as evidence of scholarly accomplishment, all this may be admitted at once. This does not, however, prove that examinations ought to be given up; for these are evils of the kind that belong to all human routine. If, on the other hand, we mean that they interfere with the full and free working of our academic discipline, then they should be abandoned or so modified as to escape this charge. The principal problems under this head are: how frequently may examinations wisely be held? by whom should they be set? what form should they take? what shall depend upon them?

So far as discipline is concerned, the most important question is as to the relation between the teaching and the examining functions. To what extent should they be kept in the same hands, and how far may they wisely be separated. On the one side we have the example of most European countries, where examinations are, as a rule, infrequent, occurring only at a few critical points in the student's career and held by some authority quite independent of his own special teachers. On the other hand we have our own American tradition of tolerably frequent examinations, covering small and detached pieces of work and conducted entirely by the men who have done the preparatory teaching. The advantage of the European system is that the student stands in no commercial relation to the teacher. He has nothing to get from him except a knowledge of his subject; the teacher as such has no legitimate influence upon the examination. The evil of the system, an evil so great that it has led many intelligent critics to condemn it from top to bottom is just in the opposite sense: the examination influences the teacher. Almost inevitably teaching under this system tends to become a cram, and the teacher to degenerate into the slave of an examining board in which he has no part. The disciplinary effect is to give the student a false conception of learning as of a mechanical process, a thing of so much "reading" and so much facility at putting results into tangible shape.

The apparent advantage of our American method is that the teacher is nominally far more free to teach as he will, but his relation to the student is subjected to a severe handicap. He may do his best as teacher, but he cannot conceal the fact that he is also the examiner, upon whose personal equation depends in great part the academic fate of his pupils. They may have every respect for his learning and his character, but, if he is a "hard marker" they will beware of him. In any case they will be far too much concerned to find out "what he wants them to do" than with the subject itself.

In regard to frequency a similar comparison may be made. In Europe the examination generally covers a considerable period of study and determines by one, two, or three great tests the future of the candidate. With us official and recorded examinations are generally held at the close of each brief stage of progress, and the candidate's final standing is determined by some crude process of averaging. The theory of the European examination is that it is a test of the candidate's learning and power after completing a considerable course of study. The American theory is that examinations are a kind of taking account of stock as one goes along, a theory which easily degenerates into the notion that a subject once "passed" is so much "worked off" to be set aside forever. The European plan tends to diminish the importance of the teaching process, especially in the earlier stages. The American plan tends to over-emphasize it. The former lays stress on the element of power; the latter on the element of regular acquirement. In Europe the examination is a spur to effort only in that meaning of a far off goal we have already tried to make clear. In America the use as a daily spur is what chiefly recommends it, and we have sometimes been led to the logical conclusion that the more we have of such a good thing the better.

To put this distinction in another way, we may distinguish between examinations as a means of instruction and as a basis of record. These two purposes have obviously nothing in common, and yet in practice they have been rather hopelessly confused. It seems to be generally assumed that the results of all examinations must be tabulated, kept in the official records and used at the discretion of "the office" for its manifold devices. A moment's thought will convince anyone that no such necessity exists. Examinations as a means of instruction have their own proper and useful place. Every teacher should be at liberty to employ this mechanism as he would any other to accomplish some pedagogic end, but he should be at liberty also to keep the results to himself or impart them to his students or destroy them, as may seem best to him. They need not be made a matter of official record. To enforce this distinction it might be well to designate such exercises by some specific name, as, for example, "repetitions," reserving the word "examinations" for the larger and more formal recorded tests by which some honor is to be conferred, promotion granted, or scholarships assigned. The educational value of such repetitions, oral or written, has been in danger of eclipse through the great increase of instruction by lectures. The experience of the late William James, who said that he found himself lecturing more and more because that was the line of least resistance is doubtless typical of all teachers who have passed through the transition from the required curriculum to the system of free choice of studies. We have all felt on the one hand the immense gain in the possibilities of real instruction, but on the other we have all seen with increasing regret the growing incapacity of students to express in words the results of their studies. The kind of repetitions I have here in mind would go far to diminish this evil. They could be made valuable supplements to the word of the teacher provided only that they do not come to be regarded as so many clubs to diligence or threats of punishment. The old-fashioned "recitation" with all its pedagogic horrors had at least this merit that it gave to a real teacher the opportunity to bring out of the better student some kind of intellectual reaction. Its fatal defect was that it tended to sacrifice everything to the mechanical reproduction of a given task. It is gone for good, and no teacher who is also a scholar can regret it. The highest discipline will not suffer if we can keep the idea of repetition on the level of our best instruction freed from all penitential suggestion.

As to those examinations upon which academic standing, in any sense of the word, is to be based: according to what truly disciplinary principle can they be regulated? The answer has already been suggested. They must be so planned as to direct the student's attention steadily toward real and remote ends, not toward fictitious and immediate ones. To accomplish this purpose they should be few in number; they should represent the completion of considerable pieces of work and they should involve the element of power as well as that of learned acquisition. Further, they should be conducted partly by those teachers who have been preparing the candidates and partly by other examiners. This mixed body should prepare questions, examine and estimate the answers and conduct oral examinations when these are to be used.

There is, of course, room for wide differences both of opinion and of practice. What constitutes a suitable basis for examination? What is a considerable piece of work? How shall the shares of the immediate teachers and the other experts be distributed? I venture to make these definite suggestions: First, that for all purposes of academic record the examining body in any subject should be the department which has that subject in charge. The teacher in any branch of the subject is, of course, a member of the department and would have weight in its councils in proportion to his special knowledge in his branch. His idiosyncrasies would be balanced by the larger view of his colleagues, and thus the relation of his branch to the whole subject would be made more effective. Second, the unit of examination should be a subject or a branch of a subject. It should not be the "course" of any teacher or the text-book of any author, or the work of any fixed period of residence. The purpose of this suggestion is, that the mind of the student may be kept continually on the realities of his work. He should be made to feel from the beginning that he is a fellow-worker, though a humble one, in a great field, where he has many companions. He should be reminded in every useful way, that the particular "course" he may be following at the moment is not a natural unit, but only one man's contribution to a larger whole.

Third, the examinations in each subject should be treated as one system with stages graded according to extent and difficulty. Requirement for a degree — assuming that degrees are still to be retained — could be expressed in terms of so many stages of examinations passed in so many subjects. A suitable balance between specialization and "general culture" could be secured by regulating the proportion of higher examinations to lower and the amounts of time given to special and to general instruction. A higher degree of specialization would be gained by demanding a greater amount of examination in the upper grades; a wider range of general excellence would be attained by requiring more examination in the lower grades. For example: supposing a scheme of four examination stages, a conceivable requirement for the bachelor's degree might be, that the candidate should pass the fourth stage in one subject, the second in this and three others and the first in these and four others. That would mean in all fourteen examinations in eight subjects and covering, say, four years. The candidate would in this case have passed eight first examinations, four seconds, one third, and one fourth; that is, he would have studied while in college eight different subjects, would have carried three of these into a second stage of advancement and one into a fourth. A slight variation could be made by dropping one first and adding one third. A higher degree of specialization would be gained by reducing the number of firsts and carrying, say two subjects through the fourth stage. Under this plan a great variety of combinations would be possible while still preserving the desired balance between specialization and wide election. It would avoid many of the crudities which result from unrestricted choice among individual courses given by men who are not only teaching any fragment of learning in any way they please, but, through their sole control of examinations, limit in many subtle ways the very freedom of choice they seem to represent.

Such a plan is not an imitation of any European model. It avoids the danger of a system of cramming towards a set of examinations in which the teacher has no share. It would stimulate the teacher to do his best because it brings his instruction to the test of publicity of a kind for which he has the greatest respect, publicity before his equals and his superiors. Without some such departmental coöperation the teacher goes on year in and year out examining, as it were, his own work and never brought under the wholesome criticism of those best qualified to judge it. At the same time the plan avoids the danger of petty and fragmentary instruction, since all teaching would be coördinated and directed toward some reasonably remote end. Experiments already made in substituting a system of granting degrees upon examination rather than upon any "accumulation of credits" give encouraging promise of still greater success when our academic communities shall once have worked themselves free of their obsolete paternalistic traditions.

The separation between the educational and the bookkeeping functions of the college affects our general subject of academic discipline chiefly at two points, first, in its effect upon the relation of the student to his teachers and second, as it influences his choice of studies. As to the former, there is no more striking result of the system of freedom, so far as it has been honorably applied, than the change which has come over the whole attitude of the student toward his teachers. In proportion as they have ceased to be taskmasters and have become more really interpreters between him and the various subjects of learning he has come to think of them as older fellow-workers with himself. In many ways his attitude has become more intelligently critical, and this greatly to the profit of his instruction. He has learned something of the great art of discriminating between what is valuable and what is not. He shows a certain impatience with the merely conventional and becomes somewhat too clever in dodging when he expects a period of "padding" or commonplace. His personal curiosity is aroused. He develops an instinct at asking inconvenient questions. He lets the teacher know by many unmistakable signs when he finds him dull or obscure. He ventures to set up opinions of his own, sound or otherwise, and to defend them in personal encounter.

All this has reacted most powerfully and most profitably upon the teacher. Even men who on principle opposed every stage of advance in the method of freedom have found their academic careers infinitely brightened and sweetened by this changed attitude of their pupils. Instead of dealing with an unsifted mass of half unwilling youth they have gained the right to assume that every man before them is there because he has deliberately chosen to be there. They may, therefore, appeal to the best in him and confidently expect a response. This is the great gain of the past generation in education, that we have won this right to treat our students as fellow-workers by giving them in return the right to come to their work as a privilege. We have made an immense advance in the spirit of instruction by putting the realities of science in place of formal demands for the performance of specific tasks.

But, if we are to realize due results from our system of freedom we must keep this open and frank relation of the student and his teacher free from every admixture of baser stuff. It is idle to offer confidence and sympathy with one hand while with the other we are scoring up an account on which the academic destiny of our younger colleague may depend. We may affect as much indifference as we please about the bookkeeping; *he* will not forget it. If he finds himself really getting into friendly relations with us he will be afraid of seeming to be "swiping" us for some material gain. If he shows too much interest in our subject, he is afraid of boring us and so of injuring himself. He is constantly tempted to study our idiosyncrasies to find out "what we want," to calculate his chances of success by what he imagines are our peculiar standards. In short, the personality of the teacher, the most important incident in all formal education, is set in a totally false light, is perverted from its true influence and, instead of aiding our system of freedom as it ought, is in danger of becoming a positive check upon it.

There can be no more damning comment upon a system of so-called academic freedom than the phrases one hears so often: "My degree depends upon my mark in Professor X's course," or, "If Professor Y gives me an "A" I shall get this or that honor." Professorial human nature is not equal to such a strain and ought not tȯ be subjected to it. There is no remedy but to sever as completely as possible all connection between the teaching and the bookkeeping functions of the university college. If we must have degrees, honors, promotions and all the rest of it — and there are many who would be glad to get rid of them altogether — they must be assigned by some process which will leave our teachers free to enter into any effective relation with their pupils without fear on the one side or favor on the other.

To sum up our suggestions as to the best way to maintain that idea of discipline for which the university college offers a specially inviting opportunity: Give the student a free choice of studies modified only by what we may fairly call natural limitations. Put no artificial barriers in his way. Keep before him real, scholarly aims. Hold him to fair, rigid and not too frequent tests of his acquirement and his working power. Let him learn the lesson of failure by finding that it hurts promptly, and he may safely be trusted to respond heartily to our reasonable expectations. It is upon this faith in the essential right-mindedness of our selected youth that every attempt to use freedom as a means of discipline must ultimately rest.

GENTLEMAN AND SCHOLAR[1]

THERE died not long ago in an academic community a man of whom men said, with singular unanimity, "He was a gentleman and a scholar, and he was the last of his kind." We are prone to call certain figures the last of their kind. Cato was "the last of the Romans," Maximilian I, Bayard, Sidney, and I know not how many others, were each "the last of the knights," and so on. What we mean by the phrase is that when a certain type of man has become well fixed and has done its special service in the world, there comes a time when it inevitably gives way to some new type. In the period of transition, while the two are in conflict, it is as if the older type became intensified in the persons of those who have to maintain it against the assaults of new and strange ideals. Instinctively they gather themselves together for the shock. They seem to feel the foundations of all true things slipping away, and they brace themselves to resist with all the tenacity of a faith founded upon generations of experience. They become therefore to the men of a new day even more strongly marked specimens of their type than those earlier men who really founded it, but who were not forced by opposition into quite so clear a consciousness of their own quality.

The man whom we carried to his grave was eminently formed by such a process of transition. He stood for a conception of scholarship which had dom-

[1] Reprinted from *The Atlantic Monthly*, June, 1900.

inated the world for many generations. In naming
him thus instinctively "gentleman and scholar" and
saying that he was the "last of his kind" we did not
mean that scholars had ceased or were likely to cease
to be gentlemen; nor did we mean that gentlemen
would no longer turn to the profession of the scholar.
The phrase was meant to convey rather the idea of a
certain necessary and inevitable connection of the two
things — scholarship and gentle living. This man had
not begun life as a "gentleman," and then sought scholarship as an adornment, a kind of decoration suited to
his class. Nor had he, because he was a scholar, come
to put on the outward seeming of a gentleman as being
the appropriate livery of his profession. Both these
devices are familiar to the observer of academic types.
We know the man of refined tastes and easy fortune
who comes into the scholar's life from above — choos-
ing it rather than chosen by it, and expecting to gather
its rewards without going through its sacrifices of
drudgery and obscurity. We know also the man of
parts, capable of hard work and gifted with all the
technical qualities of the scholar, who is driven into
the formal relations of cultivated intercourse without
ever really grasping its spirit or sharing its refining
influence.

The man whose memory we are recalling would
never have suggested even the inquiry whether he was
gentleman first and scholar afterward or the reverse.
One felt that the very distinctive quality in his type
was the inseparable interfusion of the two. His outward man gave instant assurance not merely of the

gentleman, but of the refining touch which a true spirit
of scholarship ought to add. His dress, his gait, his
bearing all combined to give the impression of careful
dignity which yet had no suggestion of effort. He wore
no uniform of a class, but was equally far from following the caprices of fashion. His linen was scrupulously
neat, but it would have been hard to name its precise
brand. His clothes were always of sober black, neither
of antique nor of the latest fashion. His high hat, of no
particular mould, was always carefully brushed, and
his ivory-headed cane suited his measured but busi-
nesslike step. His manner was cordial, but not effu-
sive; his greeting always expressing a hint of surprise,
as if he had been suddenly called out of his own world
of thought, but was glad to meet the human being who
had called him.

Modest as some women, he was firm in his opinions,
and knew how to express them in language that was
always forcible and often seemed to him on reflection
to have been violent. Then, with what eager haste he
would try to repair the wrong of which no one could
ever have suspected him — to take away the sting no
one but himself ever felt. "Old-fashioned" he undoubtedly was, in the fair sense that most good fash-
ions maintain themselves to a ripe old age, but one
never quite thought of him as a piece of the antique
world, so fresh and vital was his interest in all that was
best and finest in the new world around him. As to his
whole outward bearing among men there could be but
one natural expression for it — the grand simple name
of gentleman.

So was it also with his scholarship. It sat upon him lightly, as something into which he had grown by a natural evolution. How he had got it no one ever thought of inquiring. In what schools he had been taught, what academic degrees he had gained, to what faction of scholars he belonged — these were all indifferent things. Even the question, now so often asked, and not always quite relevant: "What has he done?" was never asked of him. What he had "done" was of no importance compared with what he *was*. He had never written a book. He could only with difficulty be persuaded to do now and then some little editorial work. His ideal of what books ought to be was so high that his modesty shrank from the risk of adding to the stock of the world's mediocrity. There was so much always to be learned, and, as he came to know more and more, his own attainment seemed ever so much the more inadequate, that he simply and naturally went on always making himself a fuller man, and pouring out his surplus upon the unresponsive youth in the intimate circle of the class-room and the study.

It would have been impossible for him to describe his method in learning or in teaching. It probably never occurred to him that he had any method. What he did was to keep himself always busy reading, and ordering what he read in such fashion as would best serve him in giving it out again to untrained minds. That was all there was of it, and if he had been asked how he did it, he would have flashed upon his inquirer with some bit of epigram that would have been worth a volume of pedagogic lore. Only now and again, in the fierce aca-

demic battles of his later years, as the new ideals of
scholarship began to shape themselves in discussion, he
would speak with no uncertain voice in defense of
principles which were only clearly revealed to him
when others began to crowd them from their place.
He died with his harness on, vigorous and beautiful
to the last, reverenced by those who fancied themselves
the prophets of better ideals, as embodying, after all, a
something they could hardly ever hope to reach.

One thing there could be no doubt of: the ideal he so
clearly set forth has pretty well passed from our sight.
Again let me say that this does not mean an inevitable
and general divorce between scholarship and gentle
living. It does not rest upon any single or narrow definition either of the gentleman or the scholar. It means
that the two are no longer thought of as necessarily
combined or as forming two essential parts of a single
complete and beautiful whole. The standards of
scholarship are in many ways more exacting than in the
generation now closed. The standard of the gentleman
is a thing so elusive, so dependent upon the unreason-
ing sentiment of a day or of a nation, that one would
hardly venture to formulate it; but it would be rash to
say that it is lowered in any essential degree. The
change has come, not in a lowering of these two ideals,
but in a separation of them. The gentleman may or
may not be a scholar; the scholar may or may not be
a gentleman.

With the phrase "gentleman and scholar" have been
disappearing at about equal pace certain others of
similar suggestion — "the education of a gentleman,"

"a liberal education," "an educated man." One hardly dares use these phrases to-day, so sure is one to be called upon with a certain accent of contempt to define them in terms that will be acceptable to all hearers. Until our generation we thought we knew what an educated man, in the ordinary use of language, was. He was a man who knew, or had known, certain things, and it was assumed that in the process of acquiring these things his mind had gained a certain kind of power and an openness to certain orders of ideas which made this man, in distinction from others not so disciplined, a man of education. By virtue of this academic discipline — assuming, of course, that he had done his part in the process — he entered into a fellowship of unspeakable value to himself. He became one in an order of men who had enjoyed a great and precious privilege, and were therefore bound to justify themselves by doing so much the better whatever work they might have to do in the world. Nothing was more common than to hear it said of a man, "He is an admirable lawyer, or doctor, or engineer, or architect, but he is not an educated man." He might have been trained in the school of life infinitely more effectively than he could have been in any college, but it was felt, and by no one probably more keenly than himself, that a certain kind of capacity and certain orders of ideas were lost to him forever by reason of that lack. This thing lacking, such as it was, he and others agreed to call "an education."

If we try to analyze this somewhat vague conception, we find that the essential quality of this earlier education was that it was in no sense professional. That is what men tried to express by the word "liberal," a word one hesitates now to use, because one fears to be understood as thereby describing all other education as "illiberal." No such opposition was ever intended, nor was it felt by the generations which came and went under those conditions. They rejoiced in the privilege of spending a certain period of youth in studies and in a mental attitude which had in view no direct practical use of what they were acquiring; in other words, no professional or technical aim. At the conclusion of that period they were not, and knew they were not, fitted to carry on any given work of life. They did believe, however, that they had made the best preparation for living, no matter what specific line of work they might follow. If, at that moment, they were to enter the world of scholarship, they were without technical training in any field. That was all to come, and they were as ready to begin the necessary professional discipline in their way as were the lawyer, the physician, and the engineer in theirs.

What they had had was a chance to fix solidly in their mental character the largeness and the beauty of the intellectual life. They had had time to think and to ripen without concern as to just whither their thinking and their unconscious development were leading them. No matter into what direction they might now turn their activity, they were bound to carry with them that essential thing which, for lack of a better name, we agreed to call the liberal spirit. If they had made a proper use of their chance they could never be *mere* specialists in their field. Their special and technical skill must always be infused with that higher and larger spirit of culture to which the professional spirit is always and necessarily more or less antagonistic. Expressed in terms of the inner life, such a scholar was, and was felt to be, a gentleman. No one cared what his origin might be. There was no fixed type to which he was forced to correspond. There might be endless diversity in his outward expression of himself; only, through all diversity and with every allowance made for original advantage or disadvantage, there was the inevitable stamp of the gentleman and the scholar.

Unquestionably the origin of this typical man is to be found in the traditions of English scholarship. It is only a few months since an English scholar said to the writer in all seriousness: "Education in England is intended for the sons of gentlemen, and if by chance any one else gets possession of it, he is sure to find himself bitterly reminded that he has gone out of his class." He was using the word "gentleman" in its narrowest sense, and his statement, if it were true, as I do not believe it is, would be an indictment against English education more fatal than any that could be pronounced. It serves, however, to show that there still survives, though here expressed in a degrading and perverted form, the idea of an essential connection between the notions of gentle breeding and intellectual culture. Its expression by my English friend was perverted, because it assumed the man of gentle birth who let himself be educated as a necessary decoration of his class.

But behind this perversion there lies the long history of an association of the two ideas from which we in American have derived our now rapidly fading tradition. English scholarship has, as a matter of fact, not only been largely in the hands of gentlemen, technically so called, but when men outside that mysterious circle have become scholars, they in their turn have cultivated the ideal of a necessary and vital union between life and learning. In other words, English scholarship has never been in any strict sense professional. Naturally, as we in America were forming our educational ideals, we followed largely in the same direction. To be sure we rejected, long since, the narrow use of the word "gentleman" which still widely prevails in England; but we clung fondly to the notion of the gentle life as a life not primarily devoted to a practical calling, and we still thought of it as associated almost necessarily with intellectual culture.

Within a generation, however, this tradition has been interrupted, and again, without drawing national lines too sharply, we may fairly say that the new conception of scholarship is German in its origin. German life has long been marked above all else by the quality of professionalism. The typical German is not a man of culture; he is a man of training. Above all things else the German loves a system, and will have it at any cost. So far as German scholarship has affected the world, it has done so less by the intrinsic value of its contribution than by the help it has given to other peoples in the systematic ordering of their study and thought.

A generation ago German scholarship was practically without direct influence upon American methods. Here and there an isolated scholar or writer, himself perhaps an importation, was calling attention to a new something which Germany had to offer to the world of scholarship. The discovery of German system coincided with the vast widening of the intellectual field produced by our new interest in natural science — an interest, by the way, which did not in any sense originate in Germany. "Science," "the scientific method," "truth by induction," have been the cry of the generation now coming to its close. To meet this new demand, education has had to modify its ideals. It has had to emphasize "training" instead of "culture" as its main purpose. It has come to aim at making a man fit for something in particular, rather than for anything he might afterward decide upon.

Education has felt powerfully the reaction of the immense material advance of this past generation. Not only have the subjects of education been greatly increased in number, and that chiefly in the direction of material and technical branches, but the mechanism of all education has been developed to an almost alarming extent. We have been learning from the Germans something of their own *Systemsucht*, and we have shown signs of our usual determination to better our instruction. There is not an educational nostrum from the elaborate fooleries of the kindergarten up to the highly sublimated pedagogical psychology of the "graduate schools" that we have not been willing to try.

It has been a period of great activity, and, mis-

directed as much of this activity has been, there can
be no absolute waste of serious and conscientious
effort. Great good things have come to pass and
greater are to come. Only let us ask ourselves, just
now, at the close of one generation of energy, what
shape our ideals have come to take, and whether we
may well modify them in any particular. The merest
glance at the program of our schools and colleges
shows the enormous advance in all the mechanism of
education, and in the term mechanism I would include
not merely the material equipment, but all that great
chapter of our subject which in the books comes under
the head of "organization" — grouping of topics in
departments, gradation of instruction, quality of text-
books — opportunities of every sort for getting the
most out of the great educational "plant."

The only serious question before us at this moment
is whether our machinery is not too dangerously complete. When we had less machinery we were compelled to rely more upon personal quality. A perfect
machine does its work almost without human aid; set it
going, supply it with raw material, and it turns out the
finished product with inevitable success. More than
this, the highly developed machine is able by its very
perfection to give to comparatively poor material an
apparent finish, which may deceive the unwary. The
very uniformity of the machine product conceals many
a defect and irregularity. On the other hand, a comparatively poor tool working on good material may, in
the right hands, give the best results. One theory of
manual training has been that pupils ought to be re-

quired to work first with dull and ill-contrived tools,
lest they learn to depend too much on the tool, and
too little on their own skill and talent.

There is precisely the question as to our new educational methods. Not really, of course, whether we
have made our machinery too good. No one could advise going back one step along the road we have already
traversed in that direction. Let us go on even, gaining
always better apparatus, better organization, better
comprehension of detail; but while we do this let us not
forget that our ultimate salvation is never to be found
in these things. While we present to ambitious youth
the pathways of scholarship, and hang out all the
lights we can to guide him, we must guard him carefully from the delusion that he has only to march
through these pathways in order to attain the desired
goal. We may prescribe conditions and defend them
by every practicable test; but all conditions must be
graded to a certain level of capacity, and all tests must
be held within certain limits of human fairness. The
more precisely conditions are defined, and the more
formally accurate the tests applied, the more we appeal
to an average grade of capacity.

Our machinery will enable us to turn out men
trained to certain definable forms of activity, men who
can be ticketed off in groups and applied in various
kinds of work in the world. It will never give us any
guaranty that these are men of real intellectual power,
whose personal quality can of itself command respect.
Underneath all the machine work there must lie the
same quality upon which the scholar of the earlier

generation exclusively relied. He had no training by any organization whatever. If he were trained at all, he trained himself. He came to be what he was by virtue of the inner impulse which alone, maintained through years of action and intensified by time, can guarantee the quality of a man.

Obviously this quality is difficult to describe. It cannot be measured in terms of academic honors. Erasmus of Rotterdam, explaining why he felt obliged to take a doctor's degree in Italy, says: "Formerly a man was called ' doctor ' because he was a learned man; but nowadays no one will believe a man is learned unless he is called ' doctor.' " A college president seeking a professor not long since made it a *sine qua non* that the candidate should be a doctor of philosophy. Another man might know more, be more highly qualified as a man, and a more effective teacher, but he must give way to the man, very possibly of less value, who had the trade-mark of his profession. I have known many a man, whose great fundamental need was intellectual refinement and culture, sacrificed to this semi-civilized demand for a certifiable kind of expert training.

So we come round again to the point from which we started, and the ideal of the past is seen to be also the truest ideal of the present. "Gentleman and scholar" remains the best expression of the product by which the new education must justify itself before the world. The mechanical appliances are pretty well completed. It remains for us to use them and not to let them use us. The American scholar of the future is undoubtedly to be a trained man in a sense quite different from that in which the older scholar could be said to be trained. Is he to be nothing else? The question is not an idle one. It is coming to us from many sides, not by any means solely from the *laudatores temporis acti*, who might be expected to cling fondly to traditions. It comes already from institutions which have made trial of men "trained" upon no foundation of scholarly character, and found them wanting. It comes from young men who have found their own best development checked and hampered by the mechanical processes of the academic mill. And it is coming also in vague and indistinct forms from that great helpless thing, the public, which misses, to its pain, the sacred something it was wont to associate with the name of the scholar.

The answer is to be found in a return to the conception of a necessary and essential union between learning and the higher life of the spirit. This conception must be made to enter vitally into every grade of our education from lowest to highest. It must not be set in opposition to the other conception of learning as essentially applicable to some human purpose. It must be united with it, so that our youth may grow up steadily to the conviction that a gentleman is a better tool than a scrub — that he will work better, play better, and fight better; and conversely that he who will not work well, play well, and fight well, is no gentleman. In that sense I should be glad to have it said of our education, as my English friend said of his, that American education is primarily intended for gentlemen.

THE CHOICE OF STUDIES IN COLLEGE

"LEARN to do the thing you don't want to do, at the time you don't want to do it, and to do it well." This was the sole advice given by a successful New York lawyer to his son who was just setting out on his course as a student a Harvard College. "Only that work can be well and profitably done which is done of the doer's own volition and in which he finds pleasure." This in substance was the teaching of those educators who led in what we may safely call the greatest educational reform through which our country has ever passed.

Here we have two apparently irreconcilable principles either of which might govern a student's choice of studies in a college where a large freedom of election is possible. Are they irreconcilable? Must the young man at the outset of his academic life accept one or the other of these alternatives, and if so which is the more likely to give him the kind of result he has a right to expect? Or, is it possible that a rational combination of the two may best of all serve his turn? On the one hand we see the ideal of conformity to some established order, the recognition of some authority which the youth is bound to respect. On the other is the idea that he and he alone has the right to set the standard that shall guide him through the whole conduct of his collegiate years. In support of the former ideal he will have the whole force of tradition, the weight of experience, the security of conservatism. For the latter he has only himself to depend upon. To be sure, he may fortify his choice by every kind of advice he can get, but in the last resort he must make his own decisions and abide by the consequences.

I feel myself in some respects especially qualified to sympathize with both these conceptions of academic duty, because I have had the opportunity to try them both under very varied and highly instructive conditions. The first two years of my college life were passed under the old traditional compulsory system, with a fixed curriculum of studies, a strictly regulated scheme of hours, a paternalistic theory of college morals, and a rigid method of official bookkeeping. The range of studies had hardly gone beyond the conventional classics and mathematics, with a prudent sprinkling of modern languages and "science." What passed for teaching was mainly the hearing of recitations from text-books and the checking off of the student's classroom performances on a numerical rank list. During my last two years, under the presidency of Mr. Eliot, changes were gradually made in the direction of larger liberty, and I recall with the greatest vividness the sense of stimulation which they produced in young minds not at all capable of understanding their real import, but swift to respond to their generous appeal.

When, five years later, I returned to take my place on the other side of the teacher's desk, these changes had so far progressed that practically the whole of the college offering was in the "elective" column. Mean-

while the colleges of the country had all begun to feel
the breath of this new academic spirit and by the year
1880 it was clear that the principle of a large, if not a
complete election of studies was so firmly established
that it was never again seriously to be called in question. It was an inspiring experience to bear one's
modest part in this great development. The "eighties"
may fairly be described as the golden age of academic
freedom in this country. Alike with teachers and
pupils it was like a new wine, rousing them out of the
torpor of the generation just past, driving them to new
exertion and showing them ever new possibilities of
sound accomplishment. Criticism there always was in
plenty. The faint-hearted were always incredulous as
to the ultimate effect of what appeared to them a lax,
ill-regulated, haphazard way of doing things. Youth,
they insisted, would never be anything but youth. It
could never rise to the height of making wise decisions
in a matter involving so many considerations about
which youth could have no experience and only the
vaguest kind of intuitions.

The inevitable result was that scruples as to the
wisdom of a free election of studies began to gather
force and to take form in protests, investigations and
finally in administrative action of various sorts. Restraints of one kind and another were devised, whereby
the principle of freedom might be guided in "safe"
directions without being altogether sacrificed. Group-
ings of studies were attempted, within which considerable latitude of choice might be allowed. Certain
studies especially liable to neglect were shifted over

into the list of the "required" and thereby subjected
to a notable stigma as compared with the "elective"
subjects. One felt as one looked over the whole field of
this experimentation how firm the hold of the elective
idea had become. A young teacher given his choice
between a position where he would be called upon to do
required work and another where his work would be
largely elective would unhesitatingly choose the latter,
because he knew that it would give him a more stimulating response to his own scholarly and personal
effort.

Still the protest and the limiting went on. One of
the most disquieting effects of the free election was the
enormous inflation of college programs. In the absence of any clear directing principle there was no
better guide than the wish, or even the whim, of the individual teacher. Nowhere was there an authoritative
voice with the right or the power to speak a decisive
word as to the relative importance of this or that "new
course" offered out of the fresh enthusiasm of the
teacher. Such enthusiasm was the very most important asset which the scholar could bring to the service
of the college. Who should dare quench the generous
spirit that prompted the new proposal? It was the
surest proof that the college had here a man who would
grow and be a more and more valuable servant as long
as he lived. Certainly faculty committees could never
undertake any effectual control over this expansion,
for the privilege they might deny to an over enthusiastic colleague they might well be seeking for themselves
at the next turn of affairs.

Effective criticism of this inflation of programs could hardly come from any source outside the college, because outsiders could not have the technical knowledge which might make their criticism valuable. The result has been that the offerings in all departments have grown beyond all reasonable bounds. The right to announce almost any "course" has become so entrenched in college traditions that any invasion of it seems like a violation of the first principles of academic freedom. This is not the place for any discussion of the limits which might wisely be set to the widening of programs. I refer to it here only to suggest the great embarrassment of riches which confronts the young student at the very outset of his academic life and also to remind the reader how firmly fixed the elective principle has become in our American higher education.

The question of a return to the ancient system of required studies is no longer open. The only problems of interest are: what studies should be optional, upon what principles such options may be based, how they may most wisely be grouped, at what stage election should begin, and how the choice of individual students may be guided — if indeed guidance be admitted at all. These questions of detail are answered very differently and must continue to receive different answers according to the personal convictions and the corporate limitations of college guardians. Such diversity of opinion and of practice is one of the happy conditions of American education. It will be a sorry day when our federal supervision, so far wisely restricted to statistical functions, shall attempt to control local educational

effort in the interest of a standardized and therefore a
degraded ideal of our national education. Those who
can afford to try experiments are likely to keep on
doing so, and those who either cannot afford or are unwilling to experiment may safely wait for the results.

For the moment we are concerned with no one of the
specific questions just referred to, but rather with the
somewhat more general problem: given a tolerably
free elective system, are there any principles that can
safely be laid down by which all elections shall be
governed? Obviously, if we could have such principles
clearly demonstrated and formulated to general acceptance there would be little room for election. We
should only have to turn to the special category in
which the individual student belonged and by a simple
rule of thumb pick out for him the line of study he was
predestined to follow. Perhaps in some academic mil-
lenium our friends, the psychological pedagogues, will
have discovered the desired categories and furnished
us with the machinery for fitting them upon the right
boy at the right moment. For the present we are,
however, met by two primary difficulties. First, we
cannot say precisely what studies or groups of studies
will produce any given educational result, and second,
we cannot say as to any considerable proportion of
boys at any period much under the age of graduation
from college just what aptitudes and qualities of character ought to determine their choice of studies.

These obstacles to any prescription of election are
fundamental, but this has not prevented us from a vast
deal of theorizing and not a little practical experiment-

ing on the tacit assumption that such obstacles do not exist. We have built up elective systems on the supposition that principles which elude the trained speculation and observation of experts would somehow reveal themselves unto our babes. On the whole far less harm has been done by these experiments than might have been expected, and so much good has come from them, that one wonders whether, after all, we may not have been following principles without knowing it. At any rate it may be worth while to try to formulate some of the possibilities that confront students and their advisers both lay and professional.

Probably all would agree that choice of studies ought to have some relation to the ultimate occupation of the youth; but, to determine this relation in advance two things are necessary: we must know what the occupation is to be and we must be clear as to the bearing of studies upon it. As regards the first point, there are those who believe that by the age of thirteen or fourteen a boy's tastes, capacities and character are clearly enough discernible to warrant his advisers in planning for him a course of study which shall lead to some specific expertness. There are others who think that such indications are altogether misleading, vague, transitory impulses having only the value of preliminary notes of quality, to be borne in mind indeed, but not to be trusted or built upon. Those who hold this latter view maintain that such differences of endowment as can safely be depended upon to give direction to one's life are matters of later development; that, at least up to the age of entrance to college, differences are to be described in terms of general rather than of specific quality; boys are bright or stupid, diligent or lazy, quick or slow, receptive or resistant; the bright boy is bright all round, the dull boy is apt to be as dull at one thing as another. They will frankly admit that most boys find some things "easier" than others, but this, they say, is not generally indicative of anything upon which we can safely act in advising for the future. A few months or even weeks may wholly change the boy's view of a subject. What repelled him under one teacher may under another become a real joy to him. What seemed at the beginning unintelligible and was therefore hateful may become full of attraction as the boy gets deeper and deeper into its meaning. What was a mere grind so long as it stood alone begins to light up in all directions as soon as it appears in its relations to other subjects. Geniuses and dolts are barred from the discussion; the mysterious Providence that created them will take care of them. We are dealing with the normal selected boy of the high school or the academy, whose circumstances permit him to look forward to the college.

Among such boys, say the opponents of an early and decisive choice of studies supposedly leading to specific occupation, any such early decision would be a grievous wrong, not so much because it would involve him in unprofitable study, as because it would cut him off from many lines of work in which he might find success and which he will probably come to miss when it is too late. On the other hand, the friends of an early determination of choice remind us that life is shorter than it used to be; that we are preparing a generation of experts; that the "all round man" is a creature of the past; that the future belongs to the man of training rather than to the man of "education." They tell us that there is no successful work except that in which we delight, and that we cannot delight in work for which we have no taste. They call our attention to the wonderful change that comes over the spirit of a man's work when, for the first time, he finds himself really master of a given task and point us to the rapture of the man or the boy riding a hobby as the supreme, if sometimes fantastic, demonstration of their view.

From this comparison of opinions we come back to the two opposing moral views of education with which we started. If, on the one hand, it is true that the best work comes easiest and that, therefore, we ought in any extended scheme of liberal education to include a large element of study selected on the ground of natural aptitude, it is equally true on the other hand, that work done without any regard to whether we like it or not, done simply because it is given us to do and done "as by God's law" has also its great educational value. It gives to the doer something of that moral force without which no workman is thoroughly well equipped. It teaches him to do his work without thought of self. It may reveal aptitudes he has never felt or shown before and it will certainly give him a confidence in all future work which will be of infinite service to him. If we allow a too early election of studies on the ground of aptitude there is danger that it will become rather a neglect of studies on the ground of supposed inaptitude.

But let us now consider the large class of cases of fairly clear demarcation along lines of real difference in taste and capacity. Such cases may in general be brought under the one broad distinction of the "literary" from the "scientific" mind. In any school there will be boys who seem to take naturally to books and others, equally capable and intelligent, who gather their knowledge instinctively from their observation of things around them. To the former class books have an attraction in themselves; to the latter they are rather a resort for the explanation of puzzles in the world of observation. The former have an instinctive taste for literary form; the latter are interested only in what the book has to say about the thing for which they consult it. Or again, to carry this distinction out a little further: there will always be one class of boys to whom the interesting thing is always the human thing and another class who find their chief pleasure in things "natural," as we say. The former class is naturally driven to books because it is only in books that the record of human experience is to be found, and as yet they have had no chance to study human life by the way of observation. The latter have not the same need of books, because their world is all about them, and the impulse to observe and to conquer it is strong within them.

So it comes about quite naturally, that the subjects which interest the former class are history as the story of organized human life, imaginative writing as the poetry of human feeling, language because it is the expression of human thought, and philosophy because it shows them the play of the human mind upon problems which it, and it alone can solve. The latter class take more readily to mathematics as dealing with absolute relations independent of all human thought or will, to chemical or physical experiment as helping to explain the great processes of outward nature, and to geology and biology as showing the history and present conditions of the world of matter.

The boy who is always to be found curled up in a corner with a book, and the boy who is forever roaming the fields hunting for "specimens" are the types of these two great classes of mental endowment. I am not forgetting that, within these two classes are infinite varieties of capacity and that some attention must be paid to these varieties, but for the moment we may regard these two groups as sufficiently representing the most pressing alternatives in the young man's choice of studies. Let us suppose that by the age of fifteen it is tolerably clear in which of these groups a given youth belongs; how shall we advise him in his choice? Thinking first of the occupation he is likely to follow, we shall probably expect that the bookish, humanly inclined boy will become a lawyer, a clergyman, a university man, an author, a journalist or a politician — in the nobler sense of that dubious word — while the experimenting, observing, collecting kind of boy will be a physician, a professor of natural science, a practical chemist, an engineer, mining, civil, electrical, sanitary or what not, an architect or a manager of manufacturing interests. Either of them may turn out an ordinary business man in such line of work as accident may determine. We will assume that each is free to follow his natural bent as far as he will.

Now there are two diametrically opposed theories as to the proper choice of studies for youths of these marked tastes and capacities. One theory is that, since the final occupation is to be determined by natural bent, the aim of education should be to strengthen this bent as much as possible and to begin this strengthening process as early as possible. It should be taken as a providential hint and followed out at every turn. The youth to whom knowledge comes most easily and naturally through books should be given books. The tasks his soul abhors, such as measuring lines and producing chemical reactions and classifying flowers and comparing rocks, to say nothing of all mathematics beyond the multiplication table, all these he should be spared. They find no response within him, and education without the inner response is a mere mockery.

So with the youth of "scientific" tastes; why torment him with human history? He is willing to take all that for granted; or with ancient literature? it has no message for him; or with poetry which deals only with fictions, while facts, clear, palpable facts, are what he cares for; or with the idle speculations of philosophy, when things as they are so completely absorb and satisfy him. Let each follow the line of least resistance; this will carry him farther with less loss of power. His work will all be of the happy kind which alone can bring success, and success again will give strength and confidence for more work to come. At the conclusion of his studies he will be an "expert," and there will be a place waiting for him where he can apply himself with most effect in the work of the expert world.

Opposed to this theory is another equally well defined and equally dear to those who hold it. They oppose the principle of specific training because they believe that a man so trained from a very early period will be a less effective man *in his own line* than if he had made himself acquainted with a wider range of subjects and had given his mind a chance to work in a greater variety of ways. Not only, they say, would his interests in the world be thus greatly increased and widened, but the reaction of these larger interests upon his own profession would give him a kind of mastery in it which a man whose point of view during his years of preparation had been almost exclusively fixed upon one single professional end could hardly hope to attain. How complete the opposition between these two opinions is may be illustrated by an experience of the writer. Happening, in the course of conversation with a very eminent authority in education, to express the opinion that a certain youth looking forward to the medical profession would do well to follow in college chiefly studies not related to medicine, I received the reply: "Well, in my judgment a man who should give that advice would be little less than crazy." It was not a tactful answer, but it had at least the great merit of frankness. It expressed with perfect accuracy the argument for expert training. The conception of an education beyond the early secondary stage which should make every thoughtful expert a better man in his profession simply did not exist in the mind of this leader of educational thought. It represented to him an antiquated theory destined to give way rapidly before the advancing demands of the expert world.

In telling this experience I have already indicated to which side of this fundamental question my own sympathies incline. Of course, every one must admit the immense increase of specialization in every field of activity, and no thoughtful person can doubt that in truth the future of professional success belongs largely to the specialized expert. That is not the question. The question is: what is the function of education in college and secondary school, dealing with selected youths from, say, fifteen to twenty-two, in view of the fact that the best of them are destined to become ultimately more or less narrow specialists? Does this fact make it more, or does it make it less incumbent on the sub-professional education to supply a basis of liberal culture of mind and soul upon which a true specialization may be built?

At the risk of seeming a candidate for a mad-house I venture to submit that this inevitable fact of specialization lays upon our colleges more than ever the duty of holding a much needed balance between the demands of the professions and those of society, of American democratic society, upon the educated man. In our world no man can be so much a specialist that he can afford to neglect the all important fact of his American citizenship. The physician, for example, is not merely a physician. True, during the first years of stress, in which he is making his place in professional life, nothing is so important to him as success in that line and in that alone. But, as soon as his place is secure, other demands press in upon him. He becomes, as a citizen, professionally responsible for the health of his community. Public works requiring a knowledge of men and of politics claim him as professional adviser and advocate. School administration, happily not yet entirely in expert hands, needs his help. Charity organization with its infinitely complicated moral and social aspects calls upon him. The moment he turns to any one of these subjects he finds that his exclusively professional training does not take him very far. If in his formative years his interest in subjects lying apparently far beyond the reach of his future profession has not been aroused, his sympathies with human life in all its varied aspects quickened, his mind stirred to some active reflection upon the great problems of the speculative world, problems which, after all, underlie the practical working of life as it is — if on all these sides he has received no impulses during the irresponsible years of his youth he will be a less valuable physician than he ought to be. He may be doing incalculable good in his specialty, but he will find many sides of himself atrophied for lack of use, and there will be countless times when as a man among men, as a citizen of the Republic, he will miss what it is now too late for him to gain. If, however, in those earlier years he has kept himself open to all those other influences, has learned something of what history and literature and philosophy have to teach, no matter how closely his special work may have held him, when he is again brought into contact with these things he has points of sympathy which will enable him at once to take up new lines of activity and not fall out of the special service he has trained himself to give. The whole vast movement of human life takes on new meanings for him the moment he feels that his specialty is only one little part of it all, a part that needs all the rest to make its own meaning complete.

If this is true of the physician, whose work by its very nature touches so closely upon all human relations, the same may be said with even greater force of many other forms of expert training that seem to remove a man further from human contact. Take, for example, the great and almost new profession of engineering in all its multitudinous forms — the building of railways and bridges, the working of mines and all the machinery that belongs to it, the application of constantly new forces to the service of man. Is he going to be the leader in all this wonderful activity whose mind has never been allowed to take its period of non-professional, that is "liberal," wandering in fields where he knew he was not going to spend his productive years? Is it not rather to be expected that the more broadly a man is equipped in the years of formation, the more effective will be his leadership in the years of production? It is true, that the great mass of journey-work in every profession will have to be done by the men of severe and narrow training; but that is not the question for the advisers of college students. Their problem is rather this: shall these selected youths, who, if any, ought to look forward to being the leaders of their generation, be advised to get into the line of specialization as soon as possible or to prolong, as far as they dare, the precious period of wider study?

There is one widespread delusion on which a word of warning may be in place at just this point. Admitting heartily the value of wider interests men often say: Oh, there will be plenty of time for these things by-and-by. First professional success, and then, in the pleasant shadow of later life we will come round to these more genial pursuits. There can be no greater self-deception than this. The strain of professional life never grows less. Success only brings new responsibility and opens new avenues to ambition. The promised time of relaxation never comes, and our youthful enthusiasms remain a happy vision of the past. If we are ever to give our young men that wider view of study and thought which shall make specialization intelligent and effective, we must give it to them early, and we must not cut it off too soon. Once stopped, it can never be taken up again. Carried on long enough to show its real value, such "liberal" study remains as a deposit of suggestion and inspiration upon which, as occasion offers, the man may draw with ever renewed confidence.

Coming back once more to our crude division of boys into the bookish-humane-literary class and the observing-collecting-experimenting class I venture to give this general advice as to the choice of studies in school and college. For boys of both classes up to the college age, a fairly even division between the two types of subject. Momentary distaste should have but little weight in the decision at this stage. If lack of taste prevent high success in certain lines of work, no matter;

let the boy feel that this is only a natural part of his experience. He ought to expect to do better in some things than in others. Only be sure that his supposed distaste does not arise from bad teaching or from some other accidental circumstance. Save him, if possible, from the notion that he is in any way "peculiar" in his likes and dislikes. Persuade him for the present to take things as they come and to believe that if he will only work hard he can conquer even the most repellant of tasks. It is pretty safe to say that nothing he may acquire in this preliminary study will be wasted in the long account.

This leads me to say a word on one of the most subtle temptations offered to the youth and his advisers. "Development of the individual," "special attention to individual peculiarities," "special courses for individual pupils " — these are some of the catchwords of "educators" who like to talk about the "New Education," as if there were any educational nostrum that has not been tried over and over again and become "old" in its turn. The emphasis on the individual is doubtless due to a reaction against an over emphasis upon uniformity, regularity and system which was the natural accompaniment of the prodigious advance in all the mechanisms of education in the generation just passed. The public school and its natural sequence the state university could hardly have been brought to their present dimensions without some such exaggeration of the elements of uniformity. All standardization must necessarily press rather downward than upward, and it is a not unwholesome sign that thoughtful persons are reacting against it in favor of a greater regard for the individual.

What specially concerns us here is the danger of keeping the pupil's individuality in the foreground of his own thought and that of his advisers. That danger is especially to be guarded against in this whole matter of the choice of studies in college. Most youths are not exceptional in any sense that is worth very much consideration in determining the course of their academic life. They have their peculiarities, of course, and these are bound to work themselves out in the detail of their study. That is wholesome, and to the wise teacher it is the most welcome of all signs that the youth has something in him worth working for. I am only insisting that it should not be made the starting-point of educational effort.

The advocates of "individual attention" are fond of pointing back to an iron age of deadly routine, of compulsory curricula, of dreary memorizing, of unnecessary repetition, and all the rest of it. They show us by comparison the flowery paths of joy in learning, of short cuts to what is essential, of play as a form of work. They forget that learning in itself brings joy, that the essential thing reached first by the long road opens up the short cut, and that work well done becomes the most satisfying sort of play. First the learning, the patient long road, the unreluctant work, and then will come the joy, the dexterity and the sense of ease we call play. Let the youth planning his college work think of himself first as probably a very ordinary person and, on the whole, follow the well-trodden paths. As he advances along these he will certainly perceive in himself aptitudes for one or another kind of work, and may gradually trust himself more and more to their leading.

There can be no doubt that the system of rigid uniform requirement offered a premium for the display of some of the worst qualities in the teacher. It tended to elevate the brutal drillmaster to the highest place in the pedagogic hierarchy. The "successful" teacher was the one who could show the highest record of candidates for promotion, no matter by what shady methods such records were produced. And yet, as the victims of these methods look back over their school years, they see the value of much that was hateful to them at the time. They see that the really good teacher, even under a vicious system, was perfectly aware of individual capacities and incapacities and strove in his way to utilize them both for the profit of his pupils.

Thus prepared the boy will enter college with the beginnings of many subjects and with a pretty fair idea of the general kinds of work in which he may excel. With the change from school to college comes also another change, so subtle and yet so fundamental that until it takes place one is never safe in predicting very confidently as to a boy's future. The sudden increase of responsibility, the novel methods of teaching with their appeal to his own initiative and their hints of a great world of learning beyond, the stimulus of contact with superior boys from other schools and different homes, all these are likely to rouse in any youth not wholly indifferent a multitude of new ideas. Gradually his own tastes and capacities become clearer to himself and to others. His own judgment as to what he had better do becomes more decided and more trustworthy. Now he and his advisers are better able to form some plan of studies which shall enable him to get out of his college life all there is in it for him. Assuming still that our boy has shown a fairly distinct leaning towards one or the other of our two great classes of subjects, how shall this inclination now influence his choice?

Up to now he has carried on both types of work with a fair degree of evenness. He has made many beginnings, but, if he is a boy of any perception he must often have felt the unsatisfactoriness of this way of working. Often he must have thought: "Dear me! If only I might go on with this thing and not be compelled, just as I am getting into it, to switch off to something else!" Such a feeling of impatience is just the best possible hint for him that now at last the time has come when he may wisely do what he has vaguely desired to do. Now the moment has come for him to taste some of the joys of specialization. But with this come also the further questions: how far shall he specialize and along what lines? As to the extent of specialization, no precise answer can be given, but, speaking in terms of proportion, it would generally be a pity if more than one half of an undergraduate's time should be given to any one line of study. Nor should that half be the last two years of his college time. It should be so distributed throughout his four years that he can plan some definite progression from the elementary to the advanced and at the same time may continue his studies in what he will now be thinking of as his outside or "minor" interests. In general we may say that the proportion of specialization should increase but should never come to exclude more general studies. Acting upon this plan he should be able to secure a group of courses of instruction which may fairly be considered a topical unit.

If I have seemed so far to emphasize chiefly the importance of a wide and liberal choice of studies I may perhaps with the more reason dwell for a moment upon the value of specialization. In moderation its value to the undergraduate is very great. It gives him, probably for the first time in his life, a sense of power. Until now his acquirements have seemed fatally unrelated to each other and to any perceptible end. Now he sees relations shaping themselves at every turn. Whatever he does takes on meaning by its dependence upon something else. On many a little point he may even become a kind of authority among his mates, and his own proper self-respect grows accordingly. New possibilities develop themselves before him, new capacities shape themselves within him. The skill he acquires in his special work comes into play elsewhere. He feels now, as never before, the value of his teachers, and gains some notion of the ways they have gone before him.

These are not on my part *a priori* speculations but the result of long experience and observation. I recall a long procession of youths to whom this kind of specialized work was an epoch in their lives. One of the most harum-scarum victims of a foolish early training I have ever known was saved to usefulness and self-respect by the sudden discovery in himself of capacity in a certain line of effort and the sense of mastery which even such fitful application to it as he could give had brought him. I asked a youth who had apparently wasted three years of college life what had converted him into the eager and successful student of medicine he had then become. He answered: "Nine hours a day for six weeks in a chemical laboratory."

If then specialization at a rather early stage of education is desirable, how far shall the college go in insisting upon it? I incline to the opinion of those who would make it in some form a condition of the bachelor's degree. It used to be said that this degree represented only an accumulation of variegated incapacities. What this reproach meant was that the newly fledged *Baccalaureus* had been allowed to browse over so wide a field that he had gathered nowhere a substantial meal. It is on the whole an encouraging sign that college programs are more and more trying to overcome this evil. Under various forms of grouping, expressed sometimes in rather fantastic language, they are inviting students to decide, not too late, in what kind of study they would like to spend a considerable part of their college time. The plan I have elsewhere [1] suggested of making the degree depend upon the passing of a series of graded examinations is based upon this idea. By this method the holder of a bachelor's degree would make

[1] Pages 122 *sqq.*

some approach to the attractive if impossible standard of the man who "knows something about everything and everything about something." At all events he would know something about a good many things and a good deal about one of them. He will have learned to concentrate upon something, and he will have had at the same time the advantage of distribution over a rather wide range of interests.

Up to this point we have been dealing with boys whose future was so far, but only so far, indicated that we could classify them roughly into two main groups, the "literary" and the "scientific." But aside from these there are two other classes to be considered. One includes the small number of those youths whose taste and capacity point with absolute certainty, as by the finger of Destiny, to a definite profession. For these predestined specialists the choice of studies would seem to be the simplest possible. Here plainly is a "leading" not to be distrusted. To check such a divine impulse seems to be a sort of sacrilege. And, indeed, if we could be sure that with the clearly pronounced taste there went and always would go an equally pronounced capacity for work and an equally intelligent grasp of the things made attractive by taste, then surely one would be inclined to say: here at last is a case where everything ought to be done to strengthen the natural bent. Let this youth have his full swing, and take the chances.

Unfortunately, what seemed to be a rare combination of taste and capacity only too often proves to be rather taste and incapacity. Let any one familiar, for

example, with the profession of the ministry try to recall how many cases he has known of youths who
fancied themselves "called" to that honorable service
but who proved to be absolutely unfitted for its exacting demands. Their tastes pointed correctly, but their
capacities failed to respond. And, on the other side of
the house, how many a youth "of scientific tastes" has
found himself unequal to the strain of prolonged and
patient investigation or to the intelligent application of
details to conclusions. Especially misleading are the
indications of taste in the field of aesthetics. The
"artistic temperament" manifesting itself in a precocious knack at expression in whatever form, appeals
with especial force to indulgent advisers not similarly
endowed. Because they cannot understand him they
feel that this youth must be of some unusual clay, and
they hesitate to distort the model. Let him follow his
bent, they say, and trust to his genius to see him
through. They are likely to forget that of all temperaments the artistic is the least to be counted upon.
"Taste" may well prove to be only a form of laziness.
The great artists have seldom leaned very heavily on
their temperaments. They have learned their trade,
whatever it may have been, in the sweat of hard and
often uncongenial work. The greatest of them have
been artists all round, men who saw and felt the world
about them with sympathetic insight. He who hopes
to join their illustrious company should begin by laying broad and deep the foundations of a liberal education with so much of specialization as will serve to keep
his goal always before him.

Taste is an indication, not to be neglected; it is not a guide to be too closely followed. Even if we could be sure that the youth is to pursue the course of life toward which his tastes seem to point, we cannot be sure that this very life will not demand of him at every turn the kind of training he has seen fit to avoid. Life is too complicated; it will not be checked off into separate little fields. The borders cross and cross again. Even the predestined specialist needs the balance that comes from a sympathetic understanding of other men's work. If he has not that his own work will suffer. Only the genius, a part of whose endowment is precisely this intuitive sense of relation and proportion, can afford to trust entirely and from the beginning the leading of his own impulses. A safe principle in dealing with a boy of marked and irrepressible tastes would be to give him every reasonable opportunity to demonstrate their force and permanence. At the same time he should not be allowed to neglect studies seemingly unrelated to his tastes. Then, in proportion as his tastes develop into aptitudes and these again into accomplishment, he may more and more freely follow them. If he grows in wisdom as he grows in learning he will himself be the first to recognize the value of the things he had been tempted to neglect. He will come out a clearly defined specialist, but not a narrow one. As he leaves college already marked as a man of promise in his line he will be prepared to take up the advanced work of his profession with an intelligence born of respect for all learning as ultimately related to his own.

These form our first class of exceptional youths — exceptional in the distinctness of their tastes and their apparent aptitudes. The second class of exceptions includes the extreme opposites of these, the boys who have, or seem to have, no definite leanings of any sort. So devoid of such indications are they that we cannot even place them in our two chief divisions of the literary and the scientific types. Eventually they may become professional men or business men, or they may join the slowly increasing ranks of the unclassified. On the whole, perhaps this is the happiest group of all. It may well be doubted if it contains a larger proportion of the really idle and indifferent than the others; for moral distinctions run criss-cross through all varieties of taste and capacity.

These are the men of all others for whom an elective system may have the greatest value, as it may also prove the greatest snare. If we could follow the working of the minds of this more or less submerged section of our youth we should probably find that, consciously or unconsciously, they were spending more energy than they would care to confess in the effort to find out what they do like and what they are fit for. That is a perfectly rational use of energy in a young man, and it should be respected, but it cannot count for very much in the general scheme of his college life. The fleeting glimpses he may catch from time to time are pretty likely to prove mere will-o'-the-wisps, quite unsafe guides for him to follow. If he trusts them his regrets as to his choice will probably outweigh his satisfactions.

At all events let him not begin too early to trouble himself on this point. Let him make some kind of plan without special reference to his supposed likes or dislikes and then pursue this plan pretty strictly until he gets some certain evidence of its unsuitableness for him. Such a plan would have to be based upon some principle, and perhaps this would serve as well as another: At first let him follow a number of different subjects, partly in continuation of those he began at school, partly breaking new ground. Then, after a year or more, let him pursue somewhat more specially those lines in which he has had most success. It would be well if out of these he could select some group as a topical unit in which he may possibly hope for something like distinction. It will be a happiness for such a youth if he can prepare such a plan at the very outset of his college life reserving, however, the possibility of change as his knowledge of himself and of his circumstances shall increase.

Almost any plan will be better than the haphazard suggestions upon which a large part of our college elections are based. It would be idle to offer here more than the most general hints, for the choice of every youth will properly vary somewhat from that of every other; but it would not be out of place if colleges were to issue model groups of studies based upon certain different sets of conditions. That this has not been done more than it has is the proof of its exceeding difficulty. It is also one of the best justifications of a wide elective system, for if such guides were easily accessible an elective system would be a superfluous luxury.

On the other hand a free elective system is a permanent challenge to individuals — teachers, students of pedagogy, men of letters or of science, any one who can speak with a show of authority, to publish and defend such theories of election as seem to them likely to be useful. These theories can carry no greater weight than belongs to the personality of their authors. Comparison between them may be a most useful and instructive aid to those who have to advise students in specific cases. The trouble with such attempts generally has been, that they have tried to cover too wide a range of needs under one theory, or have been built up too exclusively with reference to some one determining idea. If, for example, we are given a workable scheme based upon future occupation, it would hopelessly fail to help those who have no clear idea as to what their future occupation is to be. If we could satisfy the demands of the undetermined, we should miss the needs of the specially endowed. A college course might well be sketched on the basis of carrying out to completion the work already begun in the school. We can imagine an attractive and apparently intelligent set of plans based upon psychological principles as seen in the order of development of the human faculties. Some day, perhaps, the doctrine of "educational values" will be so clearly worked out that we can prescribe effective doses of this or that subject at different stages of the long disease of youth. The more of these attempts the better, provided only that we be on our guard against the inherent weaknesses of them all. No one of them will take us very far, but taken together they will help to show how very serious a matter is this of election and how many considerations go to the making of a reasonable plan for any individual student.

Now, having thus warned the reader that all schemes of election of college studies must be taken with great caution, I venture to offer a few rather more specific suggestions. And first, I must frankly confess that as at present enlightened — or darkened, as the case may be, I believe in the traditional classical and mathematical preparation for a liberal education. I believe in it, not because it is traditional, nor on any theoretical grounds whatever, but because, having waited a life time with open mind for the coming of something better, I cannot yet perceive what that something better is. I have vivid memories of long faculty discussions as one by one the defenses of the old system were broken down and its citadel invaded by a horde of intruders varying in intellectual "values" from Elementary Greek to Iron Filing. We have waited patiently for the fruits of all this sincere and eager effort, but they have not appeared, and there are many signs that thoughtful men in every walk of life who have the interests of a true human culture at heart are turning back once more to those perennial sources of mental and spiritual quickening, the ancient literatures of Greece and Rome.

The reasons for this reaction can be stated very briefly in terms of practical value. These literatures and the civilizations they represent are the bases of the civilization in which we find ourselves. The languages in which they are written contain the roots of the language. we speak and from which we derive all our knowledge of the written word. The literature we read, the most precious inheritance of our race, is permeated throughout with reference to that classical world which has been its chief inspiration. If we desire to keep ourselves in touch with the past for the benefit of the present and the future we cannot be indifferent to these things. Our occupation with them is not a matter of mere idealism; it is a practical consideration of high importance. This is one group of reasons why the intensive study of the classic languages holds a quite peculiar position among possible subjects of liberal education.

There is another group which has a more directly pedagogical bearing upon our choice. We as speakers of English are almost without experience in the use of inflection as a means of expressing thought through language. There is no way in which a comprehension of the meanings and the possibilities of inflection can so well be attained as through the study of the Latin and Greek and the translation of their idiom into our own. Further, our English syntax, flexible and capable of expressing any desired meaning as it is, can never give us the same training in the fundamental principles of all syntax as can be gained from the study of the classic writers. There are, of course, two answers to this argument. One is a general denial; inflection, we are told, can be just as well learned from the study of German or French, and syntax can be taught by a careful analysis of our own idiom. The other answer is an "avoidance"; both these matters of inflection and syntax are nothing but a sort of logomachy, a linguistic game, interesting and amusing to the professional player but of no educational importance for the ordinary candidate for a liberal degree. Taken together these objections form the basis of the main charges against an intensive pursuit of classical studies in school and college, the charges of falseness and futility.

In reply it may be said first, that the objections are not in themselves sound. It is only partially true that the principles of inflection can be as well learned from French or German as from Latin or Greek. The modern tongues have suffered many changes, mostly in the way of simplification, which have broken up the forms of classic inflection. I am not one of those who lament such changes. On the contrary I incline to think that the loss of inflected forms is more than compensated for by the increased flexibility arising from the more liberal use of connecting particles. It is not a question of better or worse, for every language is capable of expressing any idea which its habitual users are capable of holding. It is a question of educational values, and the defenders of the classic tradition maintain that an easy familiarity with at least one highly inflected language is the very best means of acquiring that command of verbal expression which is one of the marks of our educated man.

As to the use of English for the study of syntax: I believe in it most thoroughly. I look back to the "analysis of sentences" in an old-fashioned public school as one of the most valuable contributions to my own "education." Such study ought to form a part of the training of every pupil; but we are here concerned with the selected minority who are going to the higher grades of liberal learning and who, therefore, may justly claim the privilege of going more deeply into the principles which underlie all practical detail, and these principles, so far as they relate to the structure of language, are most effectively to be studied in the classic literatures of Greece and Rome.

The process of translation from an idiom foreign to our own is an unrivalled means of training in the selection of the right word and phrase to express the precise shade of meaning we desire to convey by speech or by writing. The argument that translation from a modern language answers the same purpose fails precisely because the modern language more nearly resembles our own both in its word and phrase formation and in that subtle thing we can describe only as the spirit of the language as a whole. Such translation is "easier" and, by the same token, is less educative. Then, as to the subject matter: it ought not to be necessary to point out the extraordinary opportunity offered by the study of the classic literatures to introduce the young student from a very early stage to ideas of history, geography, religion, philosophy, and social science that will become permanent possessions. It is not wholly without reason that some enthusiastic souls have described philology as the universal science.

Here again there are two answers. One is, that all these subjects are equally suggested by the study of modern languages or, even without this, by intensive occupation with our own unrivalled literature. We reply that after all, these modern literatures are only the echoes of the great originals and that the specific mark of the truly educated man is that he has gone back to the originals in whatever field of study he may have worked. The "general reader" must perforce be satisfied with the echoes; the liberally educated man must demand something more. The second answer is, that not one in a hundred of the youths who have spent precious years in the study of Greek and Latin have gained thereby any appreciable knowledge in any of the subjects we have named. I wish there were a better reply to this answer. It is far too lamentably true; but it misses the whole point of the present contention. The reason why classical teaching has so largely failed to leave on our youth the kind of impression that would cause them to rally to its defense against all attack has been that it was such incredibly bad teaching. For the contempt into which it has fallen classical teachers have mainly themselves to thank. The question of its permanent value in a scheme of liberal education is not thereby affected at all.

In a recent conversation with a college graduate, now the father of college graduates, he grew positively enthusiastic over one of his classical teachers. This teacher was a proverbially dull and uninspiring person, and I was naturally curious to find out the cause of my friend's enthusiasm. It appeared, on inquiry, that this teacher had actually required his pupils to write a considerable quantity of Latin, and the grip on the

language thus acquired proved a source of lasting gratitude to this appreciative pupil. It caused him to single
out this man from the rest of his teachers as uncom-
monly gifted with teaching power. Now here was one
of the most elementary of pedagogic principles. To
learn a language the only way is to use it, and there is
no way of using it so effective as to write it. And yet,
so utterly bad had all this pupil's other teaching been,
that this perfectly simple act of common sense seemed
to him a positive stroke of genius.

My friend's experience is characteristic of American
classical teaching during more than two generations.
It has hardly been teaching at all. It has been a stupid
patching together of words and phrases to illustrate
rules of grammar; a shocking waste of time, ruinous to
real scholarly ambition, depressing where it ought to
have been stimulating. To make a bad matter worse
floods of annotated editions with skilfully limited
"glossaries" have been poured upon the market.
Designed to sugar the pill, they have deprived it of all
its beneficial qualities. Honestly intended to rescue
classical study from total neglect, they have done more
than everything else to bring it into disrepute. They
have contributed more than their share to the worst
trait of the modern pupil, the inability to sit down
alone to a hard job and put it through to the end. It is
no wonder that under such conditions classical study
should have seemed to the "practical" mind little
more than a game, amusing to the "coaches," but
hopelessly dull and uninteresting to the players.

A young German studying in a professional school of

one of our most important universities was asked to
give his impressions of his fellow-students. He replied:
"They are the hardest working fellows I have ever
seen, but they don't know anything. What in the
world were they doing with themselves between the
ages of six and twenty?" What he meant was that the
tools of their trade which should have been sharpened
and tempered in those years were still dull and soft.
They had studied the classics, but they could not read
them. They had "taken courses" in modern languages, but they could not handle them. In one word,
they had never been trained to do anything so well
that it had become a part of their intellectual equipment, ready to serve them whenever called upon. It is
only in the faith that these defects in our American
teaching are going to be measurably corrected that any
one could have the courage to give advice to the youths
who are coming on in our schools and beginning to
cast about them for help in the puzzling work of college
elections.

The old phrase was "classics and mathematics,"
and it used always to be said that the man who was
good at the one was likely to be good at the other also.
The disciplinary value of mathematics has been as
stoutly defended and as bitterly attacked as that of the
classic languages. To defend mathematics beyond
arithmetic, algebra and the elements of geometry, on
the score of practical utility would be an idle waste of
words. Every one knows that the immense majority
of educated men get on very comfortably without
them. It is only as discipline in the highest sense of

that much abused word, that a further occupation with mathematical studies can be urged.

In our plan of studies for the normal college youth mathematics would take a considerable place, and that for two apparently directly opposed reasons. The first of these is the obvious one that no other subject so directly conduces to absolute correctness of process, accuracy of statement, and certainty of result. No other holds the mind so rigidly to rules and so completely excludes any deviation from them. No other process offers so useful a corrective to the habit of desultory thinking. The second reason, strange as this may sound, is that mathematics tend to stimulate the imaginative faculties. Mathematical science is the most completely removed from the material realities of things. Two and two would make four even were there no objects to be added, and so it goes on. The study of mathematics is as purely idealistic a pursuit as the human mind is capable of, and surely, if there is any one thing which a liberal education should cultivate more than any other it is the capacity for a sound and rational idealism.

By imagination we do not mean idle fancy, the loose imagining of vain things. We mean the power of representing to ourselves unseen realities, of projecting ourselves into the world of possible, if unrealized experiences. This is eminently a constructive process. It is the method of the creative artist, in whatever field he may exercise his imaginative powers. It is the method also of the highest science working through the patient stages of minute experiment toward a goal set by the disciplined imagination. So I would say to the college youth: plan to go as far in pure mathematics as you can without doing violence to other subjects. Here, of course, as everywhere else it is a matter of proportion, and no rule could wisely be applied in all cases. I would only urge that no one let himself be cheated out of this valuable discipline by its apparent difficulty or its general unpopularity.

Passing to a group of subjects in which the factor of information rather than the factor of discipline is of primary importance, I should recommend to every student to acquire the elements of economic theory as the only sound basis of approach to those great economic questions which must play so large a part in the thought of all intelligent men about public affairs. The intensive study of some decisive period of the world's history ought to be of service as a supplement to the rapid surveys which the pupil brings from his school or perhaps gains in one of the early college years. It would be a pity if any youth should lose the opportunity of his college days to acquire some familiarity with the principles of formal logic and at least a nodding acquaintance with the history of the attempts of mankind to explain the phenomena of the universe by philosophic systems. An intensive pursuit, however brief, of some branch of experimental science may leave with the man a precious deposit of ideas that will be fruitful in unsuspected ways as long as he lives.

There remain the subjects forming the group of modern languages and literatures, including English, and there is no group more puzzling to the adviser. It seems almost axiomatic that the American youth should be especially attracted to these pursuits and should go as far in them as he can. Especially does it seem as if the study of English, both as language and literature, ought to occupy a large share of his attention. Following this natural indication our American colleges have worked out plans of instruction that have grown to almost threatening dimensions. The puzzle in this part of the adviser's task comes from a conflict of ideas that often proves insoluble. On the one side is the great educative value of a knowledge of foreign languages, which no one denies, while on the other side is the equally undeniable fact that the conditions of study in college are extremely unfavorable to acquiring this knowledge. In the learning of a language there are four processes, reading, writing, speaking, and understanding. Of these the last two are the most important in gaining a complete mastery, but it is precisely these two that cannot be taught in large classes and within the limitations of time inevitable in a college program. The most that can be done for the ordinary student is to help him to acquire a fair start at reading and a fair amount of skill in the composition of very simple narrative forms.

Is it worth while for the student to sacrifice much of the time that could be spent on subjects which can be well taught in college to the slight results that can be expected in the modern languages? One of these languages he will, as the saying is, "bring with him" to college. That means that he has made a beginning, probably a bad beginning, but at least he has something to start with, and I venture to suggest that for the moment he be satisfied with this. One other language he must then, if he is to acquire it at all, begin in college, and this he ought to do, unfavorable as the conditions are. Beyond this, however, I do not advise him to go in "taking courses," but there are three other ways in which he can go far towards accomplishing the very desirable end of a real command of a language other than his own.

The first is by running over to Europe for a long summer, going *alone* to some place where he will never see an English speaking person and there, with the help of a local school teacher to correct his exercises and talk with him and introduce him to other persons, spend his time in endless reading of pleasant books, translating systematically English into French or whatever the language may be, making all the acquaintances he can and compelling every one he meets to give him a lesson in understanding — not forgetting to go to the theatre every evening and to church every Sunday. In default of the opportunity to do this very pleasant thing, the next device is to devote one or two long vacations at home to such parts of the above program as may be accomplished here. That means reading foreign books, the lighter and more amusing the better, without much attention to the meanings of new words or to strange constructions. In addition to this, however, the reading of some one book with the greatest care, looking up all words and working out all puzzles of syntax. The youth who has not tried it will be amazed to find how rapidly the difficulties will smooth themselves out and how soon he will begin to feel the sense of mastery which is the greatest joy of all learning.

I suggest these summer occupations because in fact almost every self-respecting student nowadays plans to devote his summers to some kind of work which shall forward the purpose he has in mind in his scheme of life. The "summer loafer" is out of date. To gain a language by the process I have indicated is to add a tool to one's equipment for all future study and to open a delightful entrance into the charms of a literature that will be a permanent possession.

The third method is to make use of whatever elements of a foreign language the student possesses in the study of other subjects in college. There are few if any departments in which books in the foreign language cannot readily be recommended, and in many departments such books are distinctly better than those available in English. The obvious objection to this practice is the apparently great increase of time it demands, but this objection is rather apparent than real. The actual time spent over the book is undoubtedly greater than an English book would require, but taking into account the long result, remembering that one is acquiring two subjects at once, and acquiring the language in the very best possible way, it may well appear that instead of a waste there is a positive saving of time in this method. By applying it successively or at the same time to several subjects the vocabulary becomes widened, while the forms common to all writing in the given language are impressed upon the mind as is possible in no other way. The strain upon the student's persistence at the beginning is great, but it is sure to be well rewarded by notable gains, not merely in subjects, but in that supreme virtue of the student, academic character.

So we come finally to "English." The most persistent and influential advocate of a free elective system in this country always said that there was but one subject which every student should be required to pursue, and that was the study of English. As to the supreme importance of a right use of one's native tongue and a vital acquaintance with its best literature there is no disagreement among persons qualified to have an opinion. The only difference is as to the method by which these desirable ends are to be reached, and this difference is very wide. It may, perhaps, best be expressed by using for the view of one side the phrase so popular to-day in other connections, "direct action." The logic of this party is that if a thing is desirable in education the way to get it is to put it on school and college programs, give it plenty of "time" and the thing is done. In pursuance of this notion our departments of English have grown in a way that I have already characterized as threatening. Our educators "point with pride" to the proportion of the time allotment in English, and we are left to assume that the results are justifying the expenditure of energy.

Now, of course, we are not speaking here at all of the vast problem of dealing with the hordes of foreigners whom we are trying with, all things considered, amazing success to assimilate to our public institutions and to our habits of thought. In that endeavor all methods, direct and indirect, may find their justification, but all that lies outside the question of wise educational theory. The real question to-day is: have these enormous outlays of effort so far produced anything like a corresponding increase in refinement in the American speech, of correctness — if there be such a thing — in American writing and of elevation in the American taste for literature? I am not proposing to answer this question. I prefer to leave it to the conscience of those who are responsible for the immediate future of our academic programs. Upon its answer must depend their view of what is desirable in framing new and, it is to be hoped, more efficient policies.

The view of the opposite party may be illustrated by the comments of learned Englishmen. Again and again such visitors to America, studying our educational methods have expressed themselves as completely puzzled by our practice in this matter of instruction in English. "Why all this fuss about so simple a matter?" they have said. "At home we assume that an educated youth learns to speak and write his native tongue by hearing the speech of cultivated people and reading the books of the masters of English style. It is this reading that gives him the acquaintance with literature which, we agree with you, is essential to his education. He must, of course, have some systematic instruction in his early years, but after that it would seem to us an absurdity to require him to sacrifice any considerable part of his academic time to an exercise in which, after all, teaching can do so little for him. Why all this machinery of 'courses' in composition? Why these prolonged and elaborate lectures on literature? There are the masterpieces; why not let the youth read them in the only way in which they can ever do him the least good, as the best form of diversion from his more serious interests? If he enjoys them he will certainly read them, and if he does not enjoy them they will be of no mortal use to him. And as to composition, we give our youths ample opportunity for the improvement of their style in the abundant use we make of written work in the regular processes of instruction in all our subjects. We think of all our college teachers as competent to supply such correction as will suffice, without providing a special corps of tutors in English."

Here is at once a criticism and a program. I cite it only to justify my own feeling that the principle it embodies is a sound one. The few rules of English composition ought to have been made a part of the student's intellectual equipment long before he reaches the college age. He will be far from perfect in their application, as we all are and remain, so long as we live; but the correction of his most glaring defects can be most effectually made in connection with the written work which he ought, on sound pedagogical principles, to do as a part of his regular educative process. As to literature: the important thing, it seems to me, is not that he shall have read so many plays of Shakespeare, but that at some stage of his school life, he shall have been so caught up and taken out of himself by the incommunicable charm of Shakespeare that he will steal time from every duty to wander in the forest of Arden, or pace the

Rialto, or sail to Aleppo with a crew of tailless rats, or watch the waves breaking on the coast of Bohemia. If literature does not mean that to a man, it means nothing. The youth who is once brought to the pass of saying: "I've got to read three cantos of Paradise Lost before ten o'clock to-morrow," is well embarked on the road toward a hatred of all literature for the rest of his life.

Of course, in all that is here said there is no reference whatever to the professional, linguistic pursuit of language studies. For the student in these there must be as careful, analytical work as for the student in the classics or in any other branch of science. We are dealing here with the ordinary student in the liberal arts.

So far we have been concerned with those principles of choice in academic study which refer to the nature of the subjects to be pursued. There is reason for this in the fact that most of the discussions about election turn upon this point. It is seldom that the attention of the student is called to other considerations. If one could "listen in" on the conversations of advisers with their victims, one would be sure to hear chiefly a combat of words about whether this or that subject should be "taken" at this or that stage of the game, in what doses and with what probable effect upon the symptoms in the given case. Such questions are important, but I venture to believe that back of them all lie certain other principles which ought, with due regard to proportion, to enter into the final decision.

At the risk of seeming pedantic, or even scientifically pedagogical, I should like to suggest certain distinctions of intellectual process which go rather deeply beneath the surface of all education and which ought, I think, to influence the student in his election of work. It is practically true that intellectual work may be classified under three heads: acquisition, interpretation, and production. Many other terms might be used but let these suffice for the moment. In general these three processes should go on in the order named. First there must be a solid body of acquired knowledge, call it even, if one please, by the opprobrious term "information." Only after such a foundation of knowledge has been acquired can the mind healthfully go on to the process of trying to understand what one has learned. And then again, only when this process of understanding has made some notable progress can the third step of original production profitably be taken.

Further, there is a rational correspondence between these stages of intellectual effort and the normal development of the human being. Childhood, youth, and manhood are but so many names for the development of the human faculties from the stage of acquisition, through the stage of understanding to the last stage of creative production. We all know this. The child acquires knowledge with amazing rapidity and retains it with a tenacity incredible to his own later years. The youth becomes impatient with the acquisitive process and demands explanation of the puzzles of the universe. The growing man feels within him the impulse to apply his learning and his understanding to the creation of something new. Perfectly simple — so simple that in fact it has been the basis of sound educational theory from the beginning.

Unhappily there has been in recent years, and notably in our country, an increasing impatience with so self-evident a formula. Largely under the influence of imperfectly educated, one-idead, self-heralded educational prophets and prophetesses the lines between these obvious stages, both of individual development and educative effort have been almost hopelessly obscured. The child, we have been told, must not be compelled to learn things he cannot understand. The youth must not be held back by the super-imposed interpretations of other persons, but must be left free to form his own conclusions and encouraged to proceed to creative activity. We must not lean too heavily upon memory, but must let thought do its work. Creative instinct is observable in the infant and ought not to be checked in its free exercise. "Systems" based upon these "new" revelations have been launched upon a credulous world and have run their pernicious course leaving the wrecks of sound education behind them.

The worst thing about these educational nostrums is that they contain many elements of truth. It is true that the lines of demarcation we have tried to draw do vary greatly with individual character and endowment. There are men who never pass out of the stage of intellectual infancy. There are infants who display the highest qualities of mature manhood. And all the way between there are gradations of aptitude that seem to justify almost any theories of progression.

But, after all allowances for such exceptional cases have been made, there remains the solid fact that in general the best order of procedure in methods of study runs parallel with the progress of the individual in growth. This does not mean that up to a certain point the pupil should be required to do nothing but acquire knowledge, then should do nothing but interpret, and finally should confine himself entirely to "original work." It means that up to the age, say of fourteen, he should take advantage of the special aptitudes that belong to that age by piling in solidly those stores of elementary knowledge which will become the most precious possession of his maturer years. At the same time his worth-while demands — and no others — for explanation of what he learns should be rationally met, and if he happens to "create" something his sport in this direction should not be too contemptuously checked. After this stage the proportion of acquisition may be somewhat diminished and that of understanding and of production somewhat increased. In the third stage, this shifting of proportions may be carried still further. In other words, in each period all three methods may be employed, but with greatly varying emphasis.

The bearing of all this on the student's choice of studies in college is that he ought to govern himself pretty rigidly by the principle here set forth. In college also he will encounter the elements of many subjects and in such elementary study he will find himself in the infant class again. It will be his duty to sit down hard to the process of acquisition and to call upon his memory to work for him as it did in his childhood. Elsewhere he will be in the stage of interpretation and may properly try his wings in wider flights of independent thought. And then there will come a time when the best thing he can do with the greater part of his time is greatly to reduce the amount spent on acquisition, to suspend temporarily his conscious effort to interpret, and devote himself primarily to practice in the use of original materials and the production of what we like to call — it is to be hoped with becoming modesty — "contributions to learning."

Ordinarily this progression will best coincide with the progress of his academic years and his own growth in maturity, but on this point there is room for a great deal of leeway, and wise advisers will take advantage of this. The only caution I care to emphasize is that the program be not a top-heavy one. Too early production, too much weight on understanding, and too little care for the foundations, these are the dangers to which the youth of the present day is especially liable. The melancholy effects of this misplaced emphasis are visible throughout our academic world and are having their inevitable reactions upon the larger world of business and the professions.

That is one of the general principles which may properly influence the student's choice. Another is that he should select his work with due regard to the question of how far the teacher is likely to be a help to him, and how far he must rely upon himself alone. For example, what can a teacher do for the student of a modern language under the necessary conditions of college teaching? Next to nothing. If he has a theory as to how a language must be taught, he will certainly prove more of a hindrance than a help. If, as most teachers do, he leads the pupil to think that he is going to "do something" for him, to that extent he dulls the edge of the personal enthusiasm which is essential to success. I quite realize that it is difficult for the youth to apply this principle, but his advisers may at least remind him of it. They may help to save him from the waste of time involved in listening to class-room futilities when he might be spending it upon subjects in which the help of the teacher is indispensable.

This is the high privilege of the college years, the presence of men devoted to learning and anxious to do what they can to bring its contents and its methods to the youths before them. And this leads us naturally to a final consideration: that the student should govern his choice of studies largely by the quality of the men with whom it will bring him into contact. We Americans are singularly indifferent to this whole element of personality in education. So far as we think about it at all we are apt to stop with those executive officials whose names recur with fatal frequency in the newspapers or with those picturesque figures among the teaching staff who attract attention by other gifts than those belonging to the scholarly character. We send our sons to the college of their choice and expect the college to do the rest. It is the institution that impresses us, not the persons who give the institution all the quality it has.

And yet, no man has ever gone through the experiences of college life with open eyes and open mind who does not know that the most powerful influence brought to bear upon him in those plastic years is the silent force of character in the men who have been his guides. Perhaps he learns this too late. While the process is going on the institution with its hundred appeals obscures the individual. The teacher is apt to appear to him but a cog in the great machine that is expected to turn him out as a part of its finished product. It may be half a lifetime later before he discovers the hidden threads that bind up his present life of action with those distant years of preparation. Happy the teacher who hears from such a pupil the acknowledgment of his personal obligation to lighten the shadows and sweeten the memories of advancing age!

TRAVEL AS EDUCATION

IT was my great good fortune, while still a very young man, to listen to the inaugural address of Mr. Charles William Eliot as President of Harvard College. He said a great many wise and useful things, most of them far beyond the capacity of an average undergraduate to understand, still less to appreciate at their true value. There was, however, one phrase, which he used quite casually, that impressed itself on my mind so that I never forgot it. It was this: "Travel, that foolish beginning and excellent sequel to education." The reason why I was thus impressed was, I suppose, because my thoughts were already beginning to turn to the possibilities of European travel. My studies, pursued no more seriously than those of other undergraduates, were pointing to Europe as a wonderland, where the record of human life, as we were reading it in books, was to be seen in visible form in buildings, in paintings, in sculpture and monument, and where the background of all this life was to be studied in landscape, in mountain, in river and in storied field. The allurement of this early dream continued, and in due time was realized. Travel, begun as education, became a professional duty, and much experience and observation convinced me of the absolute truth of Mr. Eliot's chance remark. One can hardly do a worse thing for a boy than to drag him about Europe before he has gained all there is to be gained by study and normal living at home, and there can hardly be a better thing for a youth thus prepared and with his mind awake to historical and aesthetic perceptions, than to give him the opportunity of intelligent travel.

Three hundred years earlier, another wise and genial counsellor, Francis Bacon, had written: "Travel in the younger sort is a part of education, in the elder a part of experience." Starting, then, with the judgment of such excellent advisors, it may well seem worth while to consider frankly some of the advantages and some of the disadvantages of travel as an educational instrument. Let us ask ourselves first of all just what we mean by travel. We speak lightly of our time as a travelling age. Questions of transportation engage the attention and affect the lives of a very large proportion of our populations. It is probably true that more individuals change their place to-day than at any time before the application of steam to the movement of persons and goods. But, in the sense in which we are now using the word, is it true that there is more travel? We go with amazing rapidity and with a self-complacency still more amazing, from one end of the earth to the other. We are, as it were, shot through thousands of miles of space, and in that transition we are as indifferent to all intervening obstacles as if we were encased in walls of steel instead of the barbaric splendors of the Pullman car. Vast corporations have been organized, whose whole function it is to operate this system of projectiles, in which the artillery is the railroad, the steamship, or the airplane, and the missiles are human beings.

And now the automobile, that demon of modern society, is added to the list, the most penetrating and the most demoralizing of all, because it reaches down deepest into social strata which can least bear the strain of the spirit it represents. The "automobile spirit," the spirit of reckless haste, of carelessness about detail, of mere desire to "get there," of indifference to the rights of others, of blindness to that which is nearest. "What was that we passed just now?" says the owner to his chauffeur, "Switzerland, Sir." A marvel of mechanism, useful in its place as a servant of industry, the automobile, as an agent of travel, has so far not contributed essentially to the result we are here concerned with, its educational value. On the contrary it has gone far to breed a state of mind thoroughly hostile to every sound educational principle. The social value of the automobile will not be found in its contribution to educative travel, but in its enlargement of opportunity within a comparatively narrow range of distance. It enables the farmer's wife to break the trying monotony of her isolated existence. It ties the suburbs to the city and to each other. It brings the open country within the range of the dust- and smoke-filled citizen. Beyond these relatively narrow limits it duplicates the service of the railway and the horse, but it does not increase the opportunity for observation and reflection which is of the very essence of travel.

Travel, for our present purpose, is change of place with the definite aim of seeing and studying new things. It includes, not merely the stopping places, but all that lies between. The most complete ideal of travel

is by the "footpath way," where every step brings
the wanderer a something that belongs to that particular bit of earth and is therefore new to him. But few
of us have strength or leisure to indulge in this supreme
joy for more than a brief period and over fragments of
our journey. For most mortals travel must consist of
fairly rapid transits from one center of interest to another and of residence in these centers for a longer or
shorter time. Then from these central points we may
radiate as widely as local means of communication will
allow and thus capture after all something of the
charm of the open road. To live at Rome does not
mean merely to visit the Forum, the Coliseum, the
Vatican, and the Piazza Vittorio Emmanuele; it means
also to wander among the Alban hills, to circle the
Lake of Nemi, to climb the streets of Rocca di Papa
and to trace, if we can, the limits of Horace's Sabine
farm.

Leisureliness, then, is an element of true travel. To
see intelligently and enjoyably these chief points of the
Roman Campagna means days of wandering and rest-
ing. Then comes along your friend with the automobile, picks you up and whirls you around through the
whole region in an afternoon. He "hasn't time" for
anything more, and, in truth, this is better than nothing, but it is not travel. He would be far more of a
travelled man if he had taken the trolley to Genzano,
wandered over to Nemi and spent his time watching
the sunset from the terrace below the ancient temple.
That would have given him something to remember
which would have been a positive and a permanent
possession.

Even Bacon, however, felt that there were wise limitations to the slowness of travel. He says of his young traveller: "Let him not stay long in one city or town, more or less as the place deserves, but not long. Nay, when he stays in one city or town let him change his lodging from one end and part of the town to another; which is a great adamant (magnet) of acquaintance." For Bacon thought that the prime object of travel was to make as complete and wide an acquaintance as possible with the countries and their inhabitants. The shrewd philosopher dreaded, I suspect, the effect of too long delay in dulling the sharpness of the first fresh impression made upon his young gentleman by new sights and sounds.

If this is a fair definition of travel, we are led on to another question: who may profitably engage in it? One's instinct would perhaps be to reply: everyone who has the means and the opportunity. But it does not require great penetration or a very wide experience to convince one that means and opportunity are often ludicrously out of proportion to the capacity to profit by them. Sometimes, as we look about us on our travels there seem to be among our travelling companions none but those in whom this disproportion is the most evident thing about them. Here again Bacon has a suggestion: "He that travelleth into a country before he hath some entrance into the language, goeth to school and not to travel." He draws an obvious distinction here between travel as in itself a means of culture and travel as, if I may say so, a mere pedagogical instrument.

He names the most important objects for the traveller's attention, and most of these are of a nature to be
useful, not to the school boy, but to the youth of a
somewhat matured judgment. First of all he mentions
the courts of princes; then "the courts of justice, while
they sit and hear causes; the churches and monas-
teries, with the monuments which are there extant;
antiquities and ruins; libraries, colleges, discussions
and lectures; houses, gardens of state and pleasure;
exercises of horsemanship; fencing, training of soldiers
and the like; comedies such whereunto the better sort
of persons would resort." He adds that after all these
things the tutors or servants of the young traveller
should make diligent inquiry. It is clear that Bacon
had in mind a kind of travel quite different from mere
residence in a foreign country for the purpose of acquiring the language, and that distinction is important
for us as well. He says further: "Let him sequester
himself from the company of his countrymen and diet
in such places where there is good company of the
nation where he travelleth."

All this points in the direction in which my own
thoughts about travel for Americans have long been
tending. To gain any real advantage from travel one
must be in position to understand something of the life
of the people and to appreciate something of the memorials of their past. It is an idle waste of time for men or
women to change merely their skies without some rational points of connection with the life, the history,
and the achievements of the people whom they visit.
Such a visitor moves about, as Bacon says, "hooded"

and he "looks abroad little." I recall a case of an American family making the grand tour of Europe timing all their movements with reference to meeting another American family and playing with them a continuous series of games of whist. There is another tale; I do not vouch for its truth, but it is too good not to be true. An American family devoted to home and to each other, had long been planning a European trip, and at length the time came when they could all go. Their voyage across the unnecessarily wet ocean was accomplished with success. They landed at Liverpool in the midst of a dreary fog such as only the English shore can offer as its welcome to the traveller. They suffered much annoyance in the transfer of their luggage; they found no ice water in their rooms and no open fires in the hotel parlors and no soda fountain at the next corner. Things began to look very serious; they held a council of war, and wisely decided to return by the same steamer to the land of comforts. That family knew what it wanted, and I have always felt that they were a model for all who are tempted to travel without due appreciation of what travel has to offer them.

The tendency of our day is toward satisfaction in mere movement without due reflection on the value of the thing we imagine ourselves to be seeking. Landing from the Harwich steamer at the Hook of Holland just as the first streaks of dawn were lighting the meadows, we found ourselves in the same railway compartment with two solid, substantial American couples evidently beginning their first continental outing after many

years of successful prudence. They had neither guide-
book nor map; they did not know just where they
were; the only fixed point in their outlook was the
next coupon of their circular ticket, which assured
them that they were to stop off at The Hague and find
refuge in a first-class hotel as nominated in the bond.
Nothing else really mattered. They were sure to be
handed on from one purveyor of travelling service to
another until they should be safely landed once more
in "God's country."

Nor is this blankness of mind confined to persons of
limited opportunity. I knew a learned professional
gentleman who made the European tour with his
family for the first time, not, as he frankly confessed,
because he wished to do so or because he foresaw any
real satisfaction in the performance. He went, he said,
because it was "one of the things you have to do."
When all was over he expressed his sense of relief that
that job was done and that it had been accomplished
at a much lower price than he had anticipated. On a
Mediterranean steamer we encountered two pairs of
young men just graduated from a great American university, precisely at the age when travel ought to have
meant most to them. They were embarked on a
journey round the world, which was to occupy them
for a year. One of these pairs, dear pleasant fellows
they were, had no more understanding of what they
were about than the quaint old couples of the Dutch
railway. They were frankly bored by the whole thing
and sought relief in any form of harmless foolery that
offered itself. They had no books with them and had

done no reading in preparation for their journey. The other pair were more thoughtful youths, evidently better students, who had given serious thought to the task they had in hand, but were already appalled at the vastness of the world and of their own ignorance. They had come to feel that the whole idea of the world tour was a mistake, that they would have done much better to give their holiday year to a more limited area and to have explored that more thoroughly. Still there they were with their round-trip tickets in their pockets and they were determined to put it through. They, I think, would learn some of the lessons of real travel and would probably profit by them in future experiences.

Travel is not mere change of place; but the fact of change is in itself an element, sometimes a very important one, in the benefit of travel. We are all, I suppose, at times aware that we are subject to a kind of strain upon mind and nerves from the mere daily and hourly sight of the same things. We become adjusted too fatally well to the routine which makes up the greater part of all human living. The very outline of familiar streets, houses, fields becomes unconsciously to ourselves a burden; it seems to wear upon certain tender fibres of our nature, and we say, without knowing precisely what we mean, that we are "tired." It is a symptom of this weariness that we feel ourselves driven more and more cruelly by the demon of routine. We cling more tightly than ever to the wonted task, until by-and-by we lose the power of relaxation. But if, happily, before that crisis comes, some fortunate circumstance brings us a change of surroundings, then the very difference of outline offered to our outward eyes gives us almost at once a surprising sense of relief. If we are wise we follow the example of the tired citizen who said "California is of no use to me. No sooner am I there than I begin to want to reform the politics of Santa Barbara. In Europe I am perfectly willing to let the people run their own politics." It is well for us if we too can shift the gear from high to low and for a time let things take care of themselves.

The ocean voyage, for example, with its change from the sharp angles that meet us in our daily walks to the vast levels of the sea, brings a sense of rest and peace that works its silent miracle upon our weary souls. When we come to land again we are conscious in quite a new way of the meanings of form and color. We of New England realize perhaps for the first time the singular beauty of our own landscape. We miss the stone wall, the rough pasture, the luxuriant foliage of the elm; but in place of these the eye dwells upon other types of vegetation and other forms of human construction. This change of form and color, with its suggestions of a life different from our own is the most obvious surface charm of travel, but it is very strange how soon the eye adjusts itself to these new combinations. As one enters, for example, a town like Antwerp, with its irregular streets, its great open places, its quaint gabled houses, its strange display in the windows, its monuments of an architecture now disappearing, the entrance ways of its stately mansions with their suggestions of garden and cloister beyond, one feels a sense of refreshment and inspiration that hardly anything else can give. As one wanders through the narrow lanes of Seville, glancing in through lace-work grills into the fascinating *patios* that at once invite and repel intrusion, and brushing past the close screened windows set for the scene of true Andalusian romance, one is lifted out of his own little world of cares and transplanted into a dreamland of elusive fancies.

But then, after a few days, we realize almost with a shock how familiar these things have become to us. If we go from Antwerp to Bruges or from Seville to Cordova, quaint and altogether delightful as these must be to the open-eyed traveller, we are surprised to be so little surprised. We seem already to take these forms of life for granted, and when that happens, one of the first charms of travel begins to be dimmed, or rather, to put it more precisely, the charm of novelty yields for the moment to the more permanent charm of familiarity. For the experienced traveller learns that there are two abiding sources of pleasure in travel, the joy of seeing new things and the joy of revisiting familiar things, and between the two he is at a loss to say which is the greater. Certainly if at any moment he feels his sense of enjoyment a little dulled, he has only to shift the scene to some marked contrast in the mingling of nature with man's devices. To pass from Belgium into Holland, there to welcome the great flat spaces of the open country, the skies bending down, as one sees them in the wonderful Dutch landscape paintings, to touch the edges of the ocean, is to renew the thrill of novelty in full measure. It must be a jaded traveller indeed who could gaze without emotion westward from the train between Alexandria and Cairo, over the luxuriant meadows of the Delta to the causeway beyond, where Abraham, Isaac, and Rebecca, with their man-servants and maid-servants, their oxen and asses, sheep and camels are passing in solemn procession, silhouetted against the golden sunset sky. These are some of the uses and suggestions of the joy and profit of intelligent travelling. They enter into our general subject of travel as education in so far as they may be utilized to advance the purpose we have finally in view. If we take them in the spirit of Kipling's soldier-man:

> For to admire an' for to see,
> For to be'old this world so wide, —
> It never done no good to me, —
> But I can't drop it if I tried!

then indeed they are devoid of educational value; but if we use them by way of introduction or as continuing illustrations to our other sources of knowledge and inspiration they may prove of the highest value.

This brings us to the question of preparation for travel. So far I have rather implied that the unprepared person would better wait; but what do we mean by preparation? Coming out of the Picture Gallery at Dresden I was accosted by the father of an American family, the members of which were standing about in various stages of physical and mental dilapidation, with the inquiry: "Say, you've just come out of here; do you think there's anything in there worth paying a quarter apiece to look at?" I was staggered for a moment, but then, recalling the sound principle that every one ought to be allowed to be happy in his own way, and with inward apologies to Raphael, Holbein and the rest, I brazenly answered: "No, I don't believe there is," and the sighs of relief that went up from that stricken family were abundant assurance that my sin would be forgiven. One morning early at Luxor, I went down through the hotel garden to the river bank and there found a compatriot who had arrived the night before from one of Cook's excursion steamers gazing out in some perplexity over the lazy flow of the water. To some vacant remark of mine about the beauty of the scene he replied: "Well, say, which way does this river run, any way?" I answered that it ran northward, to our right. "Oh, it runs north, does it? Well, most rivers run south, don't they?" I named over to him several examples of familiar northward flowing streams, and after a moment's reflection he conceded: "Well, when you come to analyze it, I dunno but they do!" I think we should all agree that these by no means unusual cases reveal a distinct lack of preparation for the best advantages of travel.

On the other hand, I recall an acquaintance made many years ago in Rome with an American college professor who said that he had found everything in the Eternal City exactly as he had worked it out from books, except that the Mamertine prison lay a few feet farther to the south than he had calculated. I confess I felt that this person had been somewhat over-prepared for his Roman visit. His joy in viewing the remains of the ancient world was rather that of one who success-

fully guesses a riddle than that of a true discoverer.
Travel taken in that spirit becomes only another form
of studious research. One might reach practically all
its results without leaving one's own library. The
most accomplished oriental scholar I have known had
never set foot in the Orient. It seemed a pity that he
could not have added this stimulating experience to his
learned achievement, but it is a fair question whether
the value of his contribution to science would thereby
have been increased.

A young friend of mine with an extraordinary gift of
imaginative expression became a successful writer of
historical novels without ever having been outside his
native state. His glowing descriptions of nature and
his telling characterizations of human life were purely
works of the imagination, founded upon books, yet,
through the power of this constructive imagination,
more true to life than many a labored product of
deeper study and wider observation. He carried about
with him for years the plan of a great work centering
around a famous historic character, postponing the
actual writing until he should be able to follow in person the footsteps of his hero through all the scenes of
his dramatic career. Meanwhile he was preparing
himself by copious reading, so that his travel should
be as intelligent as possible. At last the opportunity
came; he made his journey and he wrote his book, but
not with the hoped-for success. The scenic background was a description of realities, not a picture such
as the artist evolves by the alchemy of his genius. The
dramatic narrative was abundantly documented, but

it lacked the glow of the earlier romance. In a word, the over-preparation for travel reacted upon the artistic product, which was its too specific purpose.

Much of the joy and consequently, I think, much of the profit of travel comes in the first-hand study of what we can find without this specific preparation. One of the happiest as well as one of the most delicate duties of the college teacher is the advising of young, eager students as to the use they can make of travelling fellowships. For myself, I find an increasing tendency to counsel such ardent spirits not to spend the precious months of their foreign visit in libraries or in their studies, but to go out beyond these already familiar limits into the larger fields of personal observation and comparison. Such a man does well to take as his motto: to do in Europe what he cannot do at home. For the student, no matter in what branch of science, there is a world of experiences, of traditions, of the gathered up achievements of the past, into which as an American in America it is difficult for him to penetrate. In Europe this accumulated treasure creates for him an atmosphere into which it must repay him to enter. The very best thing that a young American who has already gained all that a formal education at home can give him may acquire in a year abroad is this chance of becoming a conscious sharer in the great inheritance of European culture.

To illustrate great things by small: I was much touched by a story told by a professor in a woman's college, whose special function was to rouse the interest of her pupils in the imaginative side of literature.

She told how she had watched from day to day the expressive blankness on the face of a young girl to whom all she was saying seemed to convey only the effect of an uncomprehended mystery; till finally after many days the poor girl came to her with tears in her eyes and begged her to tell her what this strange thing was which she felt all about her, which the others seemed to comprehend but which for her still remained the unattainable. "Tell me" she said "is this the ' culture ' I have always heard about?" That is what I mean by the European atmosphere into which the American, prepared, not necessarily by a mass of statistical information, but by some anticipation of the thing as yet unattained, may enter if he will and can.

How far he can penetrate depends upon many things. Bacon says: "He must have some entrance into the language before he goeth." Now I do not mean to imply that it is impossible for a person without the command of foreign languages to gain much that is valuable of this European influence, but I can hardly urge too strongly upon those who expect to spend, let us say, a year abroad to give time beforehand, or better still during the first few months of their visit in gaining such a speaking acquaintance with at least one European language, that they can give themselves the immense instruction of independence. The traveller who is restricted to his own tongue is the slave of those who offer themselves as his servants; and the first true delights of the traveller often come when for the first time, he finds himself afloat in regions not frequented by his fellow-countrymen and compelled by very necessity to make use of his store, scanty though it be, of foreign words.

This subject of language brings me to one of the worst sentimental delusions in regard to travel as a means of education. When I returned from several years' residence abroad as a young man, I said to myself if I could ever save anyone from the error of sending children abroad for study I would go far out of my way to do so. The argument in favor of such a practice is very catching. It begins with the apparently obvious fact that the knowledge of foreign languages is a highly important thing, it continues with the further obvious supposition that a foreign language is more easily acquired in youth than at any other period of life, and it draws the conclusion that the wise thing to do for the child is to place him where he will learn the foreign language with the least expenditure of energy. I think, however, that every stage of this argumentation requires a good deal of examination. First, it is doubtful whether the acquisition of a foreign language so that it can be spoken, is for the young American a matter of the highest importance. If it could come to him in his home with the counteracting influences of American life about him it might be accepted as one of the fortunate incidents of his education; but if the price to be paid is the displacing of the child at an age of the highest sensibility into circumstances highly unfavorable to his general development as a citizen of the Republic, the advantage may very well be questioned. Personally I believe, as President Eliot said, that a foreign education is one of the worst possible introductions of the American youth into life. As to the second proposition, that childhood is the best time to learn languages — that depends very largely upon conditions. If the language comes naturally to the child before the self-conscious period, say under the age of ten, there can be no doubt that he accomplishes a certain small result with less effort than he will ever have to make again; but, for one thing, that result is in itself but slight; he acquires a child's vocabulary and a child's command of linguistic forms. Furthermore, if he applies himself to the study of the language at a somewhat later period, say before he is twenty-five, his power to make effort is proportionately immensely greater, and his sense of the importance of what he is doing gives him the motive which is worth more than any other condition of success. If one examines with some care the conditions of life abroad for a young child, boy or girl, he can readily convince himself that they are as far as possible from being desirable. It is true, provision has been made on a considerable scale to meet the demand for this kind of so-called education on the part of American families; and a crop of hybrid schools, neither foreign nor American, has sprung up all over the continent in which an American child may be taken under conditions of at least half-respectability, but the life at which tends to separate it at the most important crisis of its life from all those influences under which it would normally come, and under which those who are to be its comrades in work through life are necessarily brought. I would not advocate in the education even of a child a narrow nationalism that may make it blind to the largeness and variety of human experience. But I would have those larger impressions grow upon a foundation of attachment to the soil and to the people that are the child's own. It will be said perhaps that the sentiment of Americanism can be kept alive in the mind of a child educated abroad, and doubtless this, in a sense, is true; but I do not think that, with a good many opportunities for observation, I have ever seen an individual case in which I felt that the life of a youth had been made larger, or richer, or more effective by this means.

As to specific results: the child who has been "educated abroad" will in all probability gradually drop all occupation with the language it has partially acquired. It will only furtively and shamefacedly speak the few words it has learned, and will have no incentive to add to its vocabulary. The famous "accent" it is supposed to have achieved will pretty promptly disappear by the subtle process of disuse. There will remain a certain substructure of ability to read, but whether upon this will be built up a real edifice of literary enjoyment depends upon conditions having little or nothing to do with the early study abroad. The less — or more — fortunate mate who has pegged out his reading knowledge of French or German by the inevitable grind is likely to outdistance the travelled youth who imagines there is some mysterious charm that will guarantee him results without effort. The most appreciative reader of German literature I have known was a woman who had never set foot in Europe, but who knew the price that must be paid for any solid intellectual acquirement. It is notorious among the college teachers of European languages, that their worst pupils are the youths who have been "educated abroad." Because they can click the "r" in their throat or master the French "u," they are too likely to despise the unromantic struggle with the grammar on which alone a true command, even of the printed page, must be based.

So far as the acquisition of language at an early age is concerned, then, we may dismiss that as one of the excuses for the restlessness which likes to call itself by the name of foreign travel. But there is another fond illusion which it is the painful duty of a truth-telling monitor to shatter, and that is the notion that we can effectively combine travel with the study of history or literature or indeed of any other serious matter. Probably most of us who have travelled have fallen victims at one time or another to this pleasing fancy, but I should be surprised if experience has not generally shown us that the scheme will not practically work. Perhaps we have filled our trunks with useful books carefully chosen with reference to the places we were to visit, only to find that when we were in the presence of the objects we most wished to see and understand we could not profitably use them. The immediate question we were asking would not come to the surface of our literature at the time we needed the answer. We felt the vastness of our ignorance more keenly than ever, but our reading seemed to supply only the information we did not need just then. If we were wise we fell back on our Baedeker with the comforting assurance that he had often been in just our predicament and would know about how much it was good for us to know at this precise point.

The fact is, I take it, that the two processes, of observation and of serious study, are so different that they will not easily go on together. Observation concerns itself with a multitude of details which we have then afterward to arrange and coördinate by the more deliberate process of study. The detail must be sifted and weighed and measured before it can be of much use to us, and for this there is no time while we are still busied with the detail itself. I recall a typical case of an eager Yankee school teacher, nervously anxious to waste no moment of her precious Roman holiday, who came home to her *pension* every day tired out with sight seeing, only to hurry into the salon, where, under her favorite chair, she kept a little library of useful books. Then with feverish haste she would chase through the volumes for answers to the conundrums which the day's adventures had set for her. She seldom found them, and the sum total of her acquisition would be far less than if she had joined some merry party at a tea room and spent the evening at the theatre. So I say, while we are travelling let us travel in the fullest sense of the word, content with a sort of guidance that we may feel to be superficial, but which is all that we can profit by for the moment.

And, speaking of guidance, I hope I shall not seem too full of the milk of human kindness if I say a good word for the "personal conductor." Of the race in general I am ready to believe almost any evil thing, but I have happened to know some highly educa.ed persons, both men and women, with whom I sh ,uld regard it as a privilege to visit places through which they felt competent to guide me. They correspond in our modern world to Bacon's "tutor or grave servant" who "knoweth the country" and their assistance given at the right time and in the right way may be of great value to the intelligent traveller. One may do a vast amount of reading beforehand without touching, certainly without remembering, the precise things needed on the spot. The experienced guide, like every experienced teacher, learns to know the difficult places and how to help one over them. He is as little likely to set himself up as a substitute for real study as the true teacher is likely to propose himself as a substitute for the pupil's own activity. Especially for the first trip abroad one might do much worse than entrust oneself to such a leader. Only let him be exceedingly careful in his choice. The advantage of a book is that it can be laid aside; the personal conductor cannot, and there is always the danger that he may become an Old Man of the Sea, a terror to one's days and nights.

To the mature traveller having full possession of his faculties, with some knowledge of languages and a reasonable background of early reading, the joy of finding out for himself what he really wants to see is a great part of his experience, the part to which he looks back with the greatest interest and satisfaction. Then there is always the peculiar comfort of thinking that, if we know but little now, there is a good time coming when we can fill up all the gaps. Of course our more experienced judgment tells us that this time seldom comes, but the illusion is one of the dearest of all ages, and it will be a sorry day when we can keep it no longer. No, let us accept the fact: the process of observation is a thing by itself. It should rest upon study, and it should lead to further and more intelligent study; but while we are about it, let us not worry over our own superficiality, but enjoy it while it lasts, frankly using our eyes and our feet and rejoicing that we have them to use.

I have hinted at the weariness that is sure to befall the observant and conscientious traveller. So widely recognized is this phenomenon that names have been invented for its various phases: "travelitis," "galleryitis," "museumitis" and so on. What the novice forgets is that in travelling, as well as in other occupations, there are twenty-four hours in every day to be disposed of. He begins with a sincere desire to "make the most" of them all, and thinks he is making the most of them when he spends the greatest number of them in the direct pursuit of his main object. The Vatican galleries in the morning, two or three neighboring churches on the way home, a hurried lunch, an hour or two of reading, a walk to some point of vantage for a study of topography, a too abundant dinner, some more reading, and to bed with a strange exhilaration that starts him up on the following morning with renewed energy to repeat the program — a week or two of this, longer or shorter according to the reserve of strength, and then reaction, a dullness of the senses, a failure of the nerves to respond to the daily call and alas! in too many cases, collapse. There is no real education in such travel as this. He is the happy man who, warned in time, learns to apportion his day as he would naturally do at home between the various resources at his command, to shorten the hours of tension and lengthen those of relaxation, to vary sightseeing by rational social intercourse, to give himself definite periods of complete rest, and from time to time take the luxury of complete exemption from every sense of duty.

Bacon says: "It is a strange thing that in sea voyages, where there is nothing to be seen but sky and sea, men should make diaries, but in land travel, wherein so much is to be observed, for the most part they omit it; as if chance were fitter to be registered than observation. Let diaries, therefore, be brought into use." The ordinary traveller's diary is, I sadly fear, not so much a means of education as a record of passing and usually incorrect impressions. That even these have a value in recalling many pleasant moments and, perhaps, marking many stages in our advancement towards a right understanding of things is not to be questioned; but they might be made to serve a positive educational purpose if we could record in them just those notes of inquiry which in the pressure of travel we have no time to answer. We visit, for example, a monument to some famous person who to us has hitherto been little more than a name. It engages our attention by some artistic quality, so that we would like to keep it always before the eye of our mind, but that is not quite enough; we would like to know more about the man it commemorates; we have not time then to read about him, but a note in our diary will fix him as one of the starting-points in that wonderful reading we are so sure we are going to do when the time comes. Reading with such notes will help to bind together many scattered incidents of our journey and so weave it into the pattern of our "education."

In a word travel may most profitably be thought of as intercalated between one period of study and another, and it is a matter well worth our attention what kind and degree of study is appropriate to these two periods. One is, of course, tempted to think that the more one knows the more one enjoys, and if we are speaking of mere statistical information, like that of my schoolmaster friend in the Roman Forum, this is true, but I cannot help thinking that, so far as education is concerned, it depends a good deal upon how and when our knowledge is acquired. In the world of aesthetic impressions especially I have serious doubts whether much that passes for useful knowledge is not rather a hindrance than a help to the fullest profit in travel.

For example, to what extent is it desirable that the intending traveller should, as the phrase is, study art at home? Is it true that the more he knows about art the keener his enjoyment and the greater his profit? Supposing, for instance, that as a very young student he has heard lectures on the great painters and studied their work in reproduction under good teachers, will his travel be, in this respect, so much the more useful to him? Can he really build upon this foundation a superstructure of knowledge and understanding that will be sound and permanent? I confess to having my doubts. His teacher will, no doubt, have taught him to believe that he likes and understands Memling better than Carlo Dolce, but is this a real attainment of his own? Is his taste truly formed in any lasting sense? I think that at the outset of his acquaintance with the painters he ought to like Carlo Dolce and be repelled by Memling, and this stage of his development ought to last until he grows out of it by his own experience. Prettiness should precede power, and it is idle to pretend that we see things until they really force themselves on our inner gaze with compelling conviction. It will be a better preparation by far if the youth can have spent his time in learning some of the foundation things of human progress — history, languages and literature, gaining in this way the subtle sense of beauty and order which shall afterward guide him in his aesthetic perception, rather than have taken precious time from these things which he can do and do well to dabble with things he can do so much better afterward. If he has the many points of attachment that a liberal education ought to give there can be few things in his travels that do not have an interest of some sort for him.

On one point I feel inclined to make an exception. The understanding of architecture depends upon so many purely technical definitions and details of construction that not even a superficial enjoyment of it is possible without some knowledge of these. Moreover these are matters that can easily be learned at home, since our own architecture is not yet beyond the imitation of the great styles. Even a slight acquaintance with these technicalities immensely increases the enjoyment of architecture, and there is no form of art so pregnant with suggestions of the highest educational value. In the presence of a Gothic cathedral one is brought into relation not only with the miracle of its beauty and its constructive skill, but with the vast historical development for which it stands, with the social order that made it possible, with the religious feeling it embodies and expresses, and with the currents of active present life in which it has a part. I am almost tempted to say that if we could really understand the Gothic cathedral we should hardly need any other text-book of the Middle Ages.

Bacon's advice not to stay long in any one place puzzles me a little. I fancy that with the means of travel in his day there was a certain temptation to linger, to which we are by no means liable. Our temptation is rather to rush from one set of impressions to another before we have time to let any of them really sink in. Our caution, I think, is needed rather in the opposite direction; and yet there is a certain danger of becoming, so to speak, stale as a traveller if we allow ourselves to get too far out of the traveller's attitude and too far into that of the resident. It is fatally easy, even in a place so full of suggestion as Rome, to let oneself fall back into the little familiarities of the life of the place, and to forget that after all we are there precisely for the purpose of keeping ourselves fresh in the enthusiasms of the stranger. Most of us, I suppose, can recall the feeling of a certain superiority with which after a residence of a few days we begin to look down on the new arrival. Especially if we have emancipated ourselves from the servitude of the hotel and taken lodgings in the manner of the place, we feel ourselves entitled to be a little *blasé* in the matter of sightseeing and to affect that indifference we all feel in regard to the things best worth seeing in our own homes. Perhaps it was something of this sort that Bacon had in mind when he advised his traveller to move on pretty soon or, if he stay longer, to change his lodgings from one end of the town to the other. He puts this last bit of advice on the ground of attracting a wider acquaintance, but it is obvious that it would tend also to break up those more immediate relations that might draw the visitor from his main purpose.

On the other hand, it is clear that Bacon distinguishes very sharply between travel and sightseeing. His youth is to see the sights, but obviously the knowledge of men and manners is to be a higher object. How far can we hope to emulate the superior young man for whom the philosopher is writing? He recommends him "upon his removes from one place to another (to) procure recommendation to some person of quality residing in the place whither he removeth; that he may use his favor in those things he desireth to see or know." "As for the acquaintance which is to be sought in travel" he adds "that which is most of all profitable is acquaintance with the secretaries and employed men of ambassadors; for so in travelling in one country he shall suck the experience of many. Let him also see and visit eminent persons in all kinds, which are of great name abroad; that he may be able to tell how the life agreeth with the fame." Another sage and virtuous counsellor of youth, the admirable Major Pendennis, "would as soon have thought of not calling upon the English ambassador in a continental town, as of not showing himself at the national place of worship."

I fear but few of us are in position to profit by Bacon's advice. In the present conditions of travel it is appalling to think of the fate of eminent persons, if they were to become the victims of travellers' curiosity to see how their lives agreed with their fame. Most of us have to be content with such chance acquaintance as the accidents of travel may offer. If, however, we are by profession or through any other serious interest connected with any individuals or classes of persons, we are doing wrong if we do not put ourselves in communication with them, and if my own experience is worth anything, we may be sure of uniform courtesy and consideration. Let me tell one little incident of travel which I believe to be typical. Many years ago in Rome I attended one of the public lectures given by the late Gian Battista de Rossi, for so many years in charge of the excavations in the Catacombs. At the close of the lecture, in place of all introduction, I presented my card and told him what my occupation was. He was most polite, excused himself on the ground of pressing engagements, but said he would call upon me soon. I assumed that this was only a bit of Italian politeness and thought no more of the matter until one evening I was surprised to hear that De Rossi was at my door. He had hunted up my obscure lodging, climbed the three flights of stairs, and gave me a delightful half hour. But that was not all. He invited me to come the next day to his house and to join him in a drive on the Campagna and a visit to the Catacomb in which he was then at work. This courtesy cost him a full half day but gave me an insight into his subject which no other living man could have given. Almost without exception this was my experience whenever I sought the acquaintance of any one on the basis of a professional interest, and with due regard to his personal convenience. Libraries were freely opened for my use, university men showed me their equipments and methods, and in many cases life-long acquaintances were begun.

The moment, however, that the traveller passes out of this region of professional connection, he is pretty apt to find himself alone in the crowd. If he adopts the principle of Major Pendennis and seeks his own ambassador, he is likely to find his circle of acquaintance among his own countrymen inconveniently enlarged, but not in such ways as really add much to his knowledge of the country he is in. The American whose profession it is to live abroad may be a most charming fellow, but his angle of observation of foreign life is not the most favorable. He is neither American nor foreign, but shares the disadvantages of both characters, and is none too ready — and with reason — to admit his fellow-countrymen on the wing to his intimacy. The difficulty of really making connections with the kind of persons we would like best to know has led to various devices on the part of Americans to bring about fictitious forms of association among themselves. American churches and American clubs are to be found in the larger cities and sometimes have their use, but I cannot help thinking that such attempts to provide what is, I believe, called a "home atmosphere" for the American abroad are usually misplaced. The great majority of those for whom they are intended would be far better off in their real home on this side the water.

In default of a true "society" the modern traveller may find a very considerable resource in the European café system. There is hardly a town in Europe so small that one cannot find there a comfortable resort provided with a choice of periodicals from the principal countries and furnishing the kind of light refreshment that is particularly welcome in the long interval between lunch and dinner. In the larger cities there is a wide choice of such meeting places, where acquaintances begun perhaps accidentally may be expanded into agreeable and instructive relations. One's recollections especially of the German "*Kneipe*" with its informal good fellowship, its free discussions, often unrestrained to the point of brutality, and its entire lack of social obligation form one of the most valuable, if not always one of the most refining chapters in one's record of travel. The typical American is essentially a home keeper. He likes to have his friends about him in his own home and to visit them in theirs. It is only after some experience with the freer out of doors life of continental Europe that he learns how great a limitation this unconscious exclusiveness places upon his best intellectual development. In Europe he learns to enjoy this aspect of social life, but once at home again the old traditions, chiefly of English origin, reassert themselves, and he cannot get far beyond the stage of grumbling at conditions he is powerless to alter. Even the melancholy spectacle of a theatre audience sitting bolt upright for three hours, wasting the *entre actes* in listening to cheap music or munching caramels, moves neither public nor managers to reform. And now that the gasoline car has come, apparently to stay, the American's highest ideal is not to convey himself and his family to some delightful open air meeting place where in congenial company they could enjoy the best of music and such refreshment as each person wished to pay for, but to shut his party within the car doors and go tearing about the world in a vague pursuit of change.

The educative value of foreign travel depends upon the attitude we take toward the things other countries have to offer us. One is tempted to divide travellers into two classes, those who think of everything not their own as superior to whatever is familiar to them, and those who look down with a certain suspicion and ill-concealed contempt upon what lies outside their own narrow range of vision. The former are filled with indiscriminate admiration for everything; the latter see nothing good except as it proves the superiority of what they have left behind. The wise traveller keeps himself free from both these extremes. He is concerned chiefly to see how things really are. He would understand them if he can, in the light of their history and their relation to other things. Just as the most intolerable of companions is one who sees the world only in the light of his own experiences, so the most unbearable of travellers is he who brings everything foreign to the standards of his own country, whether it be to praise or to condemn.

I had the pleasure, during one of my visits to Italy, to be the guest of two American friends in their villas outside the walls of an ancient city. One of these friends gave us for luncheon cod-fish balls, johnny-cake, and maple syrup. His bed-rooms were furnished with the choicest products of Grand Rapids, Michigan. His purpose was, as he explained, to show his Italian friends how much better things we had in America than poor old Europe could produce. Our other host would tolerate nothing that was not precisely contemporary with the building he was restoring for occupation. Even to the hinges on the doors everything must be picked up in antique shops or gathered by long and careful research among the crumbling treasures of the land he had learned to love. Perhaps these are extreme cases; but they serve to illustrate the two tendencies of the traveller I am trying to describe. Neither of these highly cultivated gentlemen seemed to me to have hit upon the happiest solution of the traveller's problem, for that must be found in a due valuation of both the present and the past, of both that which is one's own and that which is foreign.

One of the commonest impressions of the American abroad is that all Europeans are a kind of overgrown,

over-civilized, over-developed children. They seem to
be moved far more than we are by primitive impulses of
fear, of hatred, of violent passion, especially of that
intangible thing they like to call "personal honor,"
but which appears to us only an exaggerated form of
egotistical "touchiness." We wonder good naturedly
at their devotion to the silly fictions of royalty and
nobility. We smile at their simple joy in titles and decorations. We chafe at their easy assumptions of superiority. All these things, we flatter ourselves we,
the only grown-ups in the world, have permanently
outgrown. We forget, that if it had not been for the
sentiments underlying all these puzzling phenomena
there would be little in Europe worth our while to
visit. A colleague of mine reared in the Far West could
at first hardly contain his impatience at the slowness
and conservativeness of New England. "Why don't
these Bostonians rip out their confounded crooked
streets" he said to me once "and run some nice straight
modern ones through their business sections?" Two
years afterward I visited with him a house in Lexing-
ton, Massachusetts, where for two hundred years the
same family had made its home, and where a group of
maiden sisters and bachelor brothers, themselves the
most exquisite specimens in the collection, had gathered about them roomfuls of precious memorials of the
past upon which they lived. As we came away my
friend was silent for a long time, then broke out: "Now
I know why New Englanders are conservative; they've
got something to conserve!" That is the attitude we,
as travellers, ought to try to keep if we desire to gain

from our travel the kind of education it may hold for us. It will do us good to remember that the American Spirit, splendid as it is in its readiness to "match with Destiny for beers" is, after all, not the perfect flower of the ages, but only the noble promise of the greatest things to come.

THE ACADEMIC STUDY OF HISTORY

AN ADDRESS TO STUDENTS

I PROPOSE to speak to you about the study of History in college, in the hope that what I have to say may be of some help to you in settling the perplexing question of your choice of work in this department. I shall speak of the value, the purpose and the method of historical study, and shall assume that you are all interested in getting at some principles, if such there be, which shall guide you in your future work.

It may, at first thought, seem a waste of time to talk about the value of History in a community of students who already spend every year so large a part of their energies in that field. There are many commonplaces on the subject with which I might now entertain you — such as the ennobling effect of contemplating the struggles and the victories of the great of all time, the lofty lessons we may learn from their example, and the training of the mind which may result from the study itself. The topic has always been a favorite one on academic occasions, and you will find many fine orations upon it. Even if one considers only the numbers of men enrolled in our courses of historical instruction, one must believe that our students do not need to be reminded of these things, that they are already sufficiently alive to the value of History for them and may safely be left to themselves to get out of the instruction offered them all there is in it.

And yet, I think there are still one or two points of which we all need to be reminded, lest we apply our force in the wrong ways and the wrong place. We may easily forget, in the pursuit of this or that branch of History that there is, after all, such a thing as History itself, that there is now a recognized science of historical study, with its organs, its associations, its methods, fairly well understood and producing really great results. So the first point that I would bring to your earnest attention is that History is all one thing, the continuous, uninterrupted story of man's life on this earth, as far as this life is revealed to us in trustworthy records. The program of instruction in this college has often been criticized because it contains no course specifically planned to impress upon the student this fact of the unity of History, and to furnish, either as an introduction to or the completion of your work that broad, comprehensive view of our whole science which might serve to interpret to you the meaning of its several parts. Excepting, therefore, as your individual instructors feel this need and endeavor to supply it, you are left to yourselves to fit into their proper places in the whole long story, the brief chapters you have time for in your academic life.

And this I urge you to do, because herein lies for me the chief value of this academic study of History. As you approach your topic it is spread before you in the books as a more or less ordered mass of separate events with a tedious accompaniment of dates and a wearisome amount of reference to places you never heard of. Your work presents itself to you as the act of getting, somehow or other, this mass of material into your memory, and the prospect is not an agreeable one. Nor does the thought of your work become more inspiring so long as you continue in that spirit toward it. You simply find yourself involved more and more deeply in a maze of undigested ideas, and you may even quit your study in disgust, as thousands before you have done, and vote the study of History a bore and a waste of time. For my part, I should be the last to blame you. Rather I should be inclined to put the blame of your defeat, not upon you, but only upon the fact that you had not been led to see how the detail you had been reading bore upon the final result. There is no more cruel criticism of a play or a novel than to say that its acts or its chapters do not all tell upon the solution of the plot. They must be planned so that when you close the book or rise from your seat in the theatre you feel that book or play must have moved on in just this way and no other in order to produce the result aimed at.

There is no more dreary occupation than to read chapter after chapter of an historical work in which the narrative seems to have no relation to the great current of contemporary human life and thought. There is no more fatal delusion about our study than the notion that anybody can study History for himself if only he will get the right books and read enough pages in them. This idea has been the bane of historical instruction, because it has brought so much emphasis upon this element of reading, as if, out of the multitude of words, somehow the training was to be evolved. Of course, the great mass of facts must be acquired by a process of reading and learning, and this you must in any case do for yourself. We are speaking now of the study of History in college, where you have at your service the labors of a group of men trained to help you in gaining what you cannot so readily gain by your own effort.

This is always the great problem of students under an elective system: how best to utilize the teaching force at their command. If there is any value in academic study at all — and on this point opinions differ — it is just this: that it can give something which cannot be got by the isolated scholar, and it should be the chief anxiety of every serious student to discover who will give him the most help. Now that does not mean, who will do for him the largest share of work which he might better do alone, but who will teach him to work by himself with the greatest profit.

One hears often of the value of historical study as a discipline for the mind, but I am not inclined to lay any very great weight on that part of our subject. Here, as in every other part of education, discipline comes whenever the work is done with all one's might, and one can do with the might only that in which one is honestly interested, while, conversely, one's interest increases the deeper one goes into any study. I doubt very much whether one can point very definitely to special discipline of the mind acquired by classical or mathematical, or historical study and check that off as so much clear result of his academic years. On the whole, it may well be that the mind gets the best discipline when it thinks least about it and simply goes right on acquiring and practising in the line of its work, whatever that may be. If one gains any special mental training from historical study, it is that the mind falls into the habit of weighing human motives and balancing them one against the other, so that one is less likely to be led away by false motives, less likely to think of human events as determined by single causes, and more likely to believe that all events are the resultant of very complicated causes, some of which he may see clearly, but of which many are sure to escape him.

The outcome of historical study ought to be that one should reach a middle ground between that first simple and childish impression, that History is the record of the passions and feelings of a few great men carried out into action and that other, seemingly more philosophical but hardly less narrow view which would make the men of history only the blind products and agents of forces they are powerless to direct or to control. If the mind can once get permanently into that condition of fairness, so that it can approach all questions of human life in this impartial spirit, this is certainly one gain to be set down to the credit of historical study.

And another gain there ought to be, a gain which the study of History shares with the study of the Law, and that is the power of sifting human evidence. The popular impression is that all of History is in the standard books and that it is all true, as we there find it. You all know with what reverence the English-speaking world has been accustomed to say: "Macaulay says" or "Gibbon relates," as if that settled the matter forever. There is still a sort of blind reverence for historians, chiefly among those who have least acquaintance with them, as if the mere fact of having put on paper some part of this wonderful human story entitled a man at once to our fullest confidence. On the other hand, there has been growing among intelligent persons a critical, often an over-critical attitude toward the traditions of History. Scholars have busied themselves for many years with the original records of the past in the sole purpose of discovering upon what they are based, and things have gone so far in this direction that it was possible for a famous orator, on one of the most important occasions at this university, to say that History was one-half error and the other half lies. I wonder if it ever occurred to him and to those who ape his words, that in order to be sure of errors and falsehoods we must first be sure of accuracy and truth, and that it is only by the process of sound historical inquiry that these can be ascertained. It is in that process that the discipline we are here considering may be attained.

The point firmly fixed by all this criticism is that every alleged historical fact must rest upon evidence and that the study of history must consist largely in the discovery and sifting of this evidence. It has been one of the chief satisfactions of my professional life to watch in my students the gradual disappearance of the attitude of childish faith in the printed word and the growth of a fair critical temper. The lesson they have thus learned will not be confined to History, but will go on to all the other subjects of their thought and put new life into their whole mental action.

But it will be said, and with a certain truth, that the

mental discipline which may come from the study of
History may come also and equally well from many
other kinds of study. Let us see if there are any special
gains from this science which are not shared equally by
others. I say little of the essential and permanent
charm of History arising from the mere fact that it deals
with men and what they have achieved. This charm
too it shares with poetry and romance and with the
most attractive forms of art. History should, for this
reason if for no other, claim the attention of every man
who wishes to know his kind, and there is little doubt
that it will always hold that attention. Even on this
ground it might demand a large place in an academic
program, where there should be room for all that can
tend to elevate the taste and cultivate the sense of
what is lofty as well as merely to store the mind with
useful knowledge. There is a practical side to the
study of History which should commend it especially
to the young American. It is the only study by which
we can come to a true knowledge of those principles of
government on which our state is built and on the
preservation of which our political liberties depend.

There was in America until rather recent years a
singular indifference to the value of History as a guide
for the life of to-day. Our conditions here have seemed
to be so new; the vast resources of our country have
seemed to make us so independent of all outside influence; the demands upon our activities have been so
great and so pressing, that we have imagined ourselves
quite sufficient to ourselves in every respect. The experiments of the Old World had failed to bring about

those conditions in government and in society that seemed of most value to us, and therefore we could not see why we should spend the precious time of these busy days in learning the story of that failure. Rather, we said, let us think only of the future and go on working out our own salvation in the abounding hope and courage of a young and a healthy people. A nation must make its own history. That is true; but it can never for any great length of time afford to forget that the problems of human society are ever recurring phases of the one great problem of good and free government, and that the experience of the past, however full of failures, is full also of lessons and of warnings for all who may come after.

There can be but one thing worse than a blind following of foreign traditions, and that is a blind devotion to our own. The great war has been driving this principle into the American consciousness, but long before that we had begun to wake up to its truth and the study of History had begun to take the place it deserves among the sciences taught at our higher schools, and is even making its way down into our lower instruction. From there it should enter into the living thought of our people and so become one of the great permanent forces that are molding our nation's life. There is much truth in the idea that the highest statesmanship lies in the right decision of questions as they occur rather than in the forming and carrying out of far reaching schemes of policy; but it is also true that there must be behind all successful opportunism high ideals and wise forethought or, when the moment comes, the training which shall teach men to make the right use of it will be wanting. One of the results of this awakened sense of the value of a knowledge of the past for the life of the present is seen in the rich program of historical instruction spread before you in this place.

A short generation ago the teaching of History in our colleges was done mainly by men who had some other department as their specialty but were put at this work because it was believed that any scholarly minded gentleman who had read enough books was capable of teaching History. It is not so very long since the professorship of History at Oxford was given as the reward of a successful literary career without regard to the training of the candidate in the methods of historical investigation or teaching. Now all this has pretty well disappeared. Special chairs of History have been established in all colleges of repute, and men are called to them who have served an apprenticeship in the art of historical inquiry or who have made a successful record as teachers. So you see that in entering upon this discipline you are not in the position of the isolated reader sitting down in his study to entertain himself with the story of what his fellow-men have done, but you are workmen in a wide field of inquiry, with a multitude of fellow-workers about you, with the machinery of a great science ready at your service and with well-recognized methods for getting at the kind of truth the historian seeks.

So far we have been considering the value of historical study as a reason why it may well occupy a large share of a college student's attention. How, with all these favoring circumstances shall we define its purpose? Training of the mind, a knowledge of that human life which is always the supreme interest of man, the basis of all literature and all art — these values indicate the more immediate and direct purposes you may properly have in mind as you prepare your programs of study. But beyond these there lies the more remote and more compelling purpose of becoming, by so much, better citizens of the Republic. It is not merely that the great statesman of the future must be something more than a mere opportunist. The citizen who holds no public place nor wishes to do so — if such there be in America — must learn to have such a clear grasp of political questions that he will not be the sport of every demagogue who tells him a pleasing story, but can see for himself what he would like to have done and can apply his best effort to getting it done.

If he is told that our conditions are so different from those of other peoples that we can afford to neglect their experience, he must be able to look back for himself to the history of free institutions in Greece, in Italy, in Switzerland and France, and above all in England, to estimate how these have differed among themselves and in what points we are like the peoples of these older states. If he is called upon, as any of you may be, to help in the administration of our great and growing cities, he must know something of the constitutions of Athens, of Corinth, of Venice and Florence. As he reads the history of any one of these earlier republics he will be amazed to find in how many particulars their problems were the same as ours. For example, we are brought up to believe that universal suffrage is the cure-all for every political disease. That is a very simple proposition, but its value can be tested only by one who knows something of the multitude of experiments out of which that theory has grown. The principle of universal suffrage seems to have reached its triumphant vindication in these latest days, but that very triumph is revealing, almost before it begins its activity, the weaknesses and dangers it involves. Extravagant democracy is beginning already to beget that sense of perplexity and confusion out of which men have always sought relief in the leadership of trusted individuals.

The argument against universal suffrage can be met only by men who have the power to grasp all the elements of the problem, and that power can come only through a study of the experience of the world with this very issue. Or, take the principle of the right of the majority to determine the policy of the whole community. To us Americans that seems to be almost an innate idea, so early do we begin in our childish sports to put it into practice. A study of the history of electoral methods would show us that this idea has been very slowly evolved from a long series of experiments, that it is at best only a device to carry on a political system when all other methods had failed to work.

So it would be with every great social problem. For example, the whole vexed question of the political, industrial, and intellectual status of women. It is a very simple proposition to say that a woman has a right to be anything she can be, and that all the accumulations of capital and energy which until now have been devoted mainly to the preparation of men for the work of life ought now to be equally shared by women. If one accepts that proposition without reflection one is hurried on irresistibly to the extreme conclusions of the party of the Left. At the present moment it seems as if this extreme emphasis on the question of right as against every other consideration were about to be accepted by the world calling itself civilized. If so, then we may be sure that those considerations of wisdom and expediency that are for the moment being disregarded will assert themselves again and demand a readjustment of the balance. The citizen who desires to sift out the true from the false must go back and inform himself as to the conditions of those peoples among whom the nearest approach to the desired end has been reached. He must ask himself why it is that this question comes up to us now and why it takes the forms it does. He must read the history of those communities where the equality of men and women has been realized and ask himself if the results are such as to make him wish to use his influence to extend that condition. He must inquire whether there really is any fundamental reason why difference of sex should draw any hard and fast line between rights or occupations and how far that difference has influenced the course of human history.

The same may be said of the crusade against alcohol. Under the pressure of a cruel necessity, the nations were roused to a quickened sense of a great social evil and took drastic measures to lessen it. We in America with our bolder idealism and our pathetic faith in the virtue of legislation have rushed to the extreme and abolished the evil thing without much thought of consequences. Rightly to estimate the value of arguments on both sides, we should have to inquire into the history of sumptuary laws in all countries and at all times. We should ask whether the evils aimed at were really removed, and if they were, whether the society in question was thereby on the whole advanced along the road of civic virtue. On the answer to such historical inquiries would depend our attitude toward the whole question of repressive legislation. I do not say, and I do not believe, that History would furnish complete answers to all these and similar problems, and I should be the last person to counsel the use of History as a check upon social experiment. I am only reminding you that it may contribute valuable factors to the solution of social problems, and that without this contribution no solution can ever be complete.

We come to the question of method in historical study. This may seem to you to be a subject rather for teachers than for students, but happily there is no such gulf between us that what concerns the one is not a matter of vital concern to the others. The student may receive recommendation from his teacher, but unless he is convinced that the method recommended to him is the best for him just here and now, the recommendation will not have much effect. It would be well for every student if in selecting the courses of study he proposes to follow he should allow this question of method to enter quite as largely as any other into his choice, and to do this he must, of course, inform himself as to the different possible methods. First and most obvious is the method of reading. In the English academic tradition the word "reading" is synonymous with studying. One "reads" for a degree; one joins a "reading party" for the holidays. I once heard a man of singular brilliancy in certain kinds of intellectual effort say, that his method of studying a period of history was to take a book — almost any one would do — on that period and read it through as fast as he could, then another and another in the same way, until he had exhausted his available material. Then he would read novels, plays, and poems on the same subjects, and the *residuum* of all this reading would be his knowledge of the period. I will not say that that method might not do wonders for just that man, gifted as he was with a phenomenal memory for petty details and with an imagination vivid enough to hold all this mass of scattered material together by its dramatic power. If I were to recommend it to any average student, or indeed to any man without these precise gifts, I should expect the result to be disastrous. He would probably come out of the experiment with a most curious hodge-podge of ideas without order or continuity.

This may well be called the extravagance of the reading method. A more reasonable form of it would be to choose books with greater care, to read only those written by the best equipped authors and to read them with greater deliberation. That would probably give better results; the reader would be sure that he had behind him the authority of persons of recognized merit, and, using authors of reputation known to be on opposite sides of great controverted questions, he might fairly feel that he had gone far toward gaining a real insight into the times he is studying. To be sure, he would probably have moments when he would wonder what use there is in learning what two equally learned doctors think of a given case if after all their conclusions are exactly opposite. He will perhaps hastily end his study by concluding that there is no such thing as truth in History, and that his time so far has been wasted.

There are two weak points in this reading method. One is that until it has been carried on for years one does not arrive at that historical perspective of which I have been speaking. As one reads on, book after book, his perspective instead of becoming clearer is likely to grow more indistinct. Much reading does not of necessity give the ability to make the given bit of knowledge fit into its place in the general view, and without that sort of fitting in the whole subject becomes dreary and therefore unprofitable. The method of reading, then, demands that it be supplemented by careful study and reflection upon the relations of the piece of history one is studying to the rest of the human story. And this is precisely what the college teacher can supply. Without the aid of an experienced guide it is next to impossible for the young reader of History to tell what his book really means. In the mass of detail he finds the larger movement of the time slipping away from him. He cannot see the organic connection between phenomena which seem to come from entirely different causes and to be tending toward entirely different results.

Certainly in the earlier stages of his work he must depend upon wider experience for aid in tracing out these often complicated movements. His attention once drawn to these things he is able to see how they affect all his study, but it would not have been possible for him to grasp them for himself. For example: if one wished to study the history of the Protestant Reformation, he would naturally go to books which bear that title. He would find them dealing with a certain historic period, and he would fancy that when he had got through with them he would know what the Reformation meant. It is not his fault that writers have generally neglected or passed over with scant attention many of the most important elements of that great movement and have confined themselves to the recital of events which may better be described as the outbreak of the Reformation than as the Reformation itself. Or, if he should read the whole story of the battles and the politics of our civil war, how little he would know of the real history of those years until he had been shown, as a skilful teacher could briefly show him, how all that was compressed into that crucial time was only the outburst of forces that had been gathering for a generation before. The college student is in the fortunate position of having the services of men of experience ready to his hand, and he should try to get all out of them that he can.

But when the student comes to ask himself just what he means by getting something from a teacher, he should look out that he gives himself a sound answer. He should be careful that he does not ask of a teacher to do for him just the same thing that reading might do, that is simply to pour information into him and leave him to digest it or not, as he may or can. He should make higher demands than this. He should look for the kind of teaching that lifts him up and makes him more capable of getting at things for himself. He must call for a kind of instruction different from that which the books may give. Of course this involves the question of men, and as such we are not here concerned with it; but it is also a question of subjects, and there I may point out one or two matters that might influence your choice. There are portions of History which can be dealt with by yourselves more successfully than others, and these you may well postpone or pursue less intensively while you are in college. In the others you will almost certainly fail to get at the true interest and value of study unless you can work in them under wise direction. For instance, you need help most when you are dealing with men and periods most remote from our own. I mean most remote in the nature of the institutions and modes of thought under which men lived, not necessarily most remote in time. But you may ask: why trouble ourselves about men and times so different from our own that we can draw no lessons from them? If the purpose of historical study be to make us know our own times better, why not keep as near to them as possible?

There is a certain attractiveness in that inquiry, and in fact the record of the elections in History in this college for any year shows that a great majority of our students have answered it in the way that might have been expected. They have decided that the most important periods for them to study are not the remotest but the nearest, both in time and character. Is that a wise decision? Perhaps we may profit here by the analogy of the physical sciences. If, for instance, you are studying the anatomy of the horse, whose foot has, I believe, gone through a long and perfectly traceable development from a five-toed to a one-toed condition, would you be contented to stop at the point where you find him with two or three toes and try to see how the one toe grew out of these? No, you would want to go back just as far as possible, and the farther back you went the more interesting and important your study would become. The scientist is in pursuit of the secret of the physical life. He traces the embryo back in his eager search until he reaches the point which seems only one step removed from the mystery that enwraps the transmission of life from one organism to another. We admire his infinite patience and his conviction that, though he fail in the ultimate quest, he will at least make substantial gains for the cause of truth.

We, as historical students, are dealing with life in another aspect; not with the life of the body, but with the life of the mind. Our quest is not for the origins of physical functions, nor for the relations of one form of material life to others, but for the origins and the relations of the great institutions which have shaped the lives of countless generations of men upon this earth. We are pursuing the shifting and fleeting forms which these institutions have assumed from age to age, and though we too must often stand baffled before the great mysteries of human experience, still we feel that our quest is a noble one and that, if the ultimate secret eludes us, we are making all along the way valuable contributions to the sum of human wisdom. If we allow ourselves to pause in our inquiries at a stage only a step or two removed from present conditions, we are like the naturalist who should never get beyond the outside of the egg shell, who should content himself with the mere enumeration of present forms of material life upon the earth.

The naturalist is in fact of value to the world mainly in that he is an historian, that he borrows the tools of our craft and works with them toward ends like our own. If the historical student does not learn something of ancient and mediaeval life, he has, properly speaking, not got into the subject of History at all. He is only dealing with present conditions or with those so near to the present that their educational value is hardly greater. We have all, of course, to recognize the fact of specialization in all scientific work; we know what great results have come from this and the still greater results that are to be expected from it. But we have to consider that by far the larger part of our college study is elementary and introductory to later special work and that too early specialization is sure to produce a top-heavy and one-sided development. This is especially true of History, a subject upon which the student brings very little knowledge with him when he comes to college. The problem here is to lay broad and deep the foundations of future knowledge, not to develop expertness in any one line of study.

It may well be said in reply to this, that the great majority of our students will not pursue the study of History beyond their college years, and therefore, that they ought rather to master some definite period than to spread themselves over too wide a field. If by study is meant the systematic dealing with books in academic fashion, the proposition is sound, but if we are asked to believe that our graduate is never again to busy himself with historical inquiry it may well be questioned. He can hardly fill any important place in active life in which he will not be called upon, not only to know something of the past, but to add to his knowledge. If his acquaintance extends only to the two or three generations of men just preceding his own he will be but ill-prepared to meet such demands. The problems of modern European politics, for instance, cannot be remotely comprehended by one who has not learned to understand something of the spirit of feudal Europe. I do not mean by this that one should merely have learned the events of the history of mediaeval France, Germany, and Italy, but that one should have reached the kind of comprehension of what mediaeval life meant which an experienced teacher could help him to attain.

In these days of eager discussion as to the possibilities of international coöperation in the lessening of national enmities and the bringing about of something

like the poet's "Parliament of Man" there is especial
need of an historical perspective based upon the most
complete command of all that History has to teach.
What shall we think of the guileless indifference to
facts of men who tell us that because the states of this
Union do not maintain armies and lines of fortresses
and diplomatic mechanisms, therefore the nations of
Europe can equally well afford to do without these
burdens? As if these new communities, carved out of
the wilderness were in any sense comparable to those
ancient political units knit together by ties of blood and
by institutions welded through centuries of common
experience, strengthened by struggle, glorified by heroic
example, celebrated in poetry and song. Such a perversion of ideas is possible only to men who have never
read History beneath the surface, or who have forgotten in partisan zeal the lessons they had once
learned.

If now we are convinced that there are definite and
practical reasons why the study of the remote past
should interest live young men of the present, we have
still to inquire as to the best division of time in college
according to historic periods. Upon which parts of the
human story should you here in college spend the
greater part of your time and energy? That is a question that cannot be given the same answer for all men.
There will be individual tastes and preferences, and
these may wisely be considered. The real question is:
upon what parts of this study do you need most the
interpretation of the teachers and the use of the great
literary machinery that is provided for you here?

Your choice of periods ought, I think, largely to depend upon that. Consider whether in your own reading, both now and hereafter, you will be most likely to understand without instruction the men and the ideas of the eighteenth and nineteenth, not to say the twentieth century or the men of the fourth or the tenth or the fifteenth. Consider also whether, after you leave college, in the ordinary active life of the world, in the necessary contact with modern political problems you are not far more likely to be drawn into the study of the recent than of the remoter past, and whether there is not in that fact an indication of your duty here. Here you have the means to acquire the foundation upon which all such later reading can profitably be based, and without which that later acquirement will never be so thoroughly understood.

So far we have been concerned with the principle of acquisition, the first in the natural order of progression suggested by the normal development of the mind. The second principle is that of understanding. We have already touched upon this, for at no stage of progress can the attempt to understand be wholly disregarded. The late Professor J. G. Droysen in his work on historical method defines the whole object of historical study to be: "to understand by investigation" (*forschend zu verstehen*), that is, not merely to learn, but to understand what one learns. Professor Henry Adams used to say in his half serious, half whimsical fashion: "If there is anything I despise more than another, it is information." He no more meant this to be taken literally than he meant people to believe that he was a failure as a teacher of History. What he did mean was that mere information, undigested accumulation of material would surely cause intellectual ill health. It is obvious that to understand facts we must first have them; the caution needed is that the process of accumulation should not be followed too exclusively or be continued too long. The fault with the elder pedagogy was that it relied almost entirely upon acquisition and was comparatively indifferent to understanding. I well remember, when I was a student in college being called upon to finish out a paragraph of the text-book in Greek history of which the so-called instructor had given me the first line, and being set down hard because I refused to make the attempt. Such an outrage as that would, I am happy to believe, be impossible to-day; yet the temptation to think we are truly learning when we are merely cramming is always near, and we have to brace ourselves to resist it.

To understand is the absolutely first essential of all study that can be called in any sense of the word "advanced." I asked an honest colleague of mine whether he considered the instruction he was giving in one of his courses advanced instruction. "I do most certainly" he replied. And how many of your pupils do you think *get* advanced instruction?" "About one-third." Not every teacher makes so nice and so frank a discrimination between those pupils who merely acquire a modicum of information and those who really advance to the grade of understanding. I can never forget the stimulating shock of listening for the first

time, as I did in Germany, to teachers of History who
actually knew what they were talking about, who had
mastered the detail of information, who assumed that
their pupils had also made notable progress in detail
and who tried, upon this basis, to build up a real edifice
of understanding. It is all a question of order and
proportion.

My own academic experience is long enough to have
shown me more than one change in the swing of the
pedagogic pendulum. It is now nearly two generations
ago that I was taken with other candidates for entrance to college to visit the famous Boston Latin
School and see for ourselves how it ought to be done.
At the request of our teacher, a former master in that
ancient school, a luckless "first boy" was haled from
his seat to the head master's desk and once wound up
went on reciting the rules and exceptions of Andrews
and Stoddard's Latin grammar until he was red in the
face, while we poor suburbanites were dumb with
amazement and despair. That was the ideal held before us, but I have always been thankful that I never
even remotely attained to it. I am bound to add that
the prize scholar did not, as might have been expected,
turn out an incapable, but became in his turn a head
master under a more rational system. Extravagance
produced a reaction, and the generation following
swung over into the current of a pedagogic method in
which the accurate learning of the fundamentals came
to be treated with thinly disguised contempt. Everything, we were told, had been sacrificed to memory.
Henceforth only such things were to be memorized as

were absolutely essential to the rapid attainment of "efficiency."

Under this impulse of reform the element of understanding came to be emphasized to a grotesque degree. Infants in school were to have everything explained to them. No one was to be required to learn anything that he could not understand. Mental development was to take the place of mental equipment. Only the happy worker could do good work, and the way to make people happy was not to require them to do anything that was for the moment disagreeable to them. It was a halcyon period, full of noble ideals and valuable for the clearing out of many ancient rubbish heaps. But when the time came for taking account of stock, it appeared that all this interest in the understanding had come near to destroying the whole foundation of certain knowledge and quick ability to handle tools upon which any sound comprehension must rest. So again we are coming to feel in these new days a new necessity of shifting the emphasis once more. Or, to follow our train of thought, we are trying to bring about a more just proportion and a more rational order between the elements of acquisition and the elements of understanding. We want now to train the memory, to teach the gospel of hard work whether we understand it at the time or not, and then to gather up what we have learned and so order it that it will have a meaning and a lesson for us.

So we come to our third methodic principle, that of research and production. Up to this point we have been thinking of the student in his relation to an in-

structor or to a book. We now have to think of him in
relation to definite problems of inquiry. In the earlier
stages of acquisition and understanding he was in the
attitude of receptivity. Here he is in the attitude of
personal search after a desired fact or explanation of
facts. In those former capacities the impulse to work
came largely from without, from the teacher or from a
sense of honorable class fellowship. Now the impulse
is from within, a personal demand for the satisfaction
of some question already in his mind. If you were to
ask almost any thoughtful teacher in this college what
his chief difficulty in teaching is, he would not answer
that students were reluctant to learn, or that they
were stupid or did not appreciate what was done for
them. He would say that his chief obstacle to success
was the docility and receptivity of his students. As
one of my colleagues used to put it: "It's not their
wrong attitude toward their studies; it's their lack of
attitude." Another said in answer to the question how
the boys from a certain school were fitted for college:
"They are pretty well fitted to unlearn all they have
learned." And that was saying a good deal.

The method of personal research is valuable in so far
as it tends to correct the results of too much acquisition and too much explanation. Let me illustrate by
a familiar example. What would you think of a youth
who should set before himself in school the noble ambition to be the best ball player in college, and should
then spend his time in reading books about the science
of pitching and catching and in going about to the professors of that art and persuading them to give him

lectures on the finer details of their honorable profession? You all know better than that. You know that the way to learn to catch a ball every time is to catch it. At first you will fail in a majority of cases; but your object is to reduce the percentage of errors to a minimum, and you know better than any one can tell you that the place to do that is the ball-field. Of course there are many practical hints which the expert can give to the novice, but you know that all such theoretical teaching would be thrown away if there were not going on with it the training of the eye and the hand in constant practice. Now the process of learning to do one thing is about like that of learning to do another. You learn by practice. The newspapers are filled with alluring advertisements of patent ways of learning foreign languages, but the fundamental fact remains that the only way to learn a language is to use it; and the same is true of every other subject.

The method of learning by research calls upon the student to set before himself definite subjects of inquiry and to pursue them until he reaches an answer. It is comparatively new here, and it still has to contend with the mental apathy induced by the other methods we have been considering. I urge it upon your attention in regard to History because in planning your courses of study you are likely to leave little space for instruction of this sort. You are much more inclined to follow the lines of least resistance and to go on acquiring information and trying to understand it without the kind of effort required by this third process. The objection most often found in presenting its claims to students is that it is suited only for those who intend to be professional scholars or teachers. I do not, however, think this objection well founded. The professional student of History is sure to have this method forced upon his attention at a fairly early stage of his study. The moment he begins to inquire into what is going on in his field he finds that his fellow-workers the world over are engaged in one or another kind of research, and whether he will or no he must join in the same endeavor.

The general student, on the other hand, must get the benefit of such method in college if he is to get it anywhere, and he needs it especially to aid him in forming intelligent judgments upon the historical statements, be they only the reports in the daily newspapers, which he is to meet in all his future life. It is to this method that we look for that result of historical study I have already referred to as the power of weighing and sifting human evidence. There is no process so admirably adapted to save one from that slavery to the written word which is the bane of all constructive thought. I have seldom known a student in my own practice work who did not come to me at the end of the year and tell me that he thought he had learned for life the lesson never to believe anything that is written until he had convinced himself that the writer had got his information from trustworthy sources, that he was a man not likely to pervert the truth, that he was not likely to be led by blind partisanship, and so on through the catalogue of critical tests. In other words he had grown out of the attitude of receptivity into the attitude of criticism, and criticism, meaning thereby careful examination, is the absolutely essential process in the perception of truth.

Allow me to put this system or division of methodic principles in another form. I hope I shall not be accused of any desire to invent a new philosophic scheme, still less of dabbling in the "Philosophy of History" if I suggest that there is here a useful correspondence between the different stages of a man's intellectual progress and the different methods we have just been considering. There are three stages through which the normal man in his mental growth must sooner or later pass. These are, of course, the stages of childhood, youth, and manhood. They cannot be marked off by any given age. Some persons remain all their lives in the stage of childhood; others move on through the stage of youth without ever reaching manhood, and others still, rarely gifted natures, seem never to have known the earlier steps, but spring full armed into the work of life as grown-up men. But the average man, such as most of us are, passes pretty clearly through these three periods during his intellectual growth. In his early life he has most clearly marked the powers of acquisition. He learns with amazing rapidity. His mind is simply one great receiving vault, and he is a happy man who does not find that most of the ideas which are there stored up remain dead and buried, unfruitful for the future. The whole visible world is for the child but so much material from which he may add to the stock of his information.

In the second stage he begins to arrange this mass of

matter into orderly shape. He wants to know how this and that fact hang together. He insists upon learning the reasons of things. He will not only learn; he will also understand. In the third stage a new instinct arouses within him. He is no longer satisfied with receiving impressions from without and trying to understand them; he must produce something of his own. What we like to call the creative spirit makes itself felt. The man of business must no longer work for wages; he must begin to make his own ventures and to hope for his larger profits. The man of other people's books must begin to make books of his own. The student, as he reaches this stage, begins to inquire for himself and to seek the solution of this or that problem of nature and life. This is the period of research.

You now see my purpose in this rather commonplace analogy. The methods of teaching should correspond as nearly as may be to the stage at which a man finds himself in his intellectual development. But here again I must remind you that the lines between these methods are as indistinct as are those between the stages of growth. One man remains a memorizer all his life, and no one cares what he may think on the reasons of things. Another reaches the stage of great intellectual clearness but is never moved to go on to the point of individual research and productiveness. A third seems by some singular prenatal process to have gone through the earlier stages in his ancestors and begins at once to originate. Anthony Trollope begins his creative literary life at the age of forty; Tennyson has passed his climax at thirty. It is, therefore, clearly impossible to check men off into one or the other class and insist upon methods of study rigidly adjusted to a given stage of advancement. Some of the saddest results of modern experiment have come from attempts of this kind to force students into methods, either too elementary or too advanced, which were theoretically suited to their period of academic study.

My suggestion is that all of the methods here described should be used at every stage of progress, only in widely differing proportions. In the earliest mental condition, that of the child, the process of memory should preponderate, but the understanding should be quickened also within such limits as the welfare of the individual may dictate, and he should be further taught to reproduce in proper form something of that which has been given him. Nothing is more painful than to see the effort sometimes made in our lower schools to force the understanding at an age when the pupil is capable of little else than memorizing. Our reading public has recently been deluged *ad nauseam* with the lucubrations of precocious infants exploited by enterprising publishers to the grief of judicious friends of youth. In the second stage the understanding should be stimulated by every rational means, while the memory should still be cultivated by constant exercise. Here too the impulse to reproduction should be given freer scope. The pupil should be encouraged to create something, be it ever so feeble, out of his own intellectual stock. And so in the third stage he should still continue to acquire, but in lessening degree and always for definite purpose. The devouring

curiosity of the child, for which the whole world is none
too large, must give place to the teaching of experience
that, after all, only one little fragment of the world's
wisdom can be conquered by any one man. Gen-
eralizing must diminish, and specializing must begin.
The man passes out of the period of authority into the
period of independence. His method of work is now
the pursuit of definite problems. He will not cease to
learn; he can never cease to desire to understand; but
the bulk of his effort must now go in the direction of production. He may make books or he may, as a teacher,
try to make men, or as a journalist try to move the
world, or as a politician to help along his day and generation. In any case the proportion of creative effort
to acquisition and to understanding must grow constantly greater.

You see how all this applies to the problem immediately before you: how to plan your study of History in this college to the best advantage. As to age,
you are all in the period of youth. You ought to have
left your childhood behind you. Whether you have
done so or not, each of you must answer for himself,
and upon this answer will depend the sort of study you
will want to do in college and the order in which you
will pursue it. If you honestly feel that you are incapable of anything beyond the mere work of acquiring facts, then you should so choose your studies that
the power of acquisition will be called into play. Confine yourself in that case to courses, if any such there
be, in which no demand will be made upon you beyond
the learning of certain definite things without much

inquiry into their meaning in the long story of human life. But, if you are in search of some wider satisfaction, add to the work of acquisition by taking such courses, and such I know there are, in which you will be led to see the bearing of events upon each other and upon the whole course of history. Choose those periods which lie far removed as well as those which lie nearer to the present. Try to plan a longer or a shorter course of study in such a way that it will show you the connection between the remotest and the nearest phases in human development.

As to order of selection, I can only make a few general suggestions based upon what has already been said. As between subjects, I should say: choose first those which are most easily comprehended. It would be impossible to lay down any principle here that would hold for all men, but it is safe to assume that the nearer one comes to the life of to-day, the easier one finds it to understand the life of other times. But this nearness will not always be nearness in time. The life of ancient Greece and Rome is on the whole much more like the life of to-day than that of the Middle Ages is to either. Mediaeval life is marked by certain institutions altogether peculiar to itself and can be understood only by one who has some familiarity with both that which went before and that which followed it. Some advisers will tell you that the only proper order of historical study is the strictly chronological one, beginning with the most ancient; others will tell you the reverse of this. Neither of these chronological orders, it seems to me, has any real principle behind it.

I can do no better than to say that what is easier to understand ought to come before what is more difficult and leave the matter there with the suggestion I have just made.

So much for the order of choice in regard to subjects. But I think the question of method should enter here also. It should be clear from what has already been said what its application here will be. In the earlier stages of your work, even here in college, let the process of acquisition preponderate. That is the purpose of our introductory courses. In connection with those courses, let your reading not be limited to what is prescribed, but let it be as broad and as solid as possible, so that when you go on to more advanced work you may be sure of a reasonably sound foundation. Learn without the costly method of experience that the average requirements of any course in college are far below what would be profitable for the earnest student who really wants to make each course a stepping stone to something higher. Among your advanced courses, inquire carefully as to the methods pursued and let your choice be governed partly by that. For your earlier advanced work let the effort to understand preponderate, but do in every course some bit of original work. Do not allow yourself to enter your last undergraduate year without having produced a piece of written work in history. Take advantage of the very favorable arrangements of the English Department to select historical topics for your work there and get your instructor in History to help you in the first stages of collecting material and putting it into orderly shape.

You will thus gain a bit of practice that will be of service in all your future work.

And then, as you come to the later years of study, let the element of research take a larger place. A word here at once of caution and encouragement. I have said that the method you should use should depend upon the stage of your mental progress, but let me warn you also that your progress depends a good deal upon the method you have been using. If you have gone on too long in the attitude of receptivity, you will find it all the harder to change to the method of activity. You may be led to put off the time of change by a feeling that you are not quite ready for it. If you wait till you are absolutely certain, you will never be ready. One of the most marked characteristics, I suppose of all students, certainly of Harvard students — I say it with all deliberation after many years' acquaintance with them — is modesty or self-distrust. It is partly this that keeps them from venturing early enough into the creative form of study. They fear they may produce something unripe and uncalled for; and so they will. But the base-ball candidate is not deterred by his failures from keeping at it. Even if he never rise above the humblest position in the game, he knows that he is getting something valuable by the way, and there is always the chance that he may become the great man of his year.

I urge this kind of practical study whether you mean to be a specialist in History or not. It has been an interesting experience to me that several of my most devoted pupils in research went into the work knowing at the time that they were to be physicians. They believed that that kind of training was going to help in making their lives larger and better, and I trust they have not been disappointed.

In using the word History in its academic sense I have meant to include all historical instruction, whether offered in the program of the historical department or elsewhere, and I cannot too strongly recommend every student of History to make as wide excursions into the fields of literature and art as his time will allow. Much instruction in those departments is strictly historical in its character, but even that which is more purely technical is rich in suggestion and stimulation for the historical student.

THE RATIONAL EDUCATION OF THE MODERN MINISTER

AN ADDRESS TO MINISTERS

DOES the modern minister need any education at all? In view of the almost fanatical emphasis on education in our day and country such a question may well appear absurd. And yet, as one looks over the sources of supply for the ministerial profession, one is tempted to answer it in the negative. The fact is that a large proportion of Protestant pulpits are filled by young men whose professional preparation has been of the most meager description. They have passed through some secondary school or some "college" which ought to be called a secondary school and then have spent a short time at one of the so-called "Bible Colleges" and then have gone at once into the practical duties of their arduous and exacting profession. It is comparatively seldom that they have given themselves the benefit of an apprenticeship under the direction of a more experienced chief. Without the preliminary training of the young lawyer or the young physician they are thrust directly into responsibilities as serious as any they will ever be called upon to assume. Unlike these other professional beginners the young clergyman is not permitted to gain experience by practice in unimportant cases, but is called upon at once to meet the severest demands upon his ministerial character. His success or failure for life may be determined by the manner in which he responds to these first searching tests.

The contrast with other professions, however, must not be drawn too sharply. The standards of excellence in medicine and the law also can be maintained only at the cost of eternal vigilance. Our greater schools of law especially are subject to a continual rivalry from institutions having no other object than to push on as many youths as possible into legal practice with a minimum of knowledge and a plentiful lack of training in legal method. Our medical schools have to defend themselves and the profession from the incursion of quackery in all its seductive forms. The most important difference is that the great public has, or thinks it has, its own quick tests of value in law and medicine, whereas in those things of the spirit which are the concern of the young minister such tests are almost wholly lacking. The client knows whether his lawyer wins his case and the patient thinks he knows whether the doctor cures him, but the man in the pew does not, except by rather long experience, find out whether his clergyman is really competent for the service he professes to render.

There is another line of contrasts that cannot be overlooked. In medicine and in the law there is a considerable body of material which any one not hopelessly prejudiced will readily admit to be essential to the preparation of the practitioner. Anatomy and physiology, the generally accepted maxims of the common law and the statutes of the state — this minimum of theoretical knowledge will be assumed by every one, and few will question the value of having these and some other subjects well taught through systematic instruction. For the minister, it is said, there is no such body of necessary knowledge. The one essential thing for him is the Bible, and a familiarity with the text of the Bible is best acquired in the family and will be brought with the young man into his practice. All else, such is the argument for unpreparedness, must come with the practical demands of the parish. The difficulty of replying comes from the undoubted fact that many of the most efficient ministers in our Protestant bodies have won success by precisely this process. They are remembered; the greater number who fell by the wayside are forgotten.

Aside from familiarity with the Bible the popular judgment places the greatest weight upon what it likes to call the inspirational quality of the minister. "An inspired boy!" was the comment of an intelligent woman upon a youth just entering upon his ministerial career. It was a most unfortunate estimate of the young man's quality, as the sequel inevitably proved. Inspiration without training and without the saving balance of sound common sense may carry a man along over the first obstacles, until the tests of character begin to be felt, but then it will pretty certainly fail him. If the profession of the minister is to go on there must be some systematic preparation for it, and that preparation must, for the present at least, be given in organized schools specially endowed for the purpose.

That the institution of the Christian ministry is to go on and will try to do substantially the work it has

always tried to do is here assumed, in spite of all prog-
nostications to the contrary. My own conviction on
this point may be illustrated by an early experience.
A generation ago, when I was a young teacher of History in the university I was suddenly offered the newly
founded professorship of Church History in the Harvard Divinity School. I was a layman, with only a
very loose connection with a religious organization and
I had made, up to that time, no detailed study of either
the institutions or the doctrines of the historic Church.
In my preliminary conversation with President Eliot
he asked me among other things what was my feeling
in regard to the permanence of the ministerial profession. In view of the obvious rivalries of the press, of
charitable organization, of scientific study, of popular
education, did I feel that the profession of the minister
was worth maintaining in dignity and honor as a part
of the function of a great university? My reply was,
that I did not believe the time had come or was likely
to come soon when the spoken word would lose its
power over the minds of men. If the Christian ministry
under its present form should disappear to-morrow,
under some other form it would reappear the day after
to-morrow and would go on doing the same work it had
always done.

That conviction, hastily formulated and crudely expressed, has not changed with the passing of a generation in which the rivalries I have mentioned have
certainly not diminished in number nor lessened in
their manifold and welcome activities. Not forgetting
some moments of depression I draw from the expe-

rience of this generation spent in helping to prepare young men for the practice of this profession only new encouragement and hopefulness. The world is still looking for leadership, never, I believe, more eagerly than now. It complains, to be sure, that the qualities it seeks are not often found; but when it does find them it knows them, it welcomes them and it rewards them. It bears patiently with mediocrity hoping always for better things. At the close of a generation I do not hesitate to say that the standing of your profession in the community at large is as good as it was at the beginning. In some respects it is better because of the wholesome criticism to which the profession has been subjected.

Now, what is it that the community values in the office of the minister? What kind of leadership does it ask him to supply, and what does it miss when it finds fault with his service? Through this generation there has been a persistent cry that the old idea of the minister as a teacher of religion and as a persuader to right living was gone forever. Henceforth he was to be an economic counsellor, a sanitary director, a charity organizer, a pilot through the bewilderments of "social service," an apostle of "social justice," a mouthpiece for all the divine discontents that seem to foretell the overturn of our social order — anything, in short, but the interpreter to a puzzled world of the divine idea as presented in the Good News of Jesus Christ. No wonder that many an earnest youth of rich endowment, facing the prospect of such a multifarious requirement as this should have drawn back in alarm and left the field of the ministry to duller minds and less awakened consciences, while he has applied his better powers to some profession where the demand seemed to be simpler and more tangible.

Such losses to the profession are deplorable, and the more so, to my mind, because I think they result from a wrong conception of the real demand. Of course, all these functions can be better performed by men specially trained in the several fields of knowledge and experience here suggested. If the community needs instruction in economic science, it is not going to its minister to get it. If its conscience begins to prick it with a sense of duty to its badly housed and badly fed and imperfectly washed members, there are experts at hand to suggest practical remedies. It is not skill in these things that makes the minister a useful man in his community. He must have his ideas about such problems, but so must every other good and thoughtful citizen. An expert indeed he must be; but it must be in something different from any or all of these subjects. His expertness must lie in the application to all these details of those principles in belief and those sanctions for action to which we give the name of religion. His service to mankind will be in showing what these principles are and how they may be made to work in the daily experience of every man. His leadership, if he is really to lead, must consist in the constant stimulation of his hearers to live and work as religious men, as servants of something greater than themselves.

The history of the ministerial office in the Christian church shows it under three forms best described by the.words priest, prophet, and ruler. The priest is above all else the personal representative of an institution. What he says and does has force and value only as it conveys to the individual the treasure of faith and practice entrusted to the institution of the Church. The prophet is he who utters forth the truths of Christianity without reference to their institutional sanctions. His quality as a Christian man suffices to give validity to his teaching, and this teaching must find its way to the hearts of his disciples in virtue of its inherent truth, not because it accords with any prescriptions of authority. The ruler is the minister in his quality of temporal administrator, either recognized and supported by political authority or, if independent of that, maintained and sanctioned by the religious body he represents.

Historically these several characters have been united in the one person of the priest, but at different times and under differing circumstances the emphasis has been very differently placed. At the high points of clerical domination of society the prophetic character has been almost entirely subordinated to the other two. Priestly ordination and political control have combined to repress every too ardent expression of the individual spirit. Then have come great moments of revival, when men have turned against these agencies of repression and have welcomed the individual whose prophetic quality gave them promise of betterment. Then ordinations and political institutions have had to adjust themselves to the newly awakened religious consciousness, and new historic epochs have begun.

Of all such periods of revival the Protestant Reformation was the most important, and we are the sharers in its heritage. The line of cleavage between "those who go to the Mass" and "those who go to the preaching" originating in the religious divisions of the sixteenth century, has lost none of its significance to-day. In our Protestant ministry the decisive element is still the individual appeal, freed as far as may be from the dictation of any organization or the domination of any external authority.

The Protestant minister belongs in the line of "prophets," but as it was with the prophets who were before him, his prophetic quality has no formal certification. Like the "prophet" of the "Teaching" he must prove the genuineness of his gift before he can expect men to accept his leadership. Ecclesiasticism allied with Establishmentism may and will do its best to harness the prophetic force with its own bit and bridle, but it is only the feeble and the timid among the prophets who will submit to this kind of schoolmastering. The true prophet will lead; he will not ask to be led by any light, however kindly, that dims the radiance of his own honest conviction.

How eager this search for spiritual leadership is in the modern world was abundantly shown a few years ago when a new prophet of quite the ancient type appeared with a ready-made revelation, an elaborate Scripture and a commercial establishment singularly suited to capture the imagination of a business world. A few commonplaces as to conduct, a philosophy of life absurdly distorted by a cheap travesty of science, and a working organization happily freed from the accumulated rubbish of clericalism swept thousands of plain, well-meaning people into a delusive ecstasy of deliverance from all the weaknesses of their human experience. How the balance of good and evil in this singular phenomenon is to be adjusted is not yet perceived. It serves us here only to show how ready men of good will are to grasp at shadows when the substance is no longer brought home to them with convincing force.

If the modern minister is to do his part in holding men true to the best traditions of the religion he professes to serve he must prepare himself by all the training he can command to meet the complex requirements of his unique position. A prophet in the sense of an individual with a message, he is to be, but he cannot afford to forget that for this kind of prophecy there is a technique that must be learned. Sometimes it seems as if men thought the training of the minister could be all technique. "Why," said the head of a certain theological school, speaking of the class about to graduate, "they don't even know how to say 'Here endeth the First Lesson.'" No doubt there is a right way and a wrong way to do everything, but that seemed rather a false emphasis. On the other hand there is likely to be a feeling, especially among "liberally" inclined students that every technical requirement is some kind of encroachment upon that freedom of the spirit which they claim as their special right. I have known theological students who refused to write sermons as a part of their school training on the ground that this was a fictitious and necessarily insincere performance. Others have refused to take part in public prayer, because they felt it to be, as it were, a kind of dress rehearsal and therefore irreverent and unbecoming. Such objections, flippant as they seem, were based upon a truly honorable conception of the sacredness of the preacher's office. They deserved respectful consideration, but it ought not to be difficult to convince an intelligent student that unless he is willing to submit himself to systematic training he will surely become his own worst hindrance in the work he wants to do.

The minister, we have said, is not called upon to be a specialist in any branch of science, and yet, if he is to succeed in his purpose he must so far meet the temper of the modern world as to specialize in something, and at the risk of seeming vague or unpractical we have to describe his field of specialization as the kingdom of the spirit. It is a vague word, but only in the sense in which the highest things always elude precise definition. When we are told that the letter killeth, but the spirit maketh alive, we know what is meant. The Christian doctrine of a Holy Spirit, the least definable of all doctrines, is also the most easily understood. So that when we say that the minister has to prepare himself to be a leader in the things of the spirit we have, after all, set before him a fairly definite field of effort. It is true that if the young man should come to his teachers and say: " Go to, now; tell me all about the life of the spirit and how I shall make it clear to other people," he would meet and he would deserve to meet with a smiling refusal. The wise teacher would remind

him that the kingdom of God cometh not with observation. " Direct action," the favorite weapon of social
reform in our day, will not work here. The spirit cannot be isolated and experimented with like a chemical
element or the bacillus of some special disease. It can
be known only as it expresses itself through human
action and human thought. The whole activity of a
man or a society must be permeated with a spiritual
content if he or it is to take a share in bringing about
the supreme consummation of a world set free from
servitude to material things.

While, therefore, it would seem folly to suggest a
department of spiritual leadership in the curriculum of
a theological school, it cannot be too strongly emphasized that all departments should be penetrated by
this one ultimate purpose. Scholarship, eloquence,
humanitarianism, administrative skill — all these must
somehow be conceived as vehicles through which to
convey the one animating and consecrating spirit.
There can be no separation between positive acquirement and that steady refining and clarifying of the
mind which is the mark of the truly educated man.
That this refining process goes on unconsciously does
not lessen its reality. It may be only at critical moments that it becomes perceptible to the pupil or to his
teachers, but these are precisely the test moments that
prove the reality of its progress. The education of the
modern minister, just as truly as that of the ancient
one, must begin, continue and — I was about to say,
end, but caught myself in time and will say, go on as
long as he lives preserving this constant balance be-

tween the things that can be learned outright and the
things that can only be felt as the inspiration and
justification of all the rest.

We come to the more concrete part of our subject,
the definite preparation of the Protestant minister.
And here, to begin somewhat before the beginning, and
at the risk of bringing down upon myself the reproach
of undemocracy, the most damning rebuke of the
hour, I venture to express at least the wish that the
minister's education might begin a few generations
before he is born. In other, but perhaps not less blame-
worthy language, it is a pity that our " best families,"
define that as one may, should not contribute at least
their share of candidates for this profession. In saying
this I am not subscribing to the rather fatuous defense
of the English clerical system, that " it is a good thing
to have a gentleman in every parish," but I will go so
far as to say that gentle birth, in the best meaning of
that almost forgotten word, gives to a man a kind
of start in life that nothing else can supply. The
defiant democracy which begins with the assumption
that one man is as good as another, if not better, is
a poor foundation for effective leadership in the highest things. The word " background" has been played
with a good deal of late, but it serves a purpose. As
we at the university watch the constant stream of
young life flowing into the current of our academic
activities, we see now and then a youth, clean, intelligent, modest, self-contained, efficient, on whom our
first comment is: " That boy has background." We
know nothing of his antecedents, but we feel instinc-

tively a kind of quality that, bred in the bone, will come out in the flesh, and we count upon him to fulfil this promise of his birth.

Of such a youth we say: "Here is good stuff to work upon. He can give and take. If we hit him there is a good sound ring to him. Cut him and he bleeds." You cannot polish punk; even the varnish with which you try to coat it with a fictitious brilliance will not stand the wear. The Christian ministry needs men of that finer type whether they come out of palaces or tenements, from the city or the prairie. Then, upon such a foundation of quality there should be built up a structure of sound elementary training, as free as possible from the quackeries of modern educational theorists. Nothing that can be done later can ever quite make up for the lack of such an early training. To it the man owes the best he ever gets of those instinctive mental habits that are the basis of success: quick perception, ready appropriation, prompt turning from one mental occupation to another, especially the all-important capacity for voluntary concentration. These habits, the most valuable part of all education, go back to persistent practice in earliest youth.

Then, secondly, before the professional study, should come a thorough course in the liberal arts. Perhaps this may seem a quite superfluous remark, but probably few are aware how often in the recent past this seemingly natural order of progression has been reversed. Theological seminaries have opened their doors to youths of slender means more or less seriously inclined to the ministry and finding there a kind of substitute for the education they could not otherwise obtain. Afterward, if they persisted in their expressed intention and could afford the time they would go to a college and try to make up for the lack of previous liberal training. In one of the New England states there was and for aught I know there still is, an arrangement between a college of good standing and a theological school by which the college undertook to receive such half prepared candidates and do what it could for them. Out of so curiously inverted, not to say perverted, an educational scheme exceptionally gifted youths prevented by some untoward circumstance from following the natural order, may well have drawn the essentials of a preparation for effective service in the ministry, but certainly they would be the last persons to counsel it as a normal method.

Within a comparatively recent time the requirement of an academic degree as a condition of entrance into the better theological schools has set a standard to which the country as a whole is more or less reluctantly assenting. In interpreting this standard, however, there is still the widest opportunity for evasion. What kind of a degree, from what kind of a college, acquired by what kind of a course of study? — these are all questions answered very differently by institutions nominally standing on the same level. And under the specious heading of "special students" the temptation to whip the devil around this particular stump has often proved irresistible. I recall a case of a graduate of a theological school, himself a scholar of extraordinary ability, recommending to his *alma mater* a raw youth with no qualifications except a wild desire to reform everything, and never forgiving her the offense of refusing to suspend all rules and admit him to her membership. Perhaps the refusal was stimulated by the recollection that that same school had been nearly wrecked a generation earlier by listening to similar appeals and receiving into its fellowship a swarm of candidates from a bankrupt institution whose only requirement for admission had been expressed good intentions and apparently good character.

This requirement of a previous liberal education ought to be made absolute and be strictly interpreted. The loss to the profession that may come from the rejection of an occasional exceptional candidate will be more than made up by the general toning up of the whole professional standard. I am using the word "liberal" here in its proper sense of non-professional, or to adopt the somewhat extravagant language of its defenders, of "anything that is not useful." A liberal education ought to prepare for everything as truly as it seems to prepare for nothing in particular. It ought to provide a basis for further study in any direction or for what we are always speaking of as the opposite of all further study, for "life." On the solid foundations of a firm elementary training it ought to start the young man on the beginnings of many subjects and carry him pretty far along in a few. The problem for every expectant professional student is to decide what subjects will best advance his later professional purpose. I have tried elsewhere [1] to suggest certain prin-

---

[1] Pages 145 *sqq.*

ciples by which the choice of subjects in college may
be determined and have expressed my opinion that in
general these subjects should not be too closely related to the future profession.

That principle, which I should be inclined to interpret rather strictly for the lawyer, the physician or the
engineer, may be much more liberally construed for
the theologian. His professional studies will be so far
from strictly technical, that they may much more
wisely be commenced in the preparatory stage. Indeed the most truly liberalizing studies are precisely
those which the theological candidate may most profitably pursue in the years just before he enters upon
his professional work. It would be a fortunate circumstance if the youth entering college could be quite
assured of his purpose to enter the ministry of religion. It would give definiteness to his choice of
studies, and even if he should afterward change his
intention, the choice thus made would be as likely to
prove satisfactory as any other.

In what now should such a choice of college studies
for the future minister consist? I can answer this question only for myself, realizing fully that it will be very
differently answered by others equally competent.
First of all I should lay weight upon the languages,
with especial reference to facility in reading them, with
careful attention to the essentials of grammar, but not
worrying oneself too much about refinements and exceptions. Latin, with its fatally unfamiliar idiom,
ought to be conquered to the point of easy reading.
Nothing can compare with such facility for value in

every kind of study which the minister will be called upon to make. Greek, infinitely more interesting and not essentially more difficult as a language, is going to have a more immediate value in first-hand study of Scripture, but is far less important in all other respects. If one could study only one of these two languages I should say, for linguistic training, for supreme literary enjoyment, for illumination as to possibilities of expression in words, choose Greek. But for practical use as an instrument of further study in almost every subject, Latin is to be advised. Fortunately the student is not reduced to this alternative. There is time enough in the eight years of his liberal preparation for a good start in both, and further progress can easily be assured by a very slight amount of regular practice in reading matter bearing directly upon his professional interest.

As to modern languages, they ought to be learned, so to speak, "in his stride." It is idle to waste much time on them in college, where the method of instruction is necessarily of a kind least adapted to success. They must be acquired if the student is not to be crippled throughout his active life, but when once the linguistic sense has been quickened by study of the classic models, the modern idiom and the modern vocabulary seem by comparison almost absurdly easy.

As to mathematics and the physical sciences: it would be rather a pity if the future clergyman should not add something in college to the beginnings already made in the secondary school, but the proportion of these studies must necessarily be small. The weight of his attention must be placed upon those subjects which I venture to call, "without prejudice," the humane disciplines. By this we mean those studies which deal primarily with man and his works. History in all its aspects will give to the theological candidate the background for his study of the Church without which it must always lack its most essential support. Economics, theoretical and practical, will introduce him to the principles of production and exchange which underlie all social problems. Philosophy on its historical and its speculative sides will furnish his mind with the training in pure reasoning which he will sorely need when he comes to the problems of theological discussion.

Then, first, last, and always there must run through all other disciplines, the study which a great educational authority has declared to be the only one to be required of every student, the English language. I mean by this, not the "taking of courses" in literature or, beyond a rather slight minimum, in composition. I mean the constant watchfulness over the application of the few formal rules of composition in one's own speech and writing and in those of others. Especially I would emphasize the importance for the theological candidate of cultivating a civilized method of speaking, equally removed from pedantry on the one hand and from slouchiness on the other. Bearing in mind the absence of any one precise standard of English speech, it will be well worth his while to try to free his own tongue from dialectic peculiarities and to purify his vocabulary from such divagations from good usage as

tend to obscure his thought or to weaken his power of
expression. Slang, delightful as it is in its aptness to
express an idea familiar to the moment, is sure to dull
the sense of values, that finer shading of meanings
which gives at once variety and definiteness to English
style. Dialects, it is true, are the life of language, and
it would be the height of stupidity to try to check their
resistless flow, but the educated man belongs to a cos-
mopolitan fraternity, whose password is a speech free
from marked provincialisms. The cultivated man in
Germany steers carefully between his datives and ac-
cusatives; in England he watches the placing of his
aspirates; in New England he ought not to need an "r"
between a final and an initial vowel and in the South
he ought to have overcome an over-fondness for
diphthongs.

The time to give attention to these apparently trifling matters is during the years of preparation. It is
then that the subtle influences which have formed the
habits of expression can be counteracted by conscious
effort. And what is true here of speech is equally true
of writing. The first simple principles of English prose
writing can be and should be fixed in the course of a
sound elementary education. Practice in carrying out
these principles should be continuous throughout one's
whole period of study. I am not recommending the
taking of courses in composition except as they offer
opportunities for sympathetic and searching criticism.
The value of such criticism is almost entirely a matter
of personality, and it is rarely that the college instructor can rise very much above the level of rules of

thumb or some pet formulas aiming at literary "correctness." The most insidious snare of the ministerial candidate is literariness in any of its alluring forms. The moment he finds himself achieving "fine writing" is the moment for calling a halt and toning himself down to the plain standards of clearness and accuracy. It will be time enough to indulge in eloquence when the passion of his apostleship really grips him, and then there will be no question of literary workmanship. The training he has all along been acquiring will then come to his help, saving him from extravagance and showing him instinctively how to drive his message home. The weightiness of the message will be the sufficient ballast against exuberance or affectation.

I would not disparage too greatly direct academic instruction in these matters of expression, but I am convinced that its influence is feeble in comparison with that which may come from the persistent reading of the best models. It may sound superfluous to urge upon young men bound for this or any other literary profession to cultivate during their academic years the habit of reading. Two generations ago this caution would have been less needed. At that time the requirements of college were deliberately set so that abundant leisure might be left for that kind of reading which was then thought of as something lying rather beyond the scope of academic work. Meanwhile the programs of college instruction have been expanded to include every conceivable variety of intellectual occupation. Every corner of every known subject has been made the subject of special instruction. Leisure, that delightful *otium* which is neither idleness nor "grind," has pretty much disappeared from the horizon of the serious student, so that now attempts are being made to reintroduce it as a part of his regular discipline. The latest addition to the resources of a great university library is a room, luxuriously furnished and equipped with a noble selection of the best literature open freely to the use of all students. The attendant informs me that one of her chief duties is to prevent the abuse of this room for purposes of systematic study.

The effect of reading n determining one's own forms of expression must depend largely upon temperament. A reader who, so to speak, reads aloud to himself, catching the rhythm of the writer, might well find himself so absorbed by the subtlety of the style that his own writing would be a mere imitation of a model. Another, reading without ever forming to himself the writer's sentences, but catching the meaning by a kind of intuition, would receive no impression whatever from the style. Such a reader would probably do well to subject himself to instruction, hoping to acquire something of that sensitiveness to form which will help him to analyze his own efforts and gradually to improve in effectiveness. An ancient friend of mine, a man of taste, singularly detached from all human obligations, used to say that of all men he preferred the society of Unitarian clergymen, because they were the only people left who read books. Other clergymen read only what they needed for their doctrinal purposes, and the rest of the world did not read at all. It was a judgment about as true as epigrammatic judgments are likely to be, but the fragment of truth it contained is worth remarking. It was passed a generation ago, and we may well ask ourselves whether the rush of human life in the interval is likely to have made a change for the better. Certainly the clergyman can form no more valuable habit in his habit-forming years than this of serious and continuous reading.

If we have been right in assuming that the modern minister is above all else a man among men, claiming no superiority but that which comes from training and personality, it follows that beginning with his academic years, he ought to cultivate every opportunity of gaining that knowledge of other men which is the secret of social influence. He should combat with especial determination every tendency to aloofness from the interests of his mates. If these seem trifling or aimless to him, he may be sure that it is not wholly because they are really so, but partly at least because of some deficiency in himself which will work against his largest usefulness. He ought to try to identify himself with their sports, their social organizations, their petty politics, using his clearer vision, if he has it, to guide them into better and wiser ways. In such effort he will find guidance for himself and may be laying the foundations for those qualities of leadership on which his future success is to depend. Here in the little world of the college he can learn something of the great lesson of keeping oneself in the world, but always just enough above it to lift it up a little to higher levels of thought and action.

So we come to the question which is our main topic,

the strictly professional training of the modern minister. Supposing our preliminary demands to have
been met, what more is there to be required? Some
great authorities would reply: nothing more than a
continuation for as long as seems practicable of the
same kind of training in much the same subjects as
those already pursued. Such counsellors would, in
other words, be inclined to doubt the usefulness of all
schools of theology, strictly so-called. They might
favor the establishment in our universities of chairs of
dogmatic exposition, to be as free as possible from
sectarian control, but otherwise they would be contented to let the candidate for the ministry acquire his
knowledge of languages, of Church History, and of social obligations from teachers provided in the several
academic departments most closely related to his
future profession. Of course, as enlightened men of
their time, they would urge that in the appointment of
university professors, the needs of expectant clergymen should be consulted as well as those of other professional candidates. It is now about one generation
since a plan of this sort was laid before the Faculty of
Theology of an important university by a president to
whom the interests of theological study were a matter
of very deep concern. He believed that those interests
would be better served by abandoning frankly all attempts at framing a theological curriculum and turning the candidate loose in the alluring fields of history,
economics, languages, social science and what not,
requiring only that his studies should be pursued
seriously and with "high credit." It was very instruc-

tive to note the unanimity with which the Faculty, irrespective of departments, of age and of previous training, rejected the proposition.

That Faculty believed that back of all proficiency in his several studies there must be for the successful minister a professional character, and that this character could best be acquired by the pursuit of a certain group of studies under the guidance of a group of men professionally interested in their task. Within this limitation they were willing to allow the largest liberty of choice and to recognize, subject to their approval, the instruction of men not members of their group as equally entitled to credit for the theological degree. It is with this group of subjects that we are here specially concerned. It should be noted that almost all of them are in varying degrees continuing studies, begun at one or another stage of the preliminary training. The new thing about them all is their relation to the professional purpose.

First of all is the study of the Bible. No sophistry of a too ready liberalism can obscure the fact that Christianity, however we may define it, rests upon a body of written material, and it would seem to follow, beyond all cavil, that the minister of Christianity ought to be fortified, above all else, with a commanding knowledge of this literature. It ought to be fair to assume that he brings with him to his professional school a familiarity with the English version of both the ancient and the newer Scriptures, but even this is to-day a rather bold assumption. Anyone who has tested the knowledge of the Bible possessed by the Senior class in a respectable college will need no further evidence of the neglect into which the foundation documents of the religion all these youths profess have fallen. Even granting that the theological candidate will probably be rather better off in this respect, it remains true that he will need a great deal of practice before he can be sure of the kind of familiarity with the English versions that will stand by him in the emergencies of his profession. But this familiarity is far from sufficient for his best success.

In opening up again the much discussed question of study in the original languages of the Scriptures, I am aware that there is not much left to be said on either side of the argument. Against the requirement of a study of Hebrew and Greek it is alleged, with much show of reason, that the individual clergyman is not likely to reach such proficiency as will entitle his opinion to have any weight whatever in comparison with the matured judgment of the scholars who have given their best powers to provide the English versions. For all practical purposes, it is said, these versions supply him with all the knowledge of Scripture he will ever need. Why then spend the precious time of his all too short preparation in painfully acquiring the rudiments of this unnecessary learning? The argument is as specious as the dictum of the sage—let us call him Emerson — that he would never read an original if he could get a good translation. Our English versions, noble and beautiful as they are, faithful in the main to the general import of the texts, are burdened with archaisms, are influenced by the theological assumptions of the trans-

lators, and are often obscure in their manifold impli-
cations. Phrases hallowed by usage in ways never
dreamed of by their writers, demand continued interpretation by every possible scholarly aid. To give such
interpretation is the business of teachers; but even to
understand it is impossible without some fairly adequate knowledge of the original languages.

Martin Luther was right when he said:

This we cannot deny, that, although the Gospel came
and daily comes through the Holy Spirit alone, still it came
through the medium of the languages, has grown by them
and must be preserved by them. According as we love the
Gospel, let us eagerly study the languages, and let us not
forget that we cannot well hold the Gospel firm without
them. The languages are the sheath in which the dagger of
the Spirit rests; they are the casket wherein this jewel is
enshrined; the chalice wherein this drink is borne. Because
the languages have now come to the fore they are bringing
such a light and doing such mighty things that all the
world marvels. Therefore, although the Doctrine and the
Gospel may be preached by simple preachers without the
languages, yet this is a dull and weak affair and men at last
tire of it and after all fall to the ground. But where the
languages are, there all is fresh and vigorous, the text is
made clear, and Faith is ever renewed through new and
ever new words and works.[1]

I am not advocating an absolute requirement of
either Greek or Hebrew for the first degree in Theology,
but I do think it a pity that any really serious student

[1] M. Luther, *An die Ratherren aller Staedte deutsches Lands, dass sie
christliche Schulen aufrichten und halten sollen.* 1524. Weimar ed. XV,
37-42.

who desires to be something more than a "simple preacher" should neglect the opportunity of help offered by his teachers to acquire a working command of both. For a higher theological degree I would make them an ordinary requirement. I urge this careful study of the original documents fully appreciating the mass of material that has accumulated upon them to such a depth that they are almost buried out of sight, but realizing also, perhaps a little better than the enthusiastic youth, how in every time of crisis men are ready to throw off this whole superincumbent mass and go back to the first simple problem of the meaning of the Christian message. It is for such critical moments that the student should consciously prepare himself. If he is to lead then, he must get ready now.

Next to biblical studies we may fairly place that group for which there is no better name than "historical." Christianity is an historical phenomenon, originating in a profoundly interesting human situation, developed through progressive human activities, of which the making of a literature is one, and embodied in institutions that have played their often decisive part in the larger movements of humanity. It would seem, therefore, to need no argument to prove that historical studies are of the greatest importance for the student of Christianity. In fact the historical point of view as contrasted with the supernatural or inspirational theory of Christian origins and developments is a thing of quite recent times. It is rejected by vast sections of the Christian world as destructive of all those traditions they hold most precious. If the

Protestant ministry is to defend itself against such assumptions, it must be rooted and grounded in wide and, in the best sense, scientific study of the Christian past. Only by this study can it prepare itself for the insidious attacks of an agressive institutionalism on the one hand and a self-sufficient individualism on the other.

There are three branches of historical study especially important for the minister. The first is that of institutions, the events by which they have been determined, and their manifold interrelations with the parallel movement of society as a whole. A good deal of this kind of Church History can profitably be studied in college, the more the better, since it furnishes a very good thread on which to hang the study of "secular" history. It would be an excellent thing if the professional school could afford to assume such historical knowledge and go on from it to the other two branches of more purely technical inquiry. The first of these two is the history of doctrines, or, to give it a more intelligent name, the history of Christian Thought. That name is better because it expresses a more comprehensive idea of Christian progress on its intellectual side. It opens the way for an equal emphasis upon those movements of thought dignified by the reproach of "heresy" and by that very fact commends itself to those who would be repelled by any suggestion of dogmatism. I venture to refer to my own experience as witness to the illuminating effect of bringing this truly historical way of looking at the thought of Christian teachers to the attention of young minds hitherto accustomed only to the way of dogmatic teaching and docile acceptance. Instead of a series of formal creeds, elaborated by human ingenuity at critical epochs, the doctrine of Christianity, studied in this way, becomes a record of continuous honest attempts to understand and to express the ideas it had to contribute to the world's religious thought.

Stimulating to the historical sense as such study of purely Christian thought must be, the third topic under this heading will be even more so. Still more recent in time, the subject of the History of Religion has taken its place in the academic world with astonishing rapidity and gratifying success. Its mission has been to show Christianity as one among the great religions of the world, not the earliest nor the latest, not even in any abstract sense the best or the worst, certainly not the last form under which the religious instinct of mankind is to express itself. It has helped to abolish forever that hopeless distinction between "natural" and "revealed" religion, as if the ways of God to man were different at different times. It has demonstrated, as nothing else has done or could do, the essential unity of the religious principle and therefore the essential dignity of every attempt to give to this principle a form suited to the needs of a given time. The preacher of Christianity ought to find his apostleship not weakened by familiarity with other types of faith, but clarified and strengthened. On the practical side, he cannot afford to forget that the rivalry of religions is as active to-day as it ever was, and that at any moment it may flame out into a conflict beside which the clash of political structures would be the sport of children.

We come thus to the study which forms the central point of the minister's preparation, the study of what, in spite of much opposition, still figures on the programs as Systematic Theology. If the first qualification of the historian is freedom from all personal and partisan bias, no such demand can be made upon the theologian when he leaves the field of historical inquiry and passes over into that of speculative thought. If we say that the historian must be "objective," as free as possible from "subjectivity," we have to admit that the theologian must be permitted just the opposite standard. If his conclusions are to have any value whatever, they must be *his* conclusions, and not those of any one else. His foundations may be drawn from every possible source, but the structure of faith he builds upon them is his own if it is anything. The problem of the theological teacher is, therefore, a peculiarly delicate one. He cannot make his instruction impersonal, unless he is willing to look upon himself as merely the mouthpiece of an authority which has dictated to him what he may or must think, a vehicle by which the material thus received is to be handed on undiminished and uncorrupted to his hearers. That was the ancient conception of the teacher of systematic theology, the retailer of a system so complete and so well authenticated that it could be handed on from generation to generation with a minimum of intellectual effort.

The modern clergyman cannot be content with that kind of formalism. He demands an appeal to his own powers of reflection and his own sense of religious

truth. He asks of his instructors, not the formal statement of the confession with which he is to be connected
in his ministerial work, but some principle of thought
by which he can interpret for himself the content of
what is presented to him as Christian truth. It was
very instructive to observe that at a summer school of
theology held by a "liberal" faculty of theology, the
largest attendance through a series of years came from
a denomination which above all others claims for itself
a special authority in matters of faith. It would be
well for the theological candidate if he could bring
himself to regard all his other work, languages, history,
philosophy as so many contributions to this one central
object of his preparation for life. If as the result he
finds his inherited beliefs strengthened and illuminated
it will be well with him. If he finds them weakened or
even destroyed, that will be only the proof that he is on
the way to a clearer and more satisfying view. The
prevailing contempt for theological study is chiefly
owing to the dead-and-alive method with which it was
formerly conducted. Rightly interpreted it will reassert its claim to be in the true sense a "science," perhaps even in due time to take its place as the "*regina
scientiarum*" of the Erasmian age.

Whether there is as yet such a thing as a science of
Sociology is an open question into which we do not
need to enter. It is not very difficult to show that
Sociology can be understood to embrace all sciences
that have to do with human life, in other words to include the whole volume of the knowable; but that is
only a pretty game that can be played with almost any

branch of human knowledge. What concerns the theological candidate is that there is certainly a group of subjects about which much practical knowledge is attainable and which, in their application to human living, touch very nearly the daily work of the Christian minister. So insistent indeed have the claims of these subjects become in recent years, that they have seemed dangerously near to crowding out all the other branches of ministerial education. They have been an accompaniment, perhaps also a result of the rapid spread of social ideas that have seemed to place the body, its safety, its comfort, its convenience, its preservation in the forefront of our interests. From "drainage to divorce," we have had to run the gamut of social unrest and social reform. It has been a splendid display of energy, and its work seems only begun.

The question for the theological student is, how far it is worth his while to go in these apparently necessary and certainly very attractive subjects. In answering this question he ought, I think, to put away from him all thought of expertness. If he once allows that standard to rise before him, he is sure to be undone. Others will certainly get ahead of him, and his time and attention, withdrawn from other things, will be wasted. The best he can do is to inform himself as to the nature of the social problems suggested by the several topics of inquiry, make some acquaintance with their literature and with the agencies at work in the various fields, and then try to see if he can how they are all bound together by some common principle of religious obligation. If he cannot or will not do this, he had better quit the profession of the ministry altogether before it is too late and join the procession of the disillusioned who have turned to the many forms of "social service" and found there the kind of usefulness they would never have attained as messengers of a religious gospel. But, it will be asked, can this kind of spiritual interpretation of the social call be set forth in any formal instruction? Is not that something that each man must work out for himself in the long travail of his parish experience? Well, that depends almost entirely on the quality of the teacher. It is a rare man who can so lift both himself and his pupils above the raw details of the social struggle as to clear them from their manifold perplexities and show them in the perspective of their simple relation to the ministry of Christian hope. If the pupil is fortunate enough to come within the influence of such a teacher, he is not likely to go far wrong in yielding to its persuasions. If not, he will do well to keep pretty safely within the limits of the detail I have suggested and try to work out for himself the needful applications to his professional work.

We come finally to that group of studies which have to do with the outward expression of whatever the student may gain from all his other occupations. Much that might be said here has been anticipated in our references to preliminary training. The work in English writing, begun in the elementary school, continued and amplified in the high school and in college, must be carried forward with especial application to the minister's needs. If it is true that the central interest of the Protestant minister is in the moral and religious appeal to the individual, it would seem to follow without question that the center of the student's interest, so far as this matter of expression is concerned should be the preparation of the sermon. And yet I venture to think that there is no department of theological education that is likely to receive a more stepmotherly treatment than this. With the increasing emphasis upon "scholarship" that has marked the great advance in equipment in all other fields, the arts of expression have been crowded into corners. They have been degraded by association with "elocutionary" performance and, in so far as they have yielded to these depressing influences they have earned a well-merited contempt. The fact remains, however, that the minister as well as the actor must "get it across," not indeed by the same methods — God forbid! — but with equal attention to the process. "Do you think it is possible," asked the committee of a metropolitan church in the midst of a business district, "to hold a congregation any longer in this place?" "Certainly," replied the pastor who favored a removal "I could pack this church every Sunday if I would stand on my head in the pulpit." It is not the arts of the mountebank that we have to consider, but on the other hand it is idle to forget that speaking and writing are arts that can be taught and must be learned if the highest efficiency is to be attained. The clergyman who mounts his pulpit with a hang-dog expression, who never looks his congregation in the face, who mumbles his words, who misplaces his emphasis, who stumbles over his reading, who bellows about nothing and whispers the essential point, may be filled with the breath of the Holy Spirit, but what use is it if he cannot get it out?

Much hearing of sermons by many preachers should convince any one that the drift in recent years toward what is called *ex tempore* preaching needs careful watching. The argument for it is very specious. It is said that the free speaker comes more closely into touch with the listener, that there is a spontaneity about his utterance that holds the attention and wins the sympathy of an audience. That is, of course, precisely what the young preacher wants to do, and he is easily led to believe that the way to do it is to begin with free speaking. The matter of what he has to say is a secondary consideration; even the form of his speech may be overlooked. The main thing is to speak "without notes," not to hesitate, to keep going, to look the people in the face, not "to let a manuscript stand between himself and them." All that has a very seductive sound, but many a useful preacher has been wrecked upon this shoal. The analogy between the *ex tempore* speaker and the writer of "free verse" is instructive. One cannot help suspecting that the free-versifier is that because he lacks the power and the discipline to express himself in more canonical form, and the same suspicion rests upon the too ready preacher. He too may well be trying to "get by" without the effort of shaping his thought in more logical and therefore more convincing form. The whole question was never put more acutely than by the late

Phillips Brooks in an answer I once heard him make to an inquiring student who had asked him whether he thought the *ex tempore* sermon was preferable to the written one. "I don't think it makes any difference" said the great preacher "provided only that the sermon was once *ex tempore*." That touched the very root of the matter. The freely spoken sermon may lack every trace of the *ex tempore* quality, and the written sermon may glow with all the fervor of inspired utterance. It all depends upon whether at the moment of its production, in the study or in the pulpit, the preacher's own soul was on fire with the message he had to give.

I have stood for hours in the midst of standing throngs crowding the nave of a great cathedral and listening to preachers trained with all the art of a noble tradition driving home to the deepest consciousness of their hearers what they believed to be the essential truths of Christianity. Every word and sentence of those sermons was placed in accordance with prescribed rules, but they came forth in torrential floods, as if they had but that moment taken shape in the speaker's mind. Awe-stricken faces, many with streaming tears, were the witness to the convincing force of this well prepared, but seemingly spontaneous eloquence. There is no doubt that skill in *ex tempore* discourse can be cultivated and that it is worth cultivating. I am only cautioning the beginner against a false order of proceeding. Let him be sure that his gun is well loaded before he tries to fire it.

One more subject in this group of the expressive arts

remains to be considered. Under the heading of "pastoral care" or "the minister's office" or by whatever other phrase it may be described, the personal relation of the pastor to his people is the most delicate and the most elusive of all his responsibilities. What the sermon is to the congregation as a whole that is the pastoral visit or the passing word or the friendly message to the individual parishioner. One is tempted to dismiss this function of the minister without further comment as too intimate for any effective academic treatment. One fears that any formal instruction given classwise would degenerate into laying down certain "tricks of the trade" by which the novice might simulate the feeling he cannot really have and tide himself over the first and worst emotional strain of professional sympathy. It is even a debatable question whether this side of the minister's traditional activities may not well be eliminated altogether or deputed to assistants specially gifted. One cannot be everything, it is said, and the community may think itself fortunate if it secures from its clergyman one or two kinds of service, without reproaching him for failure in the rest.

The answer to these doubts and objections is this: that it is precisely in this personal contact with the pressing realities in the daily life of the men and women about him, that the minister finds the unfailing source of inspiration for all his other activities. In the experiences of his people he sees reflected the interests that are engaging the masses of society as a whole. From them he learns what subjects of study may best reward the time he has for study. In the joys and sorrows of their lives he touches the springs of motive that give the clue for the moral appeal of his sermon. From them he may draw lessons of hope and courage that will help to sustain him in the perplexities of his own exacting duties. Undoubtedly it is more true here than elsewhere that the real preparation for the work must come in the doing of it; but here too there is abundant opportunity for anticipation. There are teachers who, out of their own experience, can point out the snares that beset the path of the untried youth venturing for the first time into the intimacies of parish duty. There are cautions to be given and positive suggestions to be made on many points that would otherwise escape the novice. Better still there are encouragements and compensations to be pointed out that may remove many honest scruples and unnecessary anxieties.

And this leads me to revert for a moment to a suggestion made in passing, that the education of the minister may profitably be extended beyond the close of his academic years by something like an apprenticeship in the workshop of a senior craftsman. An apology for such a system exists indeed in the doubtful, if not wholly pernicious practice of permitting students of theology to undertake regular or substitute duties during their academic residence. Much observation leads me to think that this practice is as unwise as it would be to permit students in law or medicine to practice their professions. The time of preparation is too precious to be invaded by the all too engrossing demands of practice. Such objection does not in the least apply to the apprenticeship plan. There, working under the supervision of an experienced guide, the young man is given his opportunity to try his strength in ways suited to his stage of development. Above all he may be steered among the rocks and shoals of pastoral duty until the rudder is safe in his hands. There ought to be between every school of theology and some group of parishes a standing agreement for this prolongation of the minister's education. It would strengthen the school and it would be a guarantee to the parishes of a continuous supply of useful assistance.

These are the four groups of studies, no one of which the candidate for the modern ministry can afford to neglect. In the linguistic he prepares his foundations. In the historical he makes his background. In the social he finds the program for his systematic activities, and in the expressive he sharpens the tools he has to work with. The proportion in which each group shall enter into his preparation is a problem for every individual. The best that experience can do is to point out the values and leave the decision where finally it must always rest, in the hopeful enthusiasm of those whose experience is yet to come.

THE PLACE OF HISTORY IN
THEOLOGICAL STUDY

AN ADDRESS TO THEOLOGICAL STUDENTS

A T a recent conference of teachers and students of
History I was engaged in conversation by a person whom I judged to belong to the race of so-called
"Educators," and who proceeded to enlighten me with
his views about History. "The trouble with our History nowadays," he declared, "is that it is too retrospective," and during the rather bad quarter of an hour
which he gave me this phrase kept recurring like a
refrain in his discourse: "Our History nowadays is
too retrospective!" Precisely what he meant I did not
discover. Whether he had some vague idea that History ought to concern itself more with the present or
with the future was not clear, nor did it, in his case,
make any very great difference. He had got his phrase,
and that, for an Educator, is the main thing.

More important, however, was the remark which
I once heard made by one of my colleagues in this
Faculty that he sometimes feared that our teaching of
Theology — he was using the word in its larger meaning — was too historical. That remark I thought I
understood, and it was and is worthy of consideration.
It meant, I suppose, that we were inclined, in planning
our courses of study, to give especial weight to those
dealing with the historical aspects of our general subject, and our colleague thought that we ought to en-

large the scope of our program, so as to change the
balance of interest rather to the side of what were
coming to be called the more practical aspects of the
profession for which we were supposed to be preparing
young men.

The suggestion was a certain challenge to those who
were more specially concerned with the obviously historical side of our common work, to examine anew the
nature of their contribution to the total result and to
ask themselves whether they were in fact asking too
large a share of the attention of men who were, after
all, mainly concerned with preparing themselves to
help along in the struggle of the present and were naturally looking forward to an uncertain but infinitely
appealing future. As soon as this examination began it
became evident that the term "historical" could not
be confined to those subjects which were offered as
parts of a course in what used to be called "Historical
Theology," in other words, to the department of
Church History. If we use the word historical as im-
plying simply a relation with the past it is clear that it
applies equally well to the study of the languages in
which the fundamental documents of Christianity are
written. The mind of the student of Hebrew or Greek
is turned toward the past even though he restrict himself for the moment to the most purely linguistic aspects of his study. The dullest pupil of the dullest
teacher cannot fail to have some intuition that these
grammatical puzzles were once the living forms of expression of human beings who had something to say
and who said it so well that their words have never

been allowed to fade out of the consciousness of the generations who have followed them. No matter how blind the professional linguist may have become to the humane aspects of his study — and Heaven knows he has been blind enough — he has never been able quite to ignore them and in spite of him they have reasserted themselves whenever humanely minded persons have called attention to them. In other words the historical nature of linguistic study becomes evident the moment one gets away from the mere words to the living personality that lies behind them. The study of language, if it is a live study, is a study of history. If it is not a study of history it is a dead study.

A similar line of reflection is forced upon us when we consider the more distinctively speculative side of theological study or, if you please, theology proper. Here, obviously, is a field in which the purely subjective element of personal opinion and personal judgment plays a predominant part. There can be no such thing as a theology which is not *somebody's* theology. If it be the theology of a certain teacher, it must have its sources somewhere outside of his own mind. These sources cannot be wholly in the influences of the present, however powerful these may be. They must, therefore, be drawn from the past, and thus here again we find ourselves in the region of the historical. The speculative theologian, the moment he tries to give account to himself of the faith that is in him, is inevitably drawn away from himself into the company of those who through all the ages before him have busied themselves with the same problems. In agreement

with them he finds the support of his own conclusions.
In his differences from them he is led to sharper definitions of his own faith and to higher sanctions for his
own certainties. Individualist though he may be, he
cannot escape the past. If as a teacher he tries to make
clear to others the results of his own thought, he finds
the best method to be a comparison with the thoughts
of those who have gone before him. In other words he
is almost inevitably led into a more or less formal exposition of the history of the ideas he has formulated
for himself.

In these two important divisions of the theological
program then, the linguistic and the speculative, we
find a large historical element thrusting itself insist-
ently upon the attention of any one who busies himself
in these fields. So evident has this become to the
makers of academic programs that gradually specifically historical courses have been added to the
offerings within the narrower departmental limits.
Histories of the Hebrew people, early and late; histories of the related Semites; histories of the peoples
first reached by the teaching of Jesus; histories of
Christian doctrines; histories of philosophic systems as
adjuncts to speculative theology. Indeed signs have
not been wanting that these more specifically historical
studies might in time crowd out the other more strictly
technical subjects, or at any rate crowd them into such
narrow limits that their vitality would be seriously en-
dangered. The indifference to purely linguistic studies
which has so strongly marked all academic discussion
in the last generation has been projected into the field

of theology. We have had to be satisfied with knowing something about things instead of knowing the things themselves. A similar indifference as to theological opinions has had similar results in turning men from vigorous and independent thinking to the record of what other men have thought. In both cases the historical has been asserting itself with increasing effect as against the technical.

There remains to be considered the third division of theological studies, those commonly described as the practical studies, the duties of the minister, the administration of all that activity now known as "social service," the cultivation of the more purely religious aspects of the pastoral life. Here at least, one might suppose, would be found a region into which the historical element has not penetrated. Yet, even here the attention of students has been directed to the achievements of their predecessors in the work of the ministry, the sermons, for example, of famous preachers from Chrysostom to Brooks, the history of philanthropic experiments, the great works of meditative piety that have survived from the " ages of faith." So that, whichever way we turn, we find our studies permeated throughout by this legacy of the past. It may well be that our colleague was right in raising the question whether our program were not too historical.

Certainly since that question was raised there has been a notable change of emphasis in most of the discussions upon this point. More and more we have been reminded that the practical studies must be given a larger share in our consideration. We have even been threatened that if we failed to hear this warning our students, present and prospective, would take the matter into their own hands and simply leave on one side all those studies which seemed to them too historical to be of any use. Alluring pictures have been drawn of a preparation for the ministry in which all the "dead" things should be eliminated and only those things that were alive in the living present should be retained. The ministry, it has been said, must share with all other professions the great advance in all practical ways that has marked our century. The historical must be subordinated to the actual.

All this is inspiring and in its way admirable. This new enthusiasm of humanity, with all its crudenesses and vaguenesses, cannot fail to have its splendid reactions upon the thought and the activities of the youth who are coming under its quickening influence. None the less, but rather the more is it incumbent upon those who are more directly concerned with the study of the past from time to time to justify their existence by showing, if they can, the true practicality of the disciplines they represent. We can no longer ask young men to accept an educational system merely on the strength of its antiquity. I should like, therefore, to indicate very briefly what seem to me some of the actual values of historical study to the student of Theology.

I have been using the words "history" and "the past" as if they were almost synonymous terms, but this occupation with the past is only one of the aspects under which History has to be considered. Another of its qualities is that of causal sequence. The constant lesson of historical study is the absolute certainty of cause and effect. Nothing in history happens without preparation, and nothing happens without consequences. It is the business of the historical student to trace these preparations and these consequences as far and as accurately as he can. No date and no event stands by itself. No matter how famous it may have become, so that even by itself it seems to have value; it is really without significance until it can be set in its proper relations to all that went before and all that follows it. These things are easily stated. They sound like the commonest of commonplaces; but they are as easily forgotten. Test any historical writing by this standard and you will find that unconsciously to himself the writer has often allowed himself to slip into the easy and pleasant attitude of wonderment and to forget the stern canon of accuracy. History is not, as it has often been presented, a recital of marvels; it is the unfolding of a law. I am not saying that the historian *knows* the law by which the course of human affairs is guided. If he did he would be a god, and there would be no function for him as an historian. If the law were known there would be no need of History. The important thing is to accept the fact of law and then do what we can to interpret its action.

The constant preoccupation of the historian with this idea of an unfolding record, even though the ultimate solution eludes his grasp, begets an attitude of mind which cannot fail to be of service to the student of theology. His temptation is, I conceive, to dwell upon the unusual, the startling, the "luminous surprises" which have often been presented as the most convincing proofs of a divine order. The miraculous, with its almost universal appeal to the sense of wonder, is the ever present illusion before the mind of the theologian, drawing him away from the regular, the ordinary, the common, as from something inferior or even degrading. He is in danger of thinking that it is only the uncommon that is significant. He is tempted to search for the strange and the exceptional. The world of mysteries has an especial attraction for him. The mere fact that a given phenomenon seems to have no discoverable cause commends it to him as worthy of especial attention. He is in constant danger of slipping into the definition of faith as "belief in something you know isn't true."

It is, therefore, of great importance that in the formative period of his thought he should be on his guard against these subtle and agreeable forms of temptation; and I can suggest no better defense than a continuous and thoughtful occupation with historical study. Often in the course of my teaching I have found students to whom the slow and careful methods of the historian seemed altogether unworthy of their individual genius. They were impatient with the detail and the insistence upon accuracy. Their minds were always soaring in a higher region in which the air seemed purer and their sprouting wings seemed to find a better support. Their own exuberant fancy seemed to them much more interesting than the record of the mistakes of other people in the nearer or the remoter past.

Why take precious time to learn of other men's faults or failures? It is clear that argument could be of little avail in such cases, and I for one have never tried it very thoroughly. I have only tried to persuade such a youth to keep at it even against his will, and it has been one of the best satisfactions of my teaching life to see how, gradually, the habit of patient following out of cause and effect has modified the other habit of the student's mind. It has helped him to keep his feet upon the ground and to make him see that one must, after all, have some ground to stand on. It has helped to draw him away from the vague and the nebulous in his thinking and cause him to demand for himself a clearness which he can then perhaps learn in some measure to convey to others.

Again, History is of value to the theologian because it helps him to judge of the nature and weight of evidence. In historical study everything depends upon evidence. This first canon of historical science is absolute. It has been recognized by every historian from Herodotus down. It has been put forth with varying degrees of emphasis by the numerous writers on historical method, who have done what they could to place the study and writing of History on a scientific basis. In fact it seems almost unnecessary even to state so apparently obvious a fact. Nobody, it will be said, ever imagined that history could be created out of any one's head. Of course it rests on evidence. And yet there is no canon of the historian that has been more systematically violated than this. The violation begins with Herodotus himself, and his violations are of the type which especially interests us here. The Father of History did indeed take infinite pains to inform himself about the peoples and the events he tries to describe, but though he sought diligently for evidence he had a childlike indifference to the nature of the source from which his evidence was drawn. The more marvellous the tale, the more it interested him. He would invent nothing; he would accept nothing that was not known to his informant, but he had the largest charity as to the remoter sources from which the informant might have derived his alleged knowledge. Hearsay evidence was as good as any other, provided only it came from what was reported to be a trustworthy source. And this example was followed. In the ages of easy faith, to doubt any spoken or written word was regarded as an indication of a perverse mind. "It is written" was sanction enough for any opinion. The dominance of the religious motive during a thousand years of European history helped to stamp upon the peoples from whom we derive our civilization this character of naïf acceptance of whatever seemed to bear the imprint of authority. The sceptic was next thing to a heretic. Instead of being a guide to the truth he was thought of as a perverter of the truth.

It is only within the memory of some of us that the absoluteness of the law of evidence has come to be accepted as a standard by which historians were prepared to stand or fall, and the process is still far from being completed. There still lingers in men's minds the ancient dread of free inquiry, lest by the way some precious illusions be dissipated, some useful restraints be relaxed, some hallowed traditions be dispelled. Still we find men who should be leaders in thought using their minds freely up to a certain point and there halting and hesitating for fear of offending some ancient prejudice or encouraging too much a dangerous spirit of criticism. We find scholars using their learning and their skill in finding ways of going around the simple conclusions of science and of common sense, working out a new scholasticism to take the place of the older ones they have renounced. Against this tendency there is no better corrective than the practice of weighing the kind of evidence on which all historical conclusions must, in the last resort, be based.

Historical evidence rests entirely upon human foundations. The historical student is constantly in the attitude of a judge in a court of law. No matter what the subject or the nature of the trial, the decisions of the judge depend wholly upon the testimony of human witnesses. Every document produced in the court is the work of human hands and represents human purpose. The validity of a will, for example, depends upon the genuineness of signatures, the capacity of the testator, his freedom from alien influence, his ownership of the property he wishes to dispose of, and all these things must be certified to by oral or written evidence equally human in its character. If the will comes to trial in a court all suppositions, all personal considerations are rigidly excluded; only that which is a matter of human certainty is admitted. If, as sometimes happens, a witness demands especial consideration because the truth has been revealed to him by a special divine inspiration, the court rejects his claim with a cruel indifference. It calls him down from his superior height to the common level of human experience, or throws out his testimony as irrelevant to the case.

The same rule holds for the historical student, and the moment he departs from it he ceases to be a student of history and becomes something else. The temptation to the theologian under these circumstances is to become a miracle-monger, to play with the alluring devices which in that half world between fact and fancy where children in all ages have delighted to dwell, take the place of rule and law. It is then the cruel function of the historian to recall him, if he can, to the order of the court whose jurisdiction they would both acknowledge, the court of sound science and sound reason. But here I anticipate an objection. It will be said that this kind of a judgment must necessarily partake of the frailty of all human things, that this sanction lacks that certainty for which the theologian is seeking and which he thinks he can find in the higher testimonies of emotional experience. The reply to this is a full confession. The evidence of history is as far from being absolutely certain as is the evidence in a court of law, just as far, but no farther. Every lawyer knows, and every plain thinking man knows too, that every decision of a court, no matter how overwhelming the evidence on which it rests, is subject to the possibility of error. We acknowledge this and, in so far as we are a law-abiding folk, we accept the result and govern ourselves accordingly. It is only in communities where the sense of law is but feebly developed that an aggrieved party expresses his criticism of society by shooting the judge. Ordinarily we say "We have done our best; the safety of society demands that we now go on as if the decision uttered forth indeed the voice of God."

So it is with the decisions of the historical student. He knows that they are fallible, as are all human things; but he knows also that it is in the best interest of true science that they shall be accepted until further evidence shall be produced of such superior weight that it will correct their error. What he insists upon is that this new evidence shall be of the same *kind* as that which has been proved insufficient. Because some human evidence has been proved faulty he will not permit a resort to any other kind. He will only demand that his rule shall be more carefully or more thoroughly enforced. That is the attitude of every rational historian. Not miracles nor inspirations, nor revelations, nor the dictations of any authority whatsoever, but more documents and better authenticated ones are what he must have.

And then — Ah yes, what then? — then he prays for ever greater learning, ever wider knowledge and ever clearer insight so to interpret the witness of these documents that his conclusions shall represent not merely the closest fidelity to the rules of law, but also the largest and finest sense of the claims of equity. For after all the historian cannot forget that he too is living in the present and has a present task to do. When all the work of collection and comparison has been done — if that ever could be done — there still remains the more engaging, more difficult and more rewarding task of interpretation. It is here that the historian has most often proved recreant to the great trust he has assumed when he has undertaken to present the record of the past for the instruction of the present. For it is in the work of interpretation above all that he is in danger of forgetting the high standards of fidelity to his sources which he has in theory adopted. Standards there must be. Without them interpretation would be only guesswork, a haphazard stringing together of unrelated episodes.

Think only for a moment of what is going to happen with the records of the present struggle among the states of Europe. Already the volume of writings as to its nearer and remoter causes, its diplomacy, its military and its economic aspects, the possibilities of settlement, its influence upon world politics and world trade, has become enormous beyond the possibility of mastery by any one mind. An immense proportion of this material will become valueless when the outcome of the war is determined. Whatever has been written to inflame passion, to excite sympathy or to arouse loyalty will soon pass over into the mass of the ephemeral. When I hear an orator say of some phase of this conflict "Never again," I can only smile to think how short that "never" may be. Rumor has it that already (1916) all sailings to Europe are booked for months ahead after the termination of the war. Then will begin the readjustment, not only of the material relations of the contending parties, but of the judgments formed under the stress of conflict. Then, and then only, can the work of interpretation by the true historian begin, and it will be a generation after that before his perspective can be restored to something like its normal range.

I have mentioned standards—with some hesitation and with great reserves. When one has spent one's life trying to avoid hasty and insufficient interpretations of history, one is pretty sure to become more than cautious as to what standards one may safely follow. And here, I think, is a field for the theologian. If he is bound to deny himself the luxury of speculative or emotional intrusions into the area of the historian, he is within his rights when he makes use of the historian as a furnisher of material for his own analysis. As theologian he may properly have his own theory of the universal order. When then he applies himself to the interpretation of history he has a right to think in terms of this theory. Indeed, as a theologian, he cannot do otherwise. It is his function to justify the ways of God to men, and, conversely it is his privilege to harmonize the ways of men with God.

It has been one of the canons of the modern historical school that History must not be treated as the hand-maid of anything. By that was meant that the study of history must not be perverted to the service of any theories or causes whatever. Its record must be read and studied for itself; its evidence must be weighed on its merits, and its sequences of cause and effect must be established in accordance with this evidence. Nothing has contributed more effectively to the amazing success of modern historical science than this inflexible rule. Without it History could never have held its own in comparison with the other subjects of academic research. The ancient jibe, that History was one half guesses and the other half lies owed its origin to violations of this saving limitation.

And yet, on the other hand, no rational historian has ever forgotten that no science stands by itself alone. Every science has its own material and its own method, and it is right in jealously guarding these against encroachment and against misappropriation, but the larger interpretations of every science are not the affair of its votaries alone. They belong to the whole world of thinking men, and often they are best secured through the activities of men to whom the detail of the special science is unfamiliar. Often too these interpretations undertaken by specialists have proved specially disappointing and misleading. Who, for example would regard the alleged phenomena of psychic communication as having received any special illumination through the interpretations of Oliver Lodge the physicist or of William James the psychologist?

To this world-wide range of interpretation the historian must submit, and among other interpreters he must expect that the theologian will claim his turn. He will take his chance in the serene consciousness that the material which he offers has been presented in accordance with a sound scientific method. The historian stakes his reputation on this soundness of procedure. Is the theologian prepared to do the same? The historian confesses, as we have seen, that his results do not conform to any absolute standard of certainty. The best he can say is that they represent a high degree of probability. Is the theologian ready to make a similar admission? If he is, then the way is prepared for a harmonious coöperation of the two sciences with their different materials and different methods in an ever advancing comprehension of the mystery of human life. History will serve Theology, not as the slave serves the master, but as the hand serves the eye and the eye the hand. And Theology will serve History by holding before it an interpretation without which its own service to mankind must always remain barren and incomplete.